# JOHN

# The Storyteller's Companion to the Bible™

Dennis E. Smith and
Michael E. Williams, editors

## VOLUME TEN

## JOHN

Abingdon Press
Nashville

JOHN

*Copyright © 1996 by Abingdon Press*

*This book is printed on recycled, acid-free paper.*

**Library of Congress Cataloging-in-Publication Data**

The Storyteller's companion to the Bible.
  Includes indexes.
  Contents: v. 1. Genesis—v. 2. Exodus-Joshua—[etc.] — v. 10. John.

  1. Bible—Paraphrases, English. 2. Bible—Criticism, interpretation, etc. I. Williams,
Michael E. (Michael Edward), 1950-
BS550.2.S764      1991                220.9'505                90-26289
**ISBN 0-687-39670-0 (v. 1: alk. paper)**
**ISBN 0-687-39671-9 (v. 2: alk. paper)**
**ISBN 0-687-39672-7 (v. 3: alk. paper)**
**ISBN 0-687-39674-3 (v. 4: alk. paper)**
**ISBN 0-687-39675-1 (v. 5: alk. paper)**
**ISBN 0-687-00838-7 (v. 6: alk. paper)**
**ISBN 0-687-00120-X (v. 7: alk. paper)**
**ISBN 0-687-05585-7 (v. 10: alk. paper)**

Unless otherwise noted, scripture quotations are from *The Revised English Bible.* © Oxford
University and Cambridge University Press 1989. Used by permission.

96 97 98 99 00 01 02 03 04 05—10 9 8 7 6 5 4 3 2 1

MANUFACTURED IN THE UNITED STATES OF AMERICA

To
Barbara,
who taught me
everything I know about
storytelling, and from whom
I am still learning

(D.E.S.)

# Contributors

**Dennis E. Smith** is Associate Professor of New Testament and Associate Dean at the Phillips Theological Seminary in Enid, Oklahoma. He earned the Master of Divinity degree at Princeton Theological Seminary and a Th.D. degree in New Testament from Harvard University Divinity School. His previous publications include *Many Tables: The Eucharist in the New Testament and Liturgy Today*, cowritten with Hal E. Taussig (Trinity Press International, 1990).

**Phyllis Williams Provost** earned the Master of Divinity degree from Phillips Theological Seminary in Enid, Oklahoma, and is pastor at the Winfield-Grandview United Methodist Church in Winfield, Kansas, where she enjoys utilizing storytelling in her ministry.

**Barbara McBride-Smith** is a professional storyteller who frequently performs at storytelling festivals around the nation and serves on the board of the National Storytelling Association. She holds an M.Ed. degree in educational media and technology from Boston University and is a full-time librarian at Skyline Elementary School in Stillwater, Oklahoma, as well as an adjunct instructor of storytelling for ministry at Phillips Theological Seminary.

**Michael E. Williams** is one of the pastors at Dalewood United Methodist Church in Nashville, Tennessee. He formerly directed the Office of Preaching for The United Methodist Church. He is also a member of the National Storytelling Association and can be heard practicing the art of storytelling at storytelling festivals throughout North America.

# Contents

# A Storyteller's Companion

## Dennis E. Smith

This is the first volume to be published in the New Testament series of The Storyteller's Companion to the Bible. The project was begun by Michael E. Williams who served as editor for all of the volumes in the Old Testament series. I join the project as a coeditor of the volumes in the New Testament series. I will serve as primary editor of three of these volumes; Michael will serve as primary editor of the other two. Since we are only concerned with the narrative portions of the New Testament, we will concentrate on the Gospels and Acts, rather than on the epistles. The Revelation of John is included in volume 8 on apocalyptic literature.

Narrative analysis of the Bible has come into its own since the 1970s and now dominates the interpretation of the Gospels and Acts. At the same time, narrative preaching has also begun to receive greater prominence as a form of proclamation. Add to this the resurgence of storytelling during this same period and you have the ingredients that have gone into this series. It is an opportune time to reexamine the riches of the biblical stories.

The stories of Jesus have always been at the root of Christian theology. In fact, the earliest Christian preaching about Jesus was done in the form of stories. Those stories form the core of our Gospels. These stories have been told and retold throughout Christian history, and are deeply embedded in modern Western culture. Yet it is still possible to come to them afresh and gain new insights, especially now that we have available to us the tools of narrative analysis and storytelling.

The Gospel of John has long been a favorite of Bible students, and yet it is the most enigmatic of the four canonical Gospels. It is the most highly symbolic of all of the Gospels, yet it presents stories in a simple language and in an inviting, dramatic style. It lends itself easily to retelling. When I teach John to seminary students, I often have them act out the text of the day in a dramatic presentation or reading. We discover through this method how much John is written like a drama, with demarcated divisions into scenes and characters saying lines of dialogue to one another. We learn to appreciate the skill with which the stories have been put together. But we also come face-to-face with the complex theology of John that is embedded in all of the stories. Our goal is to understand that theology in its own context and then learn how to apply it to the present world.

The Gospel of John is its own best advertisement for the power of narrative preaching. The author was a pastor who was dealing with complex issues in his community. He chose to deal with those issues by retelling the stories of Jesus. As we analyze those stories in light of the author's purpose and point of view, we will learn to appreciate how truly skilled he was as a preacher. Our goal is to retell his stories, rather than simply explain them, and thereby to learn not only from his message but also from his method. It is hoped that this volume will provide you with the tools to do that.

## The Stories

The starting point for our study is the biblical story itself. Any interpretation of the text should start with a fresh rereading. These stories have survived for so long because of their power to stir our emotions. That power still comes across to us as we read them today. And each close reading of the text can bring new insights into its meaning. It is especially helpful to try to come to the text afresh, listening to it as if for the first time.

The Gospel of John has been divided into thirty story segments that make up the thirty chapters of the book. Most of the Gospel is included. In this way, we are able to follow John's narrative from beginning to end. All of the selections from John in the Revised Common Lectionary (1992) are found here, except for a few verses. The translation used is *The Revised English Bible,* which is a particularly dynamic translation for use by today's storytellers. You are encouraged to utilize a variety of modern translations to give you a perspective on the range of possibilities for translation that the original language of the text presents.

## Comments on the Stories

For this volume, I am serving not only as editor but also as commentator and storyteller. I first began teaching John as a graduate teaching assistant for Professor George MacRae at Harvard. That began my fascination with this Gospel. I have continued to include John in my teaching schedule over the years, first at Princeton Theological Seminary where I began my teaching career, and now at Phillips Theological Seminary. During this time, I have been intrigued by developments in scholarship on John, especially in the area of narrative analysis.

I have also been a part of the resurgence in storytelling through my involvement in the world of my wife, Barbara McBride-Smith, who is a professional storyteller, and a contributor to this volume.

Through years of collaboration with Barbara, I eventually developed my own style for retelling Bible stories. This style combines equal parts of left-brain analysis—or scholarly perspectives on the text—and right-brain insights from the art of storytelling. The left-brain side sets up the boundaries by defining the ranges of appropriate meanings of the text. The right-brain side takes that information and works with it creatively. The comments in this volume represent primarily left-brain information, but make suggestions about their right-brain possibilities.

## Retelling the Stories

To help you in developing your own stories, we have provided a sample story with each biblical text. These are intended to serve as models for how a retelling can be done, but they are not expected to exhaust the possibilities in each story. Various approaches have been used in the retellings. A common approach is to take the point of view of a character from the story and develop it further. The retelling may follow the original plotline of the biblical story, or it may expand on one detail of the plot, or it may explore the aftereffects of the original story. Many of the retellings here utilize the first-century setting as their starting point, but retellings may also be placed in modern settings as well. In some cases, a folktale or family story may be found to offer a retelling of a biblical story. The possibilities are many, and you are encouraged to develop your own retellings according to a format and style that works for you.

Three storytellers have written the stories for this volume. Phyllis Williams Provost is a recent M.Div. graduate of Phillips Theological Seminary where she studied storytelling with Barbara McBride-Smith. She first began writing stories for this volume while taking my course on the Gospel of John. Michael E. Williams is the founding editor of the Storyteller's Companion to the Bible series and has been the inspiration for the entire project. He has written stories for each Old Testament volume and continues that tradition with his contributions to this volume. I wrote the final set of stories, putting my left brain on hold and giving free rein to my underdeveloped right brain. Barbara McBride-Smith served as editor for the stories written by Phyllis and me, giving each of our stories a careful, critical reading, and providing comments that invariably made them into better stories.

## Parallel Stories

None of the biblical stories developed in a vacuum. They came out of a rich storytelling culture. The parallel stories are provided to bring to our attention the storytelling milieu out of which these stories came. Here I have collected a wide variety of materials that provide insights into storytelling traditions or models that John might have used or ways in which John's story was reinterpreted and retold in the early Christian community. The purpose is to acquaint us with the ancient world of storytelling so that we can better understand how John's stories were heard.

The parallel stories in the New Testament volumes take the place of the midrashim that are provided in the Old Testament volumes of The Storytellers Companion to the Bible. The midrashim are traditional Jewish interpretations, in story form, of biblical texts. There is not a Christian tradition of New Testament interpretation quite like the midrash tradition, although the New Testament texts themselves sometimes function as midrashim for Hebrew Bible texts.

## How to Use This Book

Bible stories share many characteristics with traditional stories. As every storyteller knows, there is no one way to tell a story, but a storyteller cannot tell a story any way he or she wants.

On the one hand, it is often difficult for people of faith to think that Bible stories can be retold imaginatively. We tend to think of the Bible in rigid terms—as having one, clear, divine meaning. But the plurality of the Gospels themselves, in which stories about Jesus were told and retold in different ways, teaches us to think of Bible stories differently—as imaginative retellings that showcase the art of the storyteller.

On the other hand, the possibilities are not endless; you can tell a story in a form that is inappropriate to the original. Successful storytelling involves a delicate balance between the meanings inherent in the original tradition, the parameters of understanding in the community within which the story is told, and the imagination of the storyteller. Bible stories have a range of meanings that are considered appropriate based on our sense for a balance between how they were understood then and how they can best be understood now. But we are remiss if we overlook the medium as a component part of the message, for the Gospels present stories that function as stories—they always have and always will. Gospel stories are created out of the tradition, but retold in an imaginative form that is constructed to fit the needs of the storyteller's community.

This book is intended to be a resource to promote the telling of Bible stories. But there is an important component that is not present within these pages. This missing element is what you, the reader, bring to the text. Your understanding, experience, and imagination are vital to your own creation of viable retellings of the biblical stories. Only in this way can these ancient stories become real and pertinent to our lives today.

# A Narrative Introduction to the
# Gospel of John

The Gospel of John is the latest of our four canonical Gospels. As is the case with all of the Gospels, we do not know who its author was, or the exact date when it was written, or even where it was written. Our best guess is that John was written sometime in the period of 80 to 90 C.E. by an unknown author or authors in the region of Syria. The book itself does not identify its author; the name "John" was attached by a later generation and does not seem to derive from actual information within the Gospel itself. For convenience' sake, however, we will continue to call the unknown author by the traditional name "John."

John shares many stories and traditions about Jesus with the other three canonical Gospels, but is more independent of them than these Gospels are of one another. In fact, John is so distinctive in its portrayal of the Jesus story that it seems likely to have derived from a Christian group that was largely isolated from the rest of Christianity. Much of the history of that group is reflected in John's story, so that the story of Jesus becomes intertwined with the church's story. In telling the story in this way, the author of John is simply being a good preacher, presenting the Gospel to his congregation in a form that fits their particular needs.

### John as Storyteller

As a preacher, the author is a master storyteller. His stories are captivating and not only draw the reader in to identify with the characters but even seems to encourage participation in the story. To appreciate his skill as a storyteller, it is helpful to remember how the Gospel would have been experienced. It was not written to be read privately by each individual, but rather was intended to be read aloud to the congregation. Consequently, the Gospel would have been experienced primarily not as a text, but as a set of stories presented orally.

Ancient people were much better listeners than we are today. Reading was usually done aloud, so they were accustomed to hearing a text rather than seeing it. Furthermore, theirs was a culture in which storytelling was a widespread phenomenon and in which the theater had developed a high level of sophistication. Our author was a skilled storyteller who knew how to use the tools of his trade to maximum effect.

### A Profile of John's Church

Based on isolated references here and there in the Gospel, we can reconstruct the occasion for its writing. Apparently there was a developing crisis in

John's church. At the time, they were a sect within Judaism and worshiped in the local synagogue. But this state of affairs was coming to an end; Christians were being banned from the synagogue, and were finding themselves adrift without a religious home. They had not yet developed the idea that they could survive outside the synagogue, yet they were not being allowed to continue as Christians within the synagogue. What were they to do? The Gospel of John is written as an extended sermon addressing their situation. It defines the issue as a crisis of faith. And it addresses that crisis by retelling the story of Jesus and drawing out the parallels between that story and their story.

## The Language of John

John is known for its extensive use of symbolic language. In the introduction alone, we are introduced to a personified being who is called "Logos" or "Word" and whose mission is to bring light to a world that is being overcome by darkness. Light and darkness emerge as key symbols throughout John. To come to faith is often described in terms of "seeing" whereas disbelief is described as "blindness." Light and darkness are also expressive of the innate dualism in John, in which two opposites are seen to be at war in the cosmos. For example, Jesus is said to be from above, and the world is the region below. Other seemingly innocuous terms also take on a symbolic meaning. For example, the term "world" carries a symbolic meaning that varies from a negative to a neutral sense. It is "the world" that God loved so much that the Son was sent (3:16). But it is also "the world" that was hostile to Jesus and to his disciples ("if the world hates you, it hated me first," 15:18).

The symbolic language of John, and the dualism that it expresses, serve to represent the degree to which its source community was experiencing alienation in its world. When a statement so strong as "the world hates you" is made, it can only derive from an experience of complete alienation from any sense of empowerment in the world. In such a situation, hope can only come from a vision that rises above the reality of this world and speaks of a reality on another level, the reality "from above."

## Characters and Characterizations

Ancient literature and drama presented characters in ways different than we tend to do today. Especially since Freud, we westerners have tended to psychoanalyze when we tell stories. We dwell on what is going on in the psyche, where often there is a battle of id, ego, and superego. For the ancients, character was considered stable—you were born with it and it never changed. Character was known by external actions; the ancients did not conceive of an inner psychological life. Translated to storytelling, this meant that characters tended to be stereotypes. For example, in ancient drama the characters were designated by the use of masks. There was a standard way in which masks would depict such regular characters as the old man, the slave, the young girl, and so on. In this way, when the audience saw which mask was being worn, no matter what the play, they knew immediately what kind of character was on stage.

The characters in John are also stereotypes. For example, Jesus is stereotyped as divine *Logos* or "Word" (1:1-18). Thus Jesus is proclaimed as "bread of life" (6:35), "light of the world" (9:5), and so on. As a divine character, Jesus knows the hearts of others, and knows what will happen in this story before it happens. He is pictured as the one who is really in charge of the events throughout the story. Consequently, when Jesus is arrested, tried, and crucified, it is by his own choice and in the manner he has chosen. This is not a portrayal of events in a "historical" form, but rather in a "spiritual" form.

The question in John remains whether, in fact, the Jesus of this Gospel is a docetic Jesus, that is, a gnostic Jesus. Is the Jesus of this story so thoroughly divine that he is no longer recognizable as having human characteristics? This is an important theological issue that was debated in the early church. It is still an important issue, for it matters whether Jesus really suffered and died as a human being, or was a divine being who could not die and therefore only "seemed" to die, as the docetists would put it. As we reinterpret John for today, this is an issue to which we must give attention. Classic Christian theology proclaims the Christ to be both fully human and fully divine. The Gospel of John is understood to be saying the same thing when it proclaims that "the Word *became* flesh" (1:14). It is significant that John does not present this idea in more explicitly gnostic terms, such as: "the Word *appeared* as flesh."

Other characters in John, such as the disciples, the various women who are mentioned, and incidental characters like Nicodemus—all are developed in specific ways to fit John's story. More often than not, they are presented as models for the types of characters to be found in John's church and, by extension, in our churches today. In this sense, these characters also are stereotypes.

Another stereotyped group of characters has significant importance for our interpretation today. These are the characters known as "the Jews." Within John's story, "the Jews" becomes a catchall term for the enemies of Jesus. It is not used purely as an ethnic term, because the church of John was made up of Jews as well. The term "the Jews" is therefore being used in a polemical way, a polemic that should be understood in the context of a first-century intertribal dispute. It should not be translated into ethnic disputes or anti-Semitism today. As stereotyped characters, "the Jews," like others in the story, such as the Romans, represent various stereotypes of enemies of the faith. Such characters today are just as likely to be found within the Christian movement as outside it.

## Theology and Irony

One of the literary methods used by John is irony. Irony is a device whereby a double meaning can be seen in events and dialogue, usually because the audience knows things that the characters do not. The standard way this functions in John is for the characters to stumble over the meaning of sayings, events, and even the identity of Jesus, while we—the audience—are given the means to understand clearly what the true meaning is.

John makes explicit use of irony in several ways. For example, the high priest states a true interpretation of Jesus but does so in ignorance of its real meaning (11:47-53). Irony is also embedded in the narrative. For example, Nicodemus continues to miss Jesus' meaning because Jesus speaks in ironic riddles, in terms with double meanings ("born from above/born again," 3:3-9).    More significantly, irony is a means for proclaiming the most profound features of John's theology. If the divine word has become flesh, but only those of faith see "his glory" or divinity (1:14), then the story of faith is one in which individuals are able to see beyond literal reality and catch the vision of the divine truth in events, or "to see the glory." Because this motif is so strong in John, the stories in John are the least realistic, and least historical, of any in the New Testament. What John wants to proclaim is a story that reveals the "glory" of God, or a divine drama, not a literal earthly version of events.

## The Plot of John

The plot of John is summarized in the prologue. The *Logos* came to his own and was rejected, but "we (i.e., John's church) saw his glory" (1:14). The plot proceeds through stories of Jesus' encounters with various characters as his "time" draws near, the time for his "glorification" (compare 2:4 and 17:1). These encounters are capsulized versions of the trials of discipleship in the community of John itself. Thus the story of Jesus is told in John in such a way that it mirrors the conflicts taking place in the community where it is told.

The archetypal story illustrating this motif is that of the blind man in chapter 9. Here the one who is healed represents the person of faith. As a result of his healing, he is threatened with banishment from the synagogue. Only when that process is complete is he able to arrive at a true level of faith. Similarly, the church of John was facing banishment from the synagogue as a result of its spiritual healing. If the church professed the faith of the blind man, then they would manifest that they truly "see" while their enemies remain "blind." Consequently the story takes place on two levels, because the world of the story mirrors the world of the faith community—John's church.

16

## Signs and Faith

Another key element of John's plot is the motif of signs and faith. In John, the miracles of Jesus are called signs. In fact, all of Jesus' words and deeds tend to be grouped under the banner of "signs." This is a rich term in John, because it points to the idea that the true meaning of Jesus is to be found at a level other that the literal level. Signs point to the "glory" or divinity of Jesus. Consequently, those of true faith see not the "flesh" but see the "glory."

This is not as easy as it sounds. Apparently the idea of signs faith had fallen on hard times when John was written, for the Gospel testifies to the idea that though there were people who believed in his signs, many of them could not be trusted (2:23-25). It seems that the whole idea of belief is being reexamined in this Gospel. The issue is not whether people profess belief in signs, but whether they exhibit their belief by their lives. More specifically, it meant being willing to break with their traditional faith and follow the dangerous path of the fledgling Christian group to an unknown future.

But where were signs to be found in the postresurrection world of John's community, a world in which the physical presence of Jesus was no more? This is an issue specifically addressed in this Gospel. For although Jesus did "many other signs . . . which are not recorded in this book" yet "those written here have been recorded in order that you may believe that Jesus is the Christ, the Son of God, and that through this faith you may have life by his name" (20:30-31). That is to say, now "sign" is present in the story. Though none of John's audience could stand with Thomas and actually see with their own eyes the resurrected Jesus as he saw him, through the story they could experience this event as if they were there. Better yet, they could experience it in its true meaning, through the eyes of faith. Indeed, in many respects the story is better than the original, because the meaning of events is often much clearer in retrospect than in real time. That is the meaning of such verses as this: "After his resurrection his disciples recalled what he had said, and they believed the scripture and the words that Jesus had spoken" (2:22). Consequently, Jesus speaks of the time of the church when he tells Thomas, "Happy are they who find faith without seeing me" (20:29).

In John's view, therefore, the "Word" that is accessible through the "words" of the Gospel he wrote is not a mere shadow of the true figure. Rather, when the story is told and comprehended with the eyes of faith, the Christ is made to be present with all "glory."

# What Are New Testament Parallel Stories?

## Dennis E. Smith

If a story is told about a modern day president in which he eventually says, "I cannot tell a lie," we might think immediately of the first such story, the one about George Washington and the cherry tree. Stories are like that. They often draw on traditional formats or motifs or plots. It is the stock-in-trade of a good storyteller to utilize shared cultural data to make her stories come alive.

The stories about Jesus work the same way. They are often adapted to standard plots, especially biblical plots. To the storytellers in the early church, the Jesus story made sense as a midrash on Old Testament stories. Did Jesus meet a woman at a well? So did Jacob and Moses. Jesus was simply following a biblical pattern, and the storyteller made sure the story fit that pattern for the listener. Motifs were also drawn from the culture at large. Was Dionysus, the Greek god of wine, famous for bringing forth wine from empty jugs? Jesus could do that, and even better—his wine would not only be the best imaginable, but would appear in prodigious quantities.

"Parallel stories" are provided here to help us trace some of the background and foreground of these stories about Jesus. They are intended to give us a sense for the different ways this story would have been heard by different Christian groups at different times in early church history. The parallel stories collected here offer a variety of types of information.

### Jewish Traditions

In some cases, similar stories are found in the Jewish tradition. In this way, we can see how the stories being told about Jesus would be similar to stories being told about rabbis in early Jewish Christian churches. Besides the rabbinic tradition, Jewish stories are also found in the hellenistic Jewish authors Philo and Josephus.

The Jewish tradition of retelling Bible stories was called midrash. Many of the rabbinic tales are midrash stories, in which a biblical story is elaborated with another story. Many of John's stories about Jesus are also midrash stories, because they represent elaborations of biblical stories in a form closely related to the rabbinic practice. A good example of this is found in John 6, in which the bread of life discourse story is constructed to parallel features of the Exodus manna story.

## Christian Traditions

John is also a part of the development of early Christian storytelling traditions. The stories of Jesus were told and retold in a variety of forms. The clearest instance of such variations can be seen in the four canonical Gospels themselves when they tell the same story about Jesus in four different ways. Other variations are found in noncanonical Christian works, and some examples of these are provided among the parallel stories. John also has had a long history of interpretation in the Christian church. The parallel stories also include examples of interpretations of John's stories in the early church. This provides a means for gauging how the stories were heard not just by the original audience, but by later audiences as well.

## "Pagan" Traditions

As a storyteller, the author of John would also draw on motifs from the culture at large. This is especially true with miracle stories, which were highly popular in the ancient world and were told about virtually every deity and emperor. The miracle stories in the Jesus tradition would have been heard in the context of these other stories from the culture.

The stories about Jesus were placed in a specific world with its own geography, politics, and social institutions. Since it was a world different from our own, it is often necessary to define aspects of that world in order to approximate better how John's stories would have been heard in his day. These kinds of details are also provided in the parallel stories because they give us a sense for the earliest level of the hearing of the story.

The storyteller, like the poet, must be able to evoke images of people and places, emotions and events, with simple expressions. Terms such as "temple" or "passover" or "Galilee" or "Samaritan" carried multiple overtones and were utilized with those overtones in mind. By skillfully drawing on images already present in the cultural parlance, the storyteller could evoke graphic word pictures and make the story come to life. In addition, through skillful interweaving of the Jesus story with biblical references, he was able to merge the world of the Bible with the world of Jesus, and then merge those worlds with the present experience of his community. These stories were intended to draw the listener in to be a part of the story itself.

20

The modern storyteller seeks for no less. The parallel stories are provided to illustrate the skill with which these stories have been constructed and the complex ways in which they would have been heard. It is our hope that this knowledge will help you to retell the Bible stories for today's world with an immediacy that rivals the ancient tellings.

# Learning to Tell Bible Stories

## A Self-directed Workshop

1. Read the story aloud at least twice. You may choose to read the translation included here or the one you are accustomed to reading. I recommend that you examine at least two translations as you prepare, so you can hear the differences in the way they sound when read aloud.

Do read them *aloud*. Yes, if you are not by yourself, people may give you funny looks, but this really is important. Your ear will hear things about the passage that your eye will miss. Besides, you can't skim when you read aloud. You are forced to take your time, and you might notice aspects of the story that you never saw (or heard) before.

As you read, pay special attention to *where* the story takes place, *when* the story takes place, *who* the characters are, *what* objects are important to the story, and the general *order of events* in the story.

2. Now close your eyes and imagine the story taking place. This is your chance to become a playwright/director or screenwriter/filmmaker because you will experience the story on the stage or screen in your imagination. Enjoy this part of the process. It takes only a few minutes, and the budget is within everybody's reach.

3. Look back at the story briefly to make sure you haven't left out any important people, places, things, or events.

4. Try telling the story. This works better if you have someone to listen (even the family pet will do). You can try speaking aloud to yourself or to an imaginary listener. Afterward ask your listener or yourself what questions arise as a result of this telling. Is the information you need about the people, places, things, or language in the story? Is it appropriate to the age, experiences, and interests of those who will be hearing it? Does the story capture your imagination? One more thing: You don't have to be able to explain the meaning of a story to tell it. In fact, those of the most enduring interest have an element of mystery about them.

5. Read the "Comments on the Story" provided for each passage. Are some of your questions answered there? You may wish also to look at a good Bible dictionary for place names, characters, professions, objects, or worlds that you need to learn more about. *The Interpreter's Dictionary of the Bible* (Nashville: Abingdon Press, 1962) and *The Anchor Bible Dictionary* (New York: Doubleday, 1992) are the most complete sources for storytellers.

6. Read the "Retelling the Story" section for the passage you are learning to tell. Does it give you any ideas about how you will tell the story? How would you tell it differently? Would you tell it from another character's point of view? How would that make it a different story? Would you transfer it to a modern setting? What places and characters will you choose to correspond to those in the biblical story? Remember, the retellings that are provided are not meant to be told exactly as they are written here. They are to serve as springboards for your imagination as you develop your telling.

7. Read the "parallel stories" that accompany each passage. These give you insights into how the story was heard or retold at various times in the early church. Do these variations on the story respond to any of your questions or relate to any of your life situations or those of your listeners? Do the alternative stories parallel cultural "stories" from today that you know of? Sometimes you may find that experiences and points of view from the past are mirrored fairly closely in the modern setting.

8. Once you have the elements of the story in mind and have chosen the approach you are going to take in retelling it, you need to practice, practice, practice. Tell the story aloud ten or twenty or fifty times over a period of several days or weeks. Listen as you tell your story. Revise your telling as you go along. Remember that you are not memorizing a text; you are preparing a living event. Each time you tell the story, it will be a little different, because you will be different (if for no other reason than that you have told the story before).

9. Then "taste and see" that even the stories of God are good—not all sweet, but good and good for us and for those who hunger to hear.

# From Heaven to Earth

*The story of Jesus begins with the descent of the Word from heaven.*

### The Story

IN the beginning the Word already was. The Word was in God's presence, and what God was, the Word was. He was with God at the beginning, and through him all things came to be; without him no created thing came into being. In him was life, and that life was the light of mankind. The light shines in the darkness, and the darkness has never mastered it.

There appeared a man named John. He was sent from God, and came as a witness to testify to the light, so that through him all might become believers. He was not himself the light; he came to bear witness to the light. The true light which gives light to everyone was even then coming into the world.

He was in the world; but the world, though it owed its being to him, did not recognize him. He came to his own, and his own people would not accept him. But to all who did accept him, to those who put their trust in him, he gave the right to become children of God, born not of human stock, by the physical desire of a human father, but of God. So the Word became flesh; he made his home among us, and we saw his glory, such glory as befits the Father's only Son, full of grace and truth.

John bore witness to him and proclaimed: 'This is the man of whom I said, "He comes after me, but ranks ahead of me"; before I was born, he already was.'

From his full store we have all received grace upon grace; for the law was given through Moses, but grace and truth came through Jesus Christ. No one has ever seen God; God's only Son, he who is nearest to the Father's heart, has made him known.

### Comments on the Story

The stage is set. The drama is ready to begin. It is not an ordinary story. It is the story of the descent of a god. To introduce the story, the storyteller chooses a device much like what his contemporaries used in Greek drama. There the story was introduced by the chorus, who explained in a poetic prologue the nature of the action that would be taking place in the drama, often indicating details that would not be known to the characters in the play itself. The prologue here has a similar purpose. It presents in poetic form the true nature of the leading character in the story, so that we as hearers (and now as readers) will understand him in a way that is inaccessible to the characters themselves. As the story proceeds, we know that it will not be about a normal human being but rather about one who is God in human form.

The prologue is actually a story in itself. It tells of the origin of a divine being in heaven, his descent to earth, and the response of those on earth. It is written in a poetic style that we call parallelism. It is a style used extensively in Hebrew poetry, such as we find in the Psalms. Parallelism expresses ideas through repetition, in which themes are repeated or contrasted in successive lines. Verses 1-2 ("In the beginning . . . ") present four phrases, all of which can be interpreted as variations on the same theme. This is called synonymous parallelism, whereby the same idea is repeated in successive lines using different words. Verse 3 ("and through him all things came to be . . . ") is another example of synonymous parallelism. Verses 4 and 5 ("In him was life . . . "), however, use another style of parallelism, in which the second line repeats a term from the first line and adds new information.

The prologue can be divided into stanzas based on the progression of thought. Stanza one ("In the beginning . . . " [vv. 1-2]) speaks of the beginning, when there is only God and the Word. The story, then, begins at the beginning of time, when the Word exists along with God. No explanation is provided for how the Word got there along with God, nor why there is another being present with God. The concept derives ultimately from Jewish wisdom theology, in which personified wisdom is present with God at the beginning and participates in creation (Proverbs 8). The transfer of the category of "wisdom" to the term "word" takes place by means of a neat exegetical maneuver. After all, in Gen. 1:1, God speaks before creation takes place. Thus to the ancient exegete, the word exists before creation. When this idea is transferred to wisdom theology, word becomes "Word" or personified "Wisdom."

In stanza two ("and through him all things came to be . . . " [vv. 3-5]) the act of creation begins. Just as Genesis says, nothing can come into being without the "word/Word" of God. But like the Genesis story, creation here takes place in a context of conflict. Whereas light is divided from darkness in Genesis, here life and light are equated as moral values brought by the Word, and their opposite is darkness, a force of evil that tries but fails to subdue them. That conflict between light and darkness that began at creation will be transferred to the human sphere and reappear in the Jesus story.

In stanza three ("There appeared a man . . . " [vv. 6-9]) we shift from the divine to the human world. Here a human character is presented for the first time, John the Baptist, the precursor of the one who is to come. This sets the stage for the movement of the story of the Word to the human level. The theme here echoes what will be emphasized later in the introductory story about John, that though he was sent by God, he was not the "light" but only came to testify to the "light."

Stanza four ("He was in the world . . . " [vv. 10-11]) speaks of the first phase of the coming into the world of the Word. It is a poetic rendering of the first half of John's Gospel. Here the term "world" has a negative connotation. Though it owed its existence to the Word through creation, it did not recognize him. Even more negative is the picture of "his own," for they reject him. This is a poetic rendering of a theme that will be emphasized in John's story, that Jesus comes to his own, "the Jews," and is rejected by them. The term "the Jews" is to be read as a symbolic term, however, referring generically to the earthly enemies of Jesus. This is true because the Christian community for whom John writes is also Jewish. The term "the Jews," therefore, cannot be read to refer to the nation as a whole. The story of that rejection is told in John 1–11, until the transition at 11:54 where it is said that "Jesus no longer went about openly among the Jews."

On the other hand, Jesus was accepted by the community of believers, who refer to themselves in stanza five ("But to all who did accept him . . . " [vv. 12-14]). They are the ones who "accept" and "put their trust in him" and therefore can be designated "children of God." It is on their behalf that the Gospel is written, and it is their voice we hear in verse 14 when it is said that the Word dwells "among us." It is they who, when faced with the paradox of Word become flesh, are able to "see his glory." This is a profound metaphor for Christian faith in John, for the believer in John is consistently the one who "sees" and recognizes the "glory" or divinity of Jesus. Their story is told throughout John, particularly in the conflict narratives, in which believers are persecuted for their faith but whose faith is founded on the "signs."

The high point of the entire poem is reached when "the Word became flesh." A parallel statement immediately follows, "he made his home among us." The concept is profound—the essence of the divine leaves the divine world, comes to the human world, and lives among humans in human form while still retaining divine status. It is the basic text for the doctrine of incarnation. It is also the centerpiece for the view that John is not, in essence, a gnostic text. For a gnostic would presumably say, "he [only] appeared in human form." John, however, says, "Word became flesh," thus emphasizing the reality of Jesus' earthly existence.

The poem closes with stanza 6 ("John bore witness . . . " [vv. 15]), a transition to the beginning of the narrative of John, and stanza 7 ("From his full store . . . " [vv. 16-17]), which provides a final theological conclusion emphasizing the contrast between the "grace and truth" offered through Jesus Christ and the law of Moses.

The prologue tells the story of the descent of the Logos from the divine to the human realm. This basic plot outline is related to a standard mythological theme of the era that had many variations. It is found in Jewish wisdom literature, in Greek philosophy, and in gnosticism. By utilizing this ancient narrative plot and widely used terminology, John is able to begin his Gospel on a level that would be recognized as profound by any ancient reader. He has, in effect, collapsed a complex set of philosophical and theological concepts of his day into the one figure of Jesus.

The word *Logos* is a Greek term that we translate as "Word" in English, but its meaning is not wholly captured by the English term. It has a rich usage in Greek philosophical speculation, where it often is used for the concept that we translate as "reason," the highest of Greek virtues. Philosophical speculation, especially among the Stoics, also uses the term to refer to a personification of the divine being. Philo the Jewish philosopher takes up this idea and refers to the God of the Old Testament as Logos.

But the idea of a personified entity present with God at creation is best understood to derive from another source—Jewish wisdom theology—as exemplified in Proverbs 1–9. Here personified Wisdom is present with God at creation and descends to earth to present the message of wisdom to a sinful humanity. Thus one of the radical features of John's theology, that there is another being present with God at creation who can be spoken of separately from God, is founded on a biblical concept.

Wisdom in Proverbs, however, is personified as "Lady Wisdom," since the term "wisdom" in Hebrew is female. John uses a masculine term in Greek, "logos," which provides a smoother transition to his masculine character, Jesus. But the concept of "Lady Wisdom" at the root of John's Christology should not be forgotten. It reminds us that the concept of the "Word" cannot be read as a gender specific term. For while "Logos" implies male, "Wisdom" denotes female. Rather it is when "Word" becomes flesh that gender is attached.

The stark contrast in John's Gospel between this world and the divine world, between light and darkness, and between the children of light and the children of darkness is very telling in the stories about Jesus and the emerging church. It was a vision that made sense in a time in which the church was experiencing a severe estrangement from its roots in this world. But when taken to an extreme, such a theology evolves into the heresy of gnosticism, as we now know through historical hindsight. As a corrective to that view, we would do well to keep John 1:14 before us: "the Word became flesh." Just as the Word was required to be fully involved in the affairs of the world in order to bring about its redemption, so also must the church define its mission today.

## Retelling the Story

IN the beginning the Word already was. The Word was in God's presence, and what God was, the Word was. (John 1:1)

"How can we know the dancer from the dance?"—W. B. Yeats, "Among School Children"

"Thou shouldst not have been old till thou hadst been wise."—The Fool, *King Lear* (1.5.47-48)

It is the time country people call first dark. Two figures sit in rocking chairs on a spacious porch. Their slow rocking reiterates the rhythm of the closing day. These ancient figures composed of shadow and silence seem almost ageless. Only their voices reveal the years of remembered trials and joys that have shaped their lives. After an extended silence such as can only be borne by long-standing friendship, a space is made for voices in the quiet tincture of evening.

"Lady Wisdom" became a prominent figure in Jewish speculation of the hellenistic and Roman periods (second century B.C.E. to first century C.E.). Her story, which can be gathered from various allusions, is an important model for John's story of the Logos. She was present with God at creation (Prov. 8:22-31, Eccles. 1:1-9), came to earth to dwell among human beings (Eccles. 24:8-10), but her preaching was rejected (Prov. 1:24). She now no longer dwells on earth but in a dwelling place known only to God (Job 28:12-14, 23). (Boring, p. 238, no. 353)

*(The two retired actors rock in rhythm, and speak slowly with several long pauses punctuating their conversation.)*

"Like the darkness at the beginning," he said.

"Before the beginning," she corrected.

"Yes, before. It's hard to remember that time before the light, the song, the dance," he added.

"But the voice was unforgettable, still haunts me," she agreed.

"Yes, the voice. It was as if the voice not only called the light forth; rather, the voice *was* the light uttered swirling into the eternal night," his voice trailed off in reverie.

"You were the light." She spoke so quietly he could hardly make out the words.

"And you were the voice," he recalled as her words finally settled in.

"And we were one. The two shall become one; isn't that what we were told? And we were . . . *are* one." Her voice was stronger now.

"And one with the One who spoke, whose voice and light we are."

"The storyteller."

"The choreographer."

"The composer."

"The Voice. That's what we all said, never a name. As if a name would have been too ordinary, too mundane for such a mystery, such a talent."

"Then we were sent out on tour. The world was our stage. We were not rich; we traveled in tents and played every wide spot in the road."

29

"We may have not been materially wealthy, but we had the best material ever. We were considered the greatest show on earth before the circus pilfered that title."

"They've taken everything that was ours and claimed it for their own, those people. They either worship you or treat you like dirt."

"But we didn't do it for the celebrity, or even the credit. There was a time, if you remember, when it was enough to simply do the dance, sing the tune, let the story tell us. It was enough that we were the Voice and the Voice was us. The light spread across the universe and that was reward enough for an eternity."

"The Voice said light and there was light."

"The Voice said world and there was a world."

"The Voice said ants and elephants, reeds and oak trees, condors and canaries, and there they were."

"The Voice said men and women in my image and they—er, we—were."

"It was the Word that took on flesh in us, not just the words, mind you, but the very Word. The first word and the last word, before all other words and after all other words."

"It was a very strange and beautiful vaudeville we played. And the storyteller. . . . "

"The choreographer."

"The composer."

"The Voice was pleased."

"*Good*, I believe, was the exact word. The voice said it was all good."

"And the Voice never took it back."

"It all was good. Even looking back after what seems like millennia it still seems good."

"We had our detractors."

"Our critics."

"Who just could not see the goodness that lay at the heart of it all."

"It was good because it was of the Voice; neither it, nor we, has any goodness but that."

"And that is enough."

"Yes, enough."

"Good night, Sophie."

"Yes it is good, Josh. Good night."

*(Michael E. Williams)*

In a Jewish midrash on Genesis 32 known as the Prayer of Joseph (second century B.C.E. to first century B.C.E.), the story of a heavenly being who comes to earth to dwell among humanity is applied to Israel (Jacob): "And when I [Jacob] was coming from Mesopotamia of Syria, Uriel, the angel of God came out and said, 'I descended to the earth and dwelt among men,' and 'I was called Jacob by name.' He was jealous, and fought with me, and wrestled with me, saying that his name preceded my name and that of every angel. And I mentioned his name to him and how great he is among the sons of God: 'Are you not Uriel, my eighth, and I Israel, an archangel of the power of the Lord and chief of the captains of thousands among the sons of God? Am I not Israel, the first minister in the presence of God, and did I not invoke my God by his unquenchable name?' " (Boring, p. 239, no. 354)

30

# John the Baptist

---

*John the Baptist testifies to Jesus.*

---

### The Story

THIS is the testimony John gave when the Jews of Jerusalem sent a deputation of priests and Levites to ask him who he was. He readily acknowledged, 'I am not the Messiah.' 'What then? Are you Elijah?' 'I am not,' he replied. 'Are you the prophet?' 'No,' he said, 'Then who are you?' they asked. 'We must give an answer to those who sent us. What account do you give of yourself?' He answered in the words of the prophet Isaiah: 'I am a voice crying in the wilderness, "Make straight the way for the Lord." '

Some Pharisees who were in the deputation asked him, 'If you are not the Messiah, nor Elijah, nor the Prophet, then why are you baptizing?' 'I baptize in water,' John replied, 'but among you, though you do not know him, stands the one who is to come after me. I am not worthy to unfasten the strap of his sandal.' This took place at Bethany beyond Jordan, where John was baptizing.

The next day he saw Jesus coming towards him. 'There is the Lamb of God,' he said, 'who takes away the sin of the world. He it is of whom I said, "After me there comes a man who ranks ahead of me"; before I was born, he already was. I did not know who he was; but the reason why I came, baptizing in water, was that he might be revealed to Israel.'

John testified again: 'I saw the Spirit come down from heaven like a dove and come to rest on him. I did not know him; but he who sent me to baptize in water had told me, "The man on whom you see the Spirit come down and rest is the one who is to baptize in Holy Spirit." I have seen it and have borne witness: this is God's Chosen One.'

### Comments on the Story

"I am not the Messiah." Those words of John the Baptist define the theme for the storyteller. How do we recognize the true Messiah? It is a timeless question, as pertinent for our time as it was for John's.

John begins his story of Jesus in a traditional way, with the testimony of John the Baptist in the wilderness. All of the Gospels start this way. Even the two that have birth and infancy narratives, Matthew and Luke, begin with John the Baptist, once they start the story proper. John uses many of the same traditional elements that the other Gospels contain, but in a highly reworked format.

31

This section in John is structured into separate scenes, which are designated as successive days. The opening scene starts at verse 19 ("This is the testimony . . .)." The scene shifts with day two at verse 29 ("The next day he saw Jesus coming"), day three at verse 35 ("The next day again John was standing . . ."), day four at verse 43 ("The next day Jesus decided to leave for Galilee . . ."), and day five at 2:1 ("Two days later . . ."). At 2:1, however, the author states that it is "two days later" since his reference is not back to the John the Baptist story in 1:19 but rather to the first call of the disciples at 1:35. This structure ties these early sections together as the introductory stories leading to the manifestation of Jesus' first sign at 2:1-11, after which the days are not counted anymore.

In the verses under consideration here, 1:19-34, John the Baptist presents his testimony. His theme is stated in verse 20, "I am not the Messiah." Apparently some people thought he was, and they were still around when this Gospel was written. To their claims that the Baptist was the Messiah, this Gospel presents a story where he vehemently denies it.

In scene one the Baptist is encountered by "a deputation of priests and Levites" who have been sent by "the Jews of Jerusalem" to inquire of him who he is. The Baptist goes through a litany denying not only that he is the Messiah, but also that he is neither Elijah nor the Prophet, two traditional biblical categories for messianic figures. Instead he affirms that he is the one proclaimed by Isa. 40:3 as the precursor to the Messiah, the "voice in the wilderness." In the synoptic Gospels it is the narrator who says that John the Baptist is the "voice in the wilderness." Here the Baptist makes that identification in his own words.

In the second scene, on "the next day" (v. 29) Jesus appears on the scene for the first time, though he is just passing by and does not interact with anyone. The Baptist sees him coming and proclaims, "There is the Lamb of God who takes away the sin of the world." This is a designation of Jesus found only in John among the four Gospels, though it is also picked up in the Revelation of John (see Rev. 5:6, for example). This concept seems to develop out of a conflation of the sacrificial lamb of Passover (Exodus 12) with the suffering servant of Isaiah 53 who dies for "our guilt" and stands before his tormentors "like a sheep led to the slaughter" (Isa. 53:6-7). Later in John's story, Jesus' death will fit his designation as "the Lamb of God who takes away the sin of the world," for it will take place at the same time that the Passover lambs are slain, as we can infer from 18:28 and 19:31.

During his monologue, John the Baptist notes that he had been sent to testify to the Lamb, but initially did not know who he was. But, he explains, "he who sent me to baptize in water had told me, 'The man on whom you see the Spirit come down and rest is the one who is to baptize in Holy Spirit.' " Interestingly, the Baptist refers to seeing the Spirit descend like a dove but does not refer to the baptism scene where the synoptic Gospels place the descent of the dove story. To put it bluntly, in this Gospel, Jesus is never baptized!

It is clear from the beginning of this Gospel that the story told is not an ordinary one. After all, it begins in heaven with the descent of the Word. And the story is about how that Word became flesh and lived among humans. That approach seems to be the reason for the peculiar way in which the John the Baptist story is told.

In the other three canonical Gospels, it is the narrator who tells us who the Baptist is (as in Mark 1:2-3). The Baptist himself does not seem to be sure about his precursor role or about who Jesus is (as in Luke 7:18-23). Furthermore, in Mark especially, no one knows who Jesus is for most of the story, and if anyone figures it out, they are told by Jesus to keep it a secret (as in Mark 1:34, 44). Yet here in John, Jesus is proclaimed openly from the outset, by John the Baptist no less, as "the Lamb of God." And the Baptist has no doubt about who Jesus is. It is this high Christology of John that also explains why there is no baptism scene. Since Jesus is divine from the outset (a conclusion drawn from many years of testimony since Jesus' death and resurrection), a baptism seems anachronistic. Matthew noticed this as well, and in his story John the Baptist protests that it should not be done (Matt. 3:13-15). John simply leaves it out.

What kind of character is John the Baptist in this Gospel? Most of the characters in John go through some kind of encounter with Jesus and must respond in faith. John the Baptist does not. This places him somewhat above the level of normal humans. Indeed, he says that he had divine guidance to help him identify the Chosen One. Consequently, John the Baptist is not presented here as a model of faith. He is rather one of God's emissaries sent to guide us to the Christ. As a divine emissary, the first words out of his mouth are significant, "I am not the Messiah." It is an important message for any generation; we must not mistake the messenger for the Messiah.

## Retelling the Story

I am a voice crying in the wilderness, "Make straight the way for the Lord." (John 1:23*b*)

The old man was a common sight on the streets of our small town. He was from a good family, one with a nice home and a comfortable income. He had gone away to college many years ago. In fact, rumor had it that he had attended a prestigious divinity school in the state capital, which was where his trouble began. He came home after his first year and never returned to study there or anywhere else. He never served a church or even attended one that anyone could remember. He never worked, never married, never shaved or cut his hair. He seldom ventured outside of the family home he had inherited from his parents. He lived like a hermit, so much so that my mother and father did not remember seeing him when they were children.

33

There were other stories in the early church in which disciples of John and disciples of Jesus debated who was the Christ. Here is an example: "And, behold, one of the disciples of John asserted that John was the Christ, and not Jesus, inasmuch as Jesus himself declared that John was greater than all men and all prophets. 'If, then,' said he, 'he be greater than all, he must be held to be greater than Moses, and than Jesus himself. But if he be the greatest of all, then must he be the Christ.' To this Simon the Canaanite, answering, asserted that John was indeed greater than all the prophets, and all who are born of women, yet that he is not greater than the Son of man. Accordingly Jesus is also the Christ, whereas John is only a prophet: and there is as much difference between him and Jesus, as between the forerunner and Him whose forerunner he is." (*Pseudo-Clementine Recognitions* 1.60 [211-31 C.E.])

After a certain time, though, he began to walk the streets of our town preaching to passersby. He was a frightening sight and I was terrified of him. Most people just ignored him as he followed them down the street shouting things like, "Turn around and see. God lives and walks in your midst. Look deeply into the eyes of those you despise and fear. There you will find God." I never knew his real name. The children of my generation knew him simply as John the Hermit.

John's hair fell over his shoulders in long, matted strands that reminded me of rope. His beard came almost to his waist, thinning to mere wisps at its end. We youngsters speculated on how he ate and we joked about the food that must have been left from previous meals in the brushy tangle of his whiskers. You could see from a distance, which was as close as we ever ventured, that his eyes were bloodshot, giving the impression that there were tiny flames flickering behind each pupil.

Though we knew that John's family, while not wealthy, had money, John dressed as if he lived on the street. His were the cast-off clothes of the Salvation Army and Goodwill. It was not that he never changed clothes. Rather, he would put on a shirt and pair of pants and wear them until they were rags, then exchange them for another set of clothes. Each set of clothes worn this way would last about a season, so John seemed always to be dressed appropriately for the weather. In the coldest part of winter he wore what was, at one time, an expensive camel hair coat that had been worn until the dirt of living had turned its beige to dark gray. While his other clothes changed each winter and summer, the coat was a constant. It would appear each autumn at the first cold snap and disappear each spring on the first balmy day.

While our town's John the Hermit would certainly attract great attention from a visitor or new resident, he became almost invisible to those of us on Franklin Street who frequented the pulpit he had carved out in his own imagination. The thing about John that rendered him so tolerable to our citizenry was that he never pushed tracts on anybody or asked for money. He simply preached his own version of repentance, or perhaps it was God's version; I am not the judge of that. I learned much later than professors from nearby seminaries and even some pastors came to study with John and apparently took him seriously. All I know is that on one fateful evening something touched my life and I have not been the same since.

We youngsters thought it great fun to taunt John, at least the bravest of us did. We would wager cold drinks or bags of popcorn at the Ben Franklin store to see who would perform some act of great courage in the face of this prophet. The challenge most frequently issued was to touch his coat. I would, on occasion, run with the frantic dedication of a child possessed, my heart pounding, hardly able to breathe while trying to touch the back of a sleeve or a coattail. The sense of danger and feeling of stark courage that followed was heady indeed, far beyond any material prize such as popcorn.

As time passed, the thrill went out of our coat-touching dares, and the degree of difficulty of the challenges began to escalate. One late afternoon a group of my friends had taunted me into accepting a dare. The dare was to run up to the door of the house in which John lived, knock on the door, and stay until he opened it. If I stayed long enough to speak to him I would be rewarded not only with each friend's entire marble collection, but also with the most valued baseball card from each of their collections: a Whitey Ford, a Mickey Mantle, and the prized Hank Aaron.

This time I did not run. I walked to the door. I was glad that my friends were some distance away so they couldn't see my hand tremble as I lifted it to rap against the door. I knocked once, then waited. Just as I raised my hand to knock a second time, the door jerked open and a hand reached out to grasp my uplifted arm. Before I knew it I was inside the house with the door closed behind me. I can remember thinking, "I am going to die. I will never see those baseball cards and marbles, because I will be dead."

With John's hand still holding onto my arm, the voice of the prophet leapt out of the darkness. "I always knew you would come," he said in a slow, gentle, almost prayerful manner. "Sit down," the voice continued as the prophet, still tightly grasping my forearm, moved me over to a sofa and into a seated position. After we both sat down, he spoke again, "God's heart is broken. Did you know that?" I wanted to answer but the constriction of my throat would let no sound through.

"That's why I do what I do, because I know the misery that God feels. It is more than a human could bear and remain sane." I could feel something wet

For the church father Clement of Alexandria, the terminology "Lamb of God" could be invoked to define the solidarity of the Christ with children. "Again, St. John, 'the prophet greatest among those born of woman' [Luke 7:28], also testifies to His childhood: 'Behold the Lamb of God.' Scripture speaks of children and little ones as 'lambs'; then in this passage, in calling God the Word, became man for us, 'the Lamb of God,' because of His desire to be like us in all things, he is speaking of Him as the Son of God, the little one of the Father." (*Paidagogos,* 1.24 [ca. 190 C.E.])

falling on my hand in drops, and I truthfully thought at first that he was drooling. I thought I would throw up right then and there.

"I knew you would come," he repeated. "I will not always be with you. But there is one coming after me who is God's own broken heart, God's baby lamb who takes away the sins of the world. He will be with you always." As he spoke these words I realized that the drops I felt were John's own tears. He was weeping for God, or for himself, or for me, or for all the little lambs who were sinned against in the world. He lifted my hands to his face, and I could feel the hot tears running into his beard. Then he opened my palm and even in the shadowy room I could tell that he was making a cross with the nail of one of his fingers. When he let go I took the opportunity to run out the door.

My so-called friends we nowhere to be seen. Oh, I collected the marbles and baseball cards the next day and was accorded a status among my peers that remained with me even through high school, as the most courageous of us all. What I did not tell them is that on that night of my youth, I came into contact with something that both terrified and fascinated me. I had been touched by the holy, though, to this day I have found no adequate way to phrase it. Let me say simply that I count that night as my baptism.    *(Michael E. Williams)*

# The First Disciples

*Jesus calls his first disciples.*

## The Story

THE next day again, John was standing with two of his disciples when Jesus passed by. John looked towards him and said, 'There is the Lamb of God!' When the two disciples heard what he said, they followed Jesus. He turned and saw them following; 'What are you looking for?' he asked. They said, 'Rabbi,' (which means 'Teacher') 'where are you staying?' 'Come and see,' he replied. So they went and saw where he was staying, and spent the rest of the day with him. It was about four in the afternoon.

One of the two who followed Jesus after hearing what John said was Andrew, Simon Peter's brother. The first thing he did was to find his brother Simon and say to him, 'We have found the Messiah' (which is the Hebrew for Christ). He brought Simon to Jesus, who looked at him and said, 'You are Simon son of John; you shall be called Cephas' (that is, Peter, 'the Rock').

The next day Jesus decided to leave for Galilee. He met Philip, who, like Andrew and Peter, came from Bethsaida, and said to him, 'Follow me.' Philip went to find Nathanael and told him, 'We have found the man of whom Moses wrote in the law, the man foretold by the prophets: it is Jesus son of Joseph, from Nazareth.' 'Nazareth!' Nathanael exclaimed. 'Can anything good come from Nazareth?' Philip said, 'Come and see.' When Jesus saw Nathanael coming towards him, he said, 'Here is an Israelite worthy of the name; there is nothing false in him.' Nathanael asked him, 'How is it you know me?' Jesus replied, 'I saw you under the fig tree before Philip spoke to you.' 'Rabbi,' said Nathanael, 'you are the Son of God; you are king of Israel.' Jesus answered, 'Do you believe this because I told you I saw you under the fig tree? You will see greater things than that.' Then he added, 'In very truth I tell you all: you will see heaven wide open and God's angels ascending and descending upon the Son of Man.'

## Comments on the Story

"What are you looking for?" Jesus says to the two strangers who follow him. It is a key question for seekers living in any age. And what they will find when they follow Jesus, according to John, will be both more marvelous and more demanding than they ever dreamed possible.

Here we have John's version of the call of the disciples. There are two scenes, divided by the writer into two days; however, these scenes are really part of a larger scheme in which five separate scenes are interconnected by the notation of successive days (1:19–2:11). Scene three in this sequence is the first scene of the call stories.

In the previous scenes, the Baptist had addressed himself to a group of priests and Levites (1:19) on one day and to an unspecified audience on the next day (1:29). Now it is the next day, and he is standing with two of his own disciples when he once more testifies, "There is the Lamb of God!" (v. 36). These two disciples immediately follow Jesus.

Only John situates the call of the first disciples in this way and identifies them as former disciples of the Baptist. There is a narrative logic to John's version, for it provides a satisfying transition from the testimony of the Baptist to the call of the first disciples. It also provides a broader definition of the role of the Baptist, since his testimony also forms the foundation for the first disciples to follow Jesus.

After responding to John's proclamation and following Jesus, the two disciples are noticed by Jesus. He turns and asks a pointed question, "What are you looking for?" The disciples' response seems unconnected, however. They ask where Jesus is staying. He responds approvingly, "Come and see," and they go and stay with him for that day. Oddly, we are never told where Jesus is staying; only that the disciples stay with him there. What are we to make of this? The conversation is ironic throughout; everything has a double meaning.

The question of Jesus, "What are you looking for?" is appropriate for any disciple just beginning the pilgrimage of faith. Also appropriate is the response of the disciples, for where Jesus "abides," to use a more traditional translation of this term, is where the true disciple should go and where he should "abide" with Jesus. It is a spiritual journey that is being emphasized here, one that is echoed again and again throughout John. The journey has practical components—the disciple must be prepared to leave his former life behind (as in the blind man story in chapter 9). It also has specifically spiritual components—the disciple must "dwell" where Jesus dwells, as is stated in John 15:5: "I am the vine; you are the branches. Anyone who dwells in me, as I dwell in him, bears much fruit; apart from me you can do nothing." The term for "dwell" in 15:5 is the same as the term for "staying" in 1:38.

In the next segment to this scene, in verses 40-42, we find out that one of the two disciples was Andrew; we never find out who the other one was. Andrew provides an example of true discipleship by finding his brother Simon Peter and telling him, "We have found the Messiah." He then brings Peter to Jesus. Jesus upon first meeting Peter pronounces those words that have become synonymous with this apostle, "you shall be called Cephas" (that is, Peter, "the Rock"). In the other three canonical Gospels, this statement follows on Peter's confession after he had been following Jesus for some time. John is unusual in placing the statement at the very beginning of Peter's encounter with Jesus. But this is consistent with the truncated form of the faith journeys of the disciples. By the time the wedding at Cana is over (2:11), they will have arrived at the appropriate level of faith to recognize the "glory" of Jesus.

In the next scene, which begins at verse 43, Jesus meets Philip and says simply, "Follow me." Philip, like Andrew, exemplifies the true disciple, for he finds another, Nathanael, and proclaims Jesus to him. Philip's proclamation is striking, for he not only identifies Jesus as the Messiah, but also identifies him as the son of Joseph and as hailing from Nazareth. This is unusual since Jesus' parentage and earthly origin are not given much importance in John's story as a whole. But it helps to introduce an important theological theme in John; for in John Jesus' origin is, in fact, a key to his identity, especially when one understands that his true origin is from heaven.

"Can anything good come from Nazareth?" Nathanael inquires. His question is full of irony, for, in fact, it is not the origin in Nazareth that defines who Jesus is. After he experiences the sign of Jesus, when Jesus exhibits divine knowledge about him, Nathanael changes his view. Now presumably he knows Jesus is not just from Nazareth but derives from heaven, for Nathanael now confesses him as "Son of God" and "king of Israel."

Jesus' final statement is addressed not only to Nathanael, but to all disciples, since it is in the plural. He says, "You [plural] will see heaven wide open and God's angels ascending and descending upon the Son of Man." The reference recalls Jacob's dream (Genesis 28). This statement of Jesus is never fulfilled directly in the Gospel. Its significance would appear to be that the sum total of the signs done by Jesus, and recorded in this Gospel, is to verify that Jesus, like the rock where Jacob had his dream, is the locus for the divine revelation to humanity.

The disciples are presented as models for proper faith. The first stage of their faith is to reject inappropriate messiahs—the Baptist is not the messiah. Rather his testimony is to the one who is greater, the Lamb of God. The disciples then must begin a pilgrimage of faith in which they leave their former associations and follow Jesus. In the process, a variety of important titles of Jesus are presented: Lamb of God, Rabbi, Messiah, Son of God, king of Israel, and Son of Man. The pilgrimage of faith is one in which the disciple proceeds beyond seeing Jesus as Rabbi to the understanding of Jesus as Son of God, as the very source for God's spirit in the world today.

## Retelling the Story

"Nazareth!" Nathanael exclaimed. "Can anything good come from Nazareth?" (John 1:46a)

Nobody expected it of Nathanael. Philip, yes, and his friends, the impetuous Andrew and Simon, of course. But not Nathanael, the model citizen, the pillar

39

of the community. Yet now here he was, leaving behind everything he had ever worked for. And for what?

It all started with the two brothers, Simon and Andrew. They had always been rather wild in their youth. Sure, they had settled down for awhile to work as fishermen. And they were pretty good at it, too. But the next thing you knew, they were off again on some wild-goose chase.

Lately they had been hanging around down by the river with an unkempt bunch of hippie types and their guru, a strange-looking fellow called John the Baptist. It seems that John was offering some kind of alternative view of the world, and the young idealistic types were flocking to him.

Simon and Andrew were always doing something like that—always looking for a better way, always wanting to reform the world, feed the hungry, save the whales, stuff like that.

The call of Jesus to his disciples here has parallels to the call of Lady Wisdom. In Prov. 1:20-33, Wisdom "cries aloud in the open air" for the wise to follow her, but many "refused to listen to my call." Wisdom 6:12-16 puts the call of Lady Wisdom in terms quite close to John's: "Wisdom . . . is readily discerned by those who love her, and by those who seek her she is found. She is quick to make herself known to all who desire knowledge of her; he who rises early in search of her will not grow weary in the quest, for he will find her seated at his door . . . she herself searches far and wide for those who are worthy of her, and on their daily path she appears to them with kindly intent, meeting them halfway in all their purposes." (from Brown, *The Gospel According to John,* 1.79)

Then this new fellow came along, named Jesus, from Nazareth of all places, and before you knew it they had latched on to him. What they saw in him is hard to comprehend. The man from Nazareth was something of a failure, a wandering teacher who barely got by on contributions from others who felt sorry for him. Apparently he had never been able to hold a steady job. But that did not matter to his groupies. They hung on every word he said.

So you could see where it was all heading. Before too long Simon and Andrew would also be wandering the streets looking for handouts—that is, unless they came to their senses and returned to their jobs as fishermen.

And then there was Philip. He was more of a stay-at-home type who tended to his duties. But he had always secretly admired the two brothers. So it should have come as no surprise that he got caught up in their latest cause.

But Nathanael? How did he get involved in this? Nathanael was known for his hard-headed pragmatism. He would not put up with any foolishness. So when Philip came to him that day and said they had finally found the Messiah, you knew Nathanael had to see right through him. There was no way the Messiah could be an itinerant preacher from a backwater community like Nazareth.

Not that Nathanael did not believe in the Messiah. Far from it. Nathanael longed with all that was in him for the day when God's chosen one would come and bring justice to the world. Nathanael may have had a gruff exterior, but inside he had a soft heart. Others may have hardened themselves against the suffering around them, but Nathanael took notice. Others might overlook the beggars at the gate, the hungry in the street, the lepers, the blind, the poor—all the forgotten ones of society—but Nathanael felt their pain. And his heart ached for them. That is why he used to dream of the coming of the Messiah.

But perhaps he had cared too deeply, because lately it had begun to wear on him. He had grown impatient with the lack of any real change in society. He had long ago lost the optimism of his youth. Now he was becoming a cynical old curmudgeon. He no longer believed that change was possible. He no longer expected the Messiah in his lifetime.

So when Philip made his remark about having found the Messiah, Nathanael just scoffed at him. All Nathanael had to do was look around him; it was clear that nothing had changed. And it did not take a great Bible scholar to figure out that Jesus was all wrong for the part. As Nathanael so eloquently put it, "Can anything good come from Nazareth?"

Now here is where the story gets a bit strange. After he actually met Jesus, Nathanael, that no-nonsense pillar of pragmatism, did a totally uncharacteristic thing—he left behind his job and his financial security to join up with the man from Nazareth. It just didn't make any sense. Jesus must have really pulled the wool over old Nathanael's eyes to make him do such a foolish thing.

The thing is, Nathanael got it right the first time. Nothing good, leastwise the Messiah, for crying out loud, can come from Nazareth! That is just not how it is supposed to work.

So Nathanael remained a mystery to everyone. The last anyone heard, he still had not come to his senses. And when you would meet him on the road, and demand an explanation for his bizarre behavior, he would just look at you with a twinkle in his eye and say, "Sometimes you have to follow your dream."

*(Dennis E. Smith)*

According to a Jewish midrash on Jacob's dream (*Genesis Rabbah* 69.3), the angels ascend and descend not upon the ladder but upon Jacob. This is similar to the language here in verse 51, where the angels ascend and descend upon the Son of Man. Another midrash (*Genesis Rabbah* 68:12) locates Jacob's true appearance in heaven while his body lies on earth. The angels therefore move between the two. This would fit the idea that the Son of Man is being proclaimed here as the connection between heaven and earth. (from Brown, *The Gospel According to John*, 1.90)

# The Wedding Feast at Cana

*Jesus does his first sign at Cana and his disciples believe.*

## The Story

TWO DAYS later there was a wedding at Cana-in-Galilee. The mother of Jesus was there, and Jesus and his disciples were also among the guests. The wine gave out, so Jesus's mother said to him, 'They have no wine left.' He answered, 'That is no concern of mine. My hour has not yet come.' His mother said to the servants, 'Do whatever he tells you.' There were six stone water-jars standing near, of the kind used for Jewish rites of purification; each held from twenty to thirty gallons. Jesus said to the servants, 'Fill the jars with water,' and they filled them to the brim. 'Now draw some off,' he ordered, 'and take it to the master of the feast'; and they did so. The master tasted the water now turned into wine, not knowing its source, though the servants who had drawn the water knew. He hailed the bridegroom and said, 'Everyone else serves the best wine first, and the poorer only when the guests have drunk freely; but you have kept the best wine till now.'

So Jesus performed at Cana-in-Galilee the first of the signs which revealed his glory and led his disciples to believe in him.

## Comments on the Story

No sooner has Jesus said, "you will see greater things than that" (1:50), than he sets about to show them. But his choice for a first miracle seems to be a strange one. After all, no one is healed, and only the disciples seem to take notice of it. We must look closely at this enigmatic miracle to see why it is so important in John.

The story of the wedding feast at Cana is a part of the larger story of the calling of the disciples. Like other stories of discipleship that will appear in John's Gospel, the motivation for faith here is response to the sign performed by Jesus (2:11). In this way, the first disciples exemplify the faith journey in its proper form as it will be presented throughout John.

The setting of a wedding feast is clearly symbolic. The fact that the bride, groom, and host of the party remain anonymous help to reinforce this point. In John's Gospel, virtually every aspect of the Jesus story is symbolic; this story is no different. The ancient mind was more attuned to its symbolic potential than we are, because stories about banquets and miraculous provisions of wine were abundant in myth and folklore. There were no supermarkets.

Jewish tradition is most pertinent here. A standard motif in Jewish messianic speculation was the messianic banquet. This was used as a potent symbol for the joys of the coming age—it would be like a great banquet with an abundant table of unending food and wine. On that day the people of God would gather to celebrate the feast of salvation, and the people would come from the nations of the earth and gather at the feast before God (Isa. 25:6-8). To specify that the messianic banquet was also a wedding banquet was not unusual. In the narrative context of John's Gospel, the wedding feast provides a standard way to indicate a meal that could easily be recognized in the culture as a feast of celebration.

Consequently, when the wine suddenly begins to run out, the double meaning of the story is still operative. Neither the wedding feast of the story nor the messianic banquet of symbol can proceed without wine, for wine is the beverage of festive celebration in the ancient world.

Though it may seem odd that Jesus' mother intervenes here, from a symbolic perspective it makes sense. Like John the Baptist, the mother of Jesus (who, incidentally, is never referred to by name in John) is a kind of divine messenger rather than a normal human being. Like the Baptist, she is not required to go through a process of faith in John's story world, and like the Baptist, she is privy to divine knowledge about events. Thus, while the story has a certain degree of verisimilitude in its depiction of apparent friction between Jesus and his mother, it is really the symbolic meaning of the story that is driving the action.

When Jesus' mother informs Jesus that the wine is depleted, she is serving as a kind of "divine advocate" (as opposed to "devil's advocate"), for, after all, Jesus ends up doing what she wants. Yet he must first reply, "My hour has not yet come." In John, the "hour" and its coming is often spoken of as the climax toward which the story is proceeding. When the hour finally does come, as Jesus pronounces at 17:1, it is clearly the event of the crucifixion, resurrection, and return to heaven that is meant. The hour is the arrival of the messianic age; since it is not yet, then it is not time for Jesus to provide the miraculous wine. But he does so anyway. In doing so under duress, he is able to symbolize the already/not-yet nature of the kingdom of God. Though the time is not right, Jesus does the miracle anyway, and, like all his miracles, its meaning consists of the way in which it prefigures eternal life in the messianic age.

While the primary background for the story's symbolism is the Jewish messianic banquet, this symbolism would also make sense to a purely Greek audience as well. For the Greeks, Dionysus, the god of wine, was one of the most powerful and ubiquitous of all the gods, since he was present in the wine at any banquet. Dionysus could provide wine in a miraculous way and was often said to have done so in Greek myth. Jesus would here be seen to be supplanting the Greek god of wine and presenting himself as "the Creator of the Fruit of the Vine" as Jews termed God in their traditional benediction over wine.

As the sign of the messianic age, the wine miracle also picks up on another motif in John. The jars of water were present for Jewish purification rituals. Jesus is seen to reinterpret Jewish ritual by replacing the water of purification with a fine wine of celebration. It is a theme that will be repeated again and again in John as Jesus will consistently reinterpret Jewish tradition. Here the primary emphasis lies on the fact that in the messianic age the need for purification is replaced by direct access to God for all people at the feast of celebration.

The banquet at the end of time, also known as the messianic banquet, was a popular motif in Jewish thought. The magnificence of the feast often included references to great quantities of wine, since it was the standard beverage for festive occasions. Here is an example: "It will happen that when all that which should come to pass in these parts has been accomplished, the Anointed One will begin to be revealed. . . . On one vine will be a thousand branches, and one branch will produce a thousand clusters, and one cluster will produce a thousand grapes, and one grape will produce a cor of wine. And those who are hungry will enjoy themselves and they will, moreover, see marvels every day." Although Jesus' hour had not yet come, he provided a foretaste of that great banquet with the miracle at Cana. (2 Bar. 29:1-8 [ca. 100 C.E.]; from Boring, pp. 249-50, no. 375)

## Retelling the Story

The master tasted the water now turned into wine, not knowing its source, though the servants who had drawn the water knew. (John 2:9)

This was the biggest event of the year in the little town of Cana. That nice Rabinowitz boy and that sweet Goldberg girl were getting married. The party would last for a week. Everybody who was anybody would be there.

Well, the big day came and everybody was there. Even Jesus and his disciples showed up. And Mary, too, Jesus' mother. Before long, Mary happened to hear one of the servants whisper to the wine steward that they were almost out of liquid refreshment.

Now there are some things in life you just don't want to do. You don't want to insult a three-hundred-pound-biker named Tank. You don't want to leave the house wearing dirty underwear. You don't want to throw up at a ceremonial dinner in a foreign country. And you don't want to run out of liquid refreshment at a Jewish wedding. The bad news began to spread.

Mary walked over to Jesus and said quietly, "Son, it's time to quit playing Clark Kent and do your stuff."

Jesus answered something like this: "Mom, don't involve me in this. You know I don't do parlor tricks."

"But, son," said Mary, "these people need help. I know you'll do the right thing." Then she turned to a servant and said, "See this man? Do whatever he tells you. Trust me."

Jesus was on the spot. Oh well, maybe this was as good a time as any to get started. He said to the servants, "You see those six water jars? Fill them up with water. Then give the steward a drink."

"Yum, Yum," said the steward. "Good stuff. Who brought *this*?" Everyone was amazed, for they knew not whence the wine had come. But the servants knew. And they applauded loudly in the kitchen. "That guy Jesus is really good," they said. "He should turn professional." And he did.

*(Phyllis Williams Provost and Barbara McBride-Smith)*

Chrysostom explained the unusual reply of Jesus to his mother in terms of his divine/human nature: "Now, when parents in no way hinder—or forbid—the things of God, it is necessary and fitting to be submissive, and not to do so is very dangerous, but if ever they make some ill-advised request, and stand in the way of a spiritual good, it is not safe to obey. . . . Because she was His Mother, after the manner of other mothers she expected as His Mother to have His obedience in all respects, while her place was to reverence and adore Him as her Lord. That is why, therefore, he then replied as He did." (Chrysostom, *Homilies on John* 21 [late-fourth century C.E.])

There were many stories in the ancient world telling about Dionysus, the god of wine, bringing forth wine in a miraculous way. One such story was told by Pausanias, who traveled through Greece in the second century C.E. He described a festival of Dionysus in which the priests of the god would put three empty pots in the ceremonial building in the presence of all interested witnesses and seal the building shut. The next day when they returned and broke the seals, they would enter to find the pots miraculously filled with wine. Variations of the same story were told in various other cities. For Christian believers, Jesus' miracle would have been seen as a form of one-upmanship, effectively claiming for Jesus powers that had formerly been relegated by the culture to Dionysus. (Pausanias, *Description of Greece* 6.26.1-2; from Boring, p. 248, no. 371)

45

# The Cleansing of the Temple

*Jesus begins his public ministry by driving animal sellers and money changers from the temple.*

## The Story

As it was near the time of the Jewish Passover, Jesus went up to Jerusalem. In the temple precincts he found the dealers in cattle, sheep, and pigeons, and the money-changers seated at their tables. He made a whip of cords and drove them out of the temple, sheep, cattle, and all. He upset the tables of the money-changers, scattering their coins. Then he turned on the dealers in pigeons: 'Take them out of here,' he said; 'do not turn my Father's house into a market.' His disciples recalled the words of scripture: 'Zeal for your house will consume me.' The Jews challenged Jesus: 'What sign can you show to justify your action?' 'Destroy this temple,' Jesus replied, 'and in three days I will raise it up again.' The Jews said, 'It has taken forty-six years to build this temple. Are you going to raise it up again in three days?' But the temple he was speaking of was his body. After his resurrection his disciples recalled what he had said, and they believed the scripture and the words that Jesus had spoken.

## Comments on the Story

Immediately after his first sign, Jesus next performs his first prophetic action in opposition to the religious complacency in his world. This story and the previous story, the miracle at Cana, introduce two of the primary motifs of John. On the one hand, there is the story of the faith of the community, exemplified in the belief of the disciples when Jesus does his first sign in Cana. On the other hand, there is the opposition between Jesus and the Jewish leaders, an opposition that is brought into focus in this story.

To be sure, the theme of conflict between Jesus and certain segments of Judaism had already been indicated in John prior to this. It is addressed in the statement, "He came to his own, and his own people would not accept him" (1:11), as well as in the symbolism whereby the jars of water for Jewish purification rituals were made into jars of new wine (2:6). There is also a degree of tension implied in the notation that the team of priests and Levites sent to question John came from "the Jews of Jerusalem" (1:19).

The story of Jesus cleansing the temple is found in the three synoptic

46

Gospels also, but in a very different context. In those Gospels, Jesus does this prophetic act as he enters Jerusalem at the end of his ministry, almost as a climax to his ministry, during the visit that will end with his crucifixion. John presents this as the first public act of Jesus (since the miracle of wine at the wedding feast is not noticed by the general public). For John, this story serves as a benchmark for all of Jesus' ministry. He is putting the world and the emerging early church on notice that Jesus' ministry involves a radical reform of Jewish traditions.

The story takes place during the Passover festival, a time when the temple would have been a focus of much activity. Those who are at the temple precincts selling animals of various kinds and changing money are performing necessary services to support the ritual of sacrifice. Yet something about their presence upsets Jesus. He attacks them with a homemade whip, driving out the animals and overturning the tables of the money changers. This characterization of Jesus puts him in the role of a prophet, much like the Old Testament prophets, who often acted out their teachings with passionate demonstrations.

Jesus' explanation for his action is somewhat obscure: "Do not turn my Father's house into a market." He sounds like he is opposed to the selling of any items at all, yet these vendors are offering an important service to the people. Jesus is certainly not opposed to the temple or sacrifice, since he refers to the temple as "my Father's house." His action, like that of the Old Testament prophet, is best seen as an attack on the complacency that he sees creeping into the religion of his people. His is a messianic zeal for the house of God.

A second theme then develops in the story. When Jesus is questioned about his actions, the question takes on a specifically Johannine tone: "What sign can you show to justify your action?" Jesus replies in a typically enigmatic way, "Destroy this temple and in three days I will raise it up again." The narrator explains that it is the destruction of his body and his resurrection after three days that he means. That will be the sign that he will do. And that sign will confirm his authority to reform the temple.

The narrator then tells us that the disciples did not understand this at the time, but they understood later, after the sign (that is, his resurrection) took place. This reference is necessary since the sign had not taken place yet, and since their faith will be built on the sign of the resurrection as well as on the additional sign that Jesus' prediction came to pass. This act of "remembering" after the fact acts as a commentary on the experience of the Johannine community. They were living in a time of conflict in which events were happening that they did not envision when they first signed on to this Christian faith journey. They can draw assurance from the fact that much about the Jesus story did not make sense until later. In fact, that is the way the spirit works, for it is only after Jesus was gone that this process would begin anyway. That is the meaning of the words of Jesus in 16:1-15, when he explains that "I did not tell you this at first, because then I was with you . . . it is in your interest that I am leaving you. If I do not go, the advocate will not come, . . . when the Spirit of truth comes, he will guide you into all the truth."

In the face of religious corruption or mediocrity, the prophet of God will be "consumed" with "zeal" for the "house of God." That zeal may lead to actions to restore worship to the standards of "spirit and truth." Those standards may be defined especially by the radical vision of discipleship that is being developed in John's Gospel. In this context, faith is not defined as belief in the content of the message, although that definition often lies behind our sense for the difference between and among Jews and Christians today. Rather, faith refers to the radical claims God makes on the life of the individual. John is talking about the difference between living in darkness and living in light, not differences in creeds. And the one who steps out on that path of faith may often find that the way will be filled with unexpected twists and turns that can only make sense in retrospect, after the journey is complete.

### Retelling the Story

After his resurrection his disciples recalled what he had said, and they believed the scripture and the words that Jesus had spoken. (John 2:22)

The first Jerusalem temple was built during the reign of Solomon and destroyed during the Babylonian conquest in 587 B.C.E. It was rebuilt after the return from exile, beginning in 520 B.C.E., but the temple in Jesus' time had been extensively remodeled by Herod the Great, beginning in 20 B.C.E., calculated by John to be forty-six years prior to the event of Jesus' cleansing. This was known as the second temple. Herod's rebuilding was actually not completed until 63 C.E. Josephus provides an account of the rebuilding: "It was at this time, in the eighteenth year of his reign . . . that Herod undertook an extraordinary work, namely the reconstructing of the temple of God at his own expense, enlarging its precincts and raising it to a more imposing height. For he believed that the accomplishment of this task would be the most notable of all the things achieved by him, as indeed it was, and would be great enough to assure his eternal remembrance. . . . And it was said that during the time when the temple was being built no rain fell during the day, but only at night, so that there was no interruption of the work. And this story, which our fathers have handed down to us, is not at all incredible if, that is, one considers the other manifestations of power given by God. Such, then, was the way in which the temple was rebuilt." (Josephus, *Antiquities,* 15.384 and 425 [ca. 90 C.E.])

Simeon had been a livestock dealer all his life, and his father before him. He always got to the temple early to claim his spot. People looked for him there. They knew him and trusted him. His cattle and sheep always met the requirements specified in the law for sacrifice. Now he could only watch in dismay as his livestock scattered into the city. He was ruined. Why? How had it happened? Who was this crazy Galilean anyway?

It was then that Simeon saw him. One of the followers of the Galilean, the one they called Thomas, was sitting alone, surveying the scene, and shaking his head dejectedly. Simeon ran over to him and said, "Hey, you, do you realize what you people have cost me?"

"I know, I know," said Thomas. "I'll send Judas over tomorrow to see if we can cover your losses."

"What was this all about?" said Simeon.

"I don't know," replied Thomas. "Something set him off—I'm not sure what. It's just that he feels so deeply . . . "

"Yeah, right! That's obvious," said

> The second temple was destroyed in the year 70 C.E. during the Jewish revolt against the Romans. It was never rebuilt. Both Christian and Jewish tradition interpreted its destruction in theological terms. Here is an example from rabbinic tradition that is not unlike the tone of Jesus' cleansing of the temple. "Rabbi Johanan ben Torta said: 'Why was the first Temple destroyed? Because of idolatry, unchastity and murder. But in the days of the second Temple, they were earnest about the Torah, and careful about tithes. Why then did the destruction come? Because they loved money, and hated one another. So learn that the hate of man for his fellow-man is a sore sin before God, and weighs as heavily as idolatry and unchastity and murder.' " (*Tosefta Menahot* 13.22; from Montefiore and Loewe, 463)

Simeon. "He seemed to think we were committing a crime or something. Doesn't he know anything about how the temple operates? We provide a service for people—we sell the animals they need to sacrifice. Without us, no one could sacrifice. And if they can't sacrifice, they can't obey God. It's as simple as that. So, don't we deserve to be paid for our services? Isn't the workman worthy of his wages?"

"Sure you are," said Thomas. "Don't take it personally. I don't think it was directed at you."

"Then what was it all about? Is he an atheist or something? Doesn't he understand the law, that sacrifice is what God commands?"

"Yes, yes, he knows that. And no, he is not an atheist. Far from it—if anything, he believes too much."

"Then what is his problem?"

Josephus recounts another story of a warning about the destruction of the temple: "But a further portent was even more alarming. Four years before the war [that is, the Jewish revolt against Rome in 66 C.E.], when the city was enjoying profound peace and prosperity, there came to the feast at which it is the custom of all Jews to erect tabernacles to God, one Jesus, son of Ananias, a rude peasant, who, standing in the temple, suddenly began to cry out, 'A voice from the east, a voice from the west, a voice from the four winds; a voice against Jerusalem and the sanctuary.' " Josephus goes on to describe his arrest and scourging, to which he would only respond, "Woe to Jerusalem!" He continued his prophecies until he saw them being fulfilled during the siege of Jerusalem, during which he also perished. (Josephus, *Jewish War*, 6.300-9 [ca. 80 C.E.])

Thomas pondered this a moment. "I don't know. It's strange. It's as if he wants people to have access to God whether they can pay for it or not."

"Yeah, wouldn't we all! Well, that is not the way the real world is, buddy! And he better get used to it."

"I know. I just hope he figures this out soon. I have felt from the beginning that he was special, but after this, I wonder. What a way to begin a ministry! I'll stick with him a while longer, but he is sure going to have to show me more than this." *(Dennis E. Smith)*

# Nicodemus

*Nicodemus misses his chance at true faith.*

## The Story

WHILE he was in Jerusalem for Passover many put their trust in him when they saw the signs that he performed. But Jesus for his part would not trust himself to them. He knew them all, and had no need of evidence from others about anyone, for he himself could tell what was in people.

One of the Pharisees, called Nicodemus, a member of the Jewish Council, came to Jesus by night. 'Rabbi,' he said, 'we know that you are a teacher sent by God; no one could perform these signs of yours unless God were with him.' Jesus answered, 'In very truth I tell you, no one can see the kingdom of God unless he has been born again.' 'But how can someone be born when he is old?' asked Nicodemus. 'Can he enter his mother's womb a second time and be born?' Jesus answered, 'In very truth I tell you, no one can enter the kingdom of God without being born from water and spirit. Flesh can give birth only to flesh; it is spirit that gives birth to spirit. You ought not to be astonished when I say, "You must all be born again." The wind blows where it wills; you hear the sound of it, but you do not know where it comes from or where it is going. So it is with everyone who is born from the Spirit.'

'How is this possible?' asked Nicodemus. 'You a teacher of Israel and ignorant of such things!' said Jesus. 'In very truth I tell you, we speak of what we know, and testify to what we have seen, and yet you all reject our testimony. If you do not believe me when I talk to you about earthly things, how are you to believe if I should talk about the things of heaven?

'No one has gone up into heaven except the one who came down from heaven, the Son of Man who is in heaven. Just as Moses lifted up the serpent in the wilderness, so the Son of Man must be lifted up, in order that everyone who has faith may in him have eternal life.

'God so loved the world that he gave his only Son, that everyone who has faith in him may not perish but have eternal life. It was not to judge the world that God sent his Son into the world, but that through him the world might be saved.

'No one who puts his faith in him comes under judgement; but the unbeliever has already been judged because he has not put his trust in God's only Son. This is the judgement: the light has come into the world, but people preferred darkness to light because their deeds were evil. Wrongdoers hate the light and avoid it, for fear their misdeeds should be exposed. Those who live by the truth come to the light so that it may be clearly seen that God is in all they do.'

51

## Comments on the Story

The Nicodemus story introduces a new theme in John. How are we to understand people who profess faith in the signs but whose actions belie their words? For John, faith in the signs is code language for true faith; it is a concept unique to John. The conclusion to the miracle at Cana defines the concept: "signs" (John's term for miracles) manifest "glory" (or the divinity of Jesus). Belief in the "signs," therefore, is to recognize who Jesus is, or, in the words of 1:14, to confront "Word [become] flesh" and to see, with the eyes of faith, not the "flesh" but the "glory."

But faith in the signs is more than just an intellectual assent. That is stated clearly in the introduction to the Nicodemus story. Here we are told that "many put their trust in him when they saw the signs that he performed . . . but Jesus . . . would not trust himself to them . . . for he himself could tell what was in people." This brief verse in many respects defines the cutting edge of what John's Gospel is all about. In his world, too many people were willing to claim faith in Jesus, but when push came to shove, many of those people were suddenly scarce. John proposes that the problem is a theological one—their faith was inadequate in the first place. And Nicodemus is exhibit A in his definition of inadequate faith that is based on signs.

In the Greek, the connection between the introductory section (2:23-25) and the beginning of the Nicodemus story is clearer than this translation suggests. Verse 25 closes with the comment that Jesus knew what was in such "people" (Greek: *anthropos*). The next verse begins with the phrase "there was such a person" (Greek: *anthropos*) thus presenting the Nicodemus story as an example of those who believed in the signs but whom Jesus could not trust.

Nicodemus emerges here as a stereotype, as a kind of "everyman" of inadequate faith. He is identified by means of other loaded terms as well, for to be a "Pharisee" and a "member of the Jewish Council" means in John that you are an enemy of Jesus. Nicodemus is also one who comes "by night," a designation that is not just incidental to the story, because it is repeated later in the Gospel when Nicodemus is mentioned again (19:39).

The play of light and darkness is a frequent symbolic theme in John. The Word came as "the light [that] shines in the darkness" (1:5) yet Nicodemus comes "by night." One can imagine this story as if it is taking place on an empty stage. A single spotlight illuminates Jesus. The only other character on stage is Nicodemus, who hovers at the edge of the light but never steps fully into the light. As the story proceeds, Nicodemus strangely fades from the scene; we are never told what happens to him. It is as if he gradually fades back into the night from which he came. The conclusion to the story supports this dramatization: "This is the judgement: the light has come into the world, but people preferred darkness to light because their deeds were evil" (3:19).

Though Nicodemus is a stereotype, he nevertheless is not a completely flat character. In fact, he is almost a sympathetic character. When he comes to Jesus he makes an honest inquiry of him, for, after all, he is a believer in the signs. Jesus, on the other hand, speaks in riddles, using a pun in Greek in which "born again" (or reborn) and "born from above" are both valid meanings of the same word (Greek: *anōthen*). Of course, the concept "born again" is a pun in itself, since it can refer either to physical or spiritual birth. Nicodemus makes what might seem to be an honest mistake; he thinks Jesus is talking about physical rebirth and he does not understand.

Why doesn't Jesus help him out a little here? Why must Jesus be so obtuse? Clearly we are not dealing with a realistic conversation but a symbolic one. The obtuseness of Jesus is a regular device in John to separate the children of light from the children of darkness. Those who have seen "the glory" will understand. They are the ones who play the role of true believers in John's story; they are stand-ins for the members of John's own community to whom the Gospel is addressed. The children of darkness, on the other hand, will show by their misunderstanding their lack of faith. This helps to explain the unusually high level of symbolic language that is so characteristic of John. It functions like a secret language, understood only by the faithful who are members of the community.

In our imaginary stage setting for this story, we envisioned a stage empty except for the two actors, Jesus and Nicodemus. At verse 9 Nicodemus says his last lines, "How is this possible?" After this, his presence is no longer indicated. In fact, we should imagine Jesus at this point turning from Nicodemus to address the audience, for his words from verse 11 on are no longer addressed to a single individual but to a group for which Nicodemus is only the representative. "In very truth," Jesus says, "we [plural!] speak of what we know, and testify to what we have seen, and yet you all [plural!] reject our testimony." The use of plural pronouns causes the story to cross over into the life and experience of the community of faith for whom the Gospel is written. The "we" here is the church, and the "you" represents the detractors of their day. Based on internal evidence in John, found especially in chapter 9, we can conclude that John's community was a Jewish Christian sect that still maintained its primary identity within larger Judaism. But now they were being persecuted and expelled from the only religious home they had ever known, the synagogue. By retelling the Jesus story in this way, they have found a way to understand and deal with the traumatic events in their own lives. Thus when Jesus speaks of testimony and rejection, he is not only speaking of events in his story, but events in the community's story as well. His story becomes their story. And Nicodemus becomes a symbol, albeit a poignant one, of what must have been a substantial group of their countrymen and women who were once considered members of the group but now had forsaken them.

The theological definition of Nicodemus's failure is concentrated on the term "born again/from above." Though he believes in the signs, he obviously lacks this level of faith. "New birth" is a powerful image for a radical change in social location. Belief must be so total that one has, in essence, been born again into a new clan, for, after all, it was one's original birth that constituted one's membership in Judaism. To put it another way, true belief in the signs, so that one sees the "glory" rather than the "flesh," is functionally equivalent to a total change in social location, a rebirth into a new community. You can't have one without the other.

How is the new birth to be judged? Obviously it cannot be judged by testimony alone, no matter how convincing it might be. Such testimonies must have come from many who "believed in the signs" among John's community. No, the new birth is judged by "deeds," and those of the darkness are identified by their "evil deeds." What evil deeds might be in mind here? They doubtless consisted of the many betrayals of the faith that the community of John was experiencing among their number. The Nicodemuses of the world might be able to say all the right things, but until they put their lives on the line for the faith, they are still people who "prefer darkness to light."

## Retelling the Story

"But how can someone be born when he is old?" asked Nicodemus. "Can he enter his mother's womb a second time and be born?" (John 3:4)

Chrysostom explained the obscure nature of Jesus' discourse with Nicodemus to be a teaching device: "Now, it was for this reason that Christ often spoke obscurely, because He wished to make His hearers more inclined to ask questions and to cause them to be more attentive. What has been said with its meaning obvious often escapes the listener, but what has been said obscurely makes him more curious and eager." (Chrysostom, *Homilies on John* 24 [late-fourth century C.E.])

I'll never forget what Old Man Nick Demos told me about the time he met this Jesus feller. He used to talk to me a lot about things he couldn't talk to nobody else about. All I done was clean up his office of an evenin'. While I was gettin' the trash out of the trash cans and dustin' the desk he would lotsa times ask me questions or tell me things.

One evenin' I was working round the office and he up and asked me, "Zeb, do you believe in God?" I allowed that I did. Then he went on, "You believe God can do anything?" I allowed that God hadn't ever had to ask my permission to do anything, but I figured that just about anything was possible with Old Jehovah.

Then he asked the downright strangest thing, "You believe that somebody could get back up inside their mama and be born all over again?" I was so bumfuzzled by the question that I didn't know what to say at first. I just couldn't feature it, if you know what I mean. Before I could answer he told me that this was what this Jesus feller said to him about gettin' born all over again from above. I said surely to goodness that what Mr. Nick was imaginin' was not what Jesus meant. Maybe it had a spiritual meanin', and he just hadn't found it yet. He didn't say anymore, and I just finished my work.

Nick Demos was a politician from the word go and served in the state legislature. He was an educated man and a lawyer. He thought about deep things that most of the rest of us never have the time or interest for. He kept up with things and read more magazines than any man I ever did see—not them trashy kind, though, but the kind that keep you up on current events. I never seen him read any religious magazines, but he sure did talk about them, to me at least. Maybe he knew that I was raised Baptist and was used to talkin' about such things without it embarrassing me.

Another night he asked, "Zeb, you believe that God loves the whole world?" Well sir, I told him, if God can love me after all the wickedness I've done and all the good I didn't do when I should've done somethin', then he can love about anybody. Sometimes I just allowed that these questions were from a midlife crisis. I think that's what they call it. I can't say for sure since I've never had the time or money for one myself.

About a year or so after that, Mr. Nick called me in his office and asked me to sit down. Well, I mean to tell you this got me scared that I had done somethin' wrong and was about to lose my job. I mean, I never before was asked to sit down to talk. It made me nervous as a cat in a roomful of rockers to sit there eye to eye, so to speak. "Tomorrow there will be a vote in my committee at the legislature on a bill to ban traveling evangelists who hold no official standing in a recognized religious body. That would include this Jesus I have spoken to you about. My constituents are leery of traveling preachers to begin with, and a vote to ban would probably be pretty popular among them. What do you think?"

Don't matter what I think or don't think, I told him. Only thing matters is what God's put on your heart to vote. "I'm inclined at this time to vote against the ban, based on my personal experience with this Jesus. I think I am finally beginning to understand what he was telling me before, about being born, I mean." Then the decision's made, I told him.

Rabbinic tradition also used the language of new birth to refer to proselytes: "Rabbi Jose ben Halafta said: 'A proselyte who embraces Judaism is like a newborn child. God cannot therefore now chastise him for deeds done or duties neglected before his new birth.' " (*Babylonian Talmud Yebamoth* 48B; from Boring, p. 259, no. 388)

Come to find out Mr. Nick not only voted against the ban in the committee, but when it came to the floor, he even got up and made a speech defendin' the good that Jesus had done. Told me once he still worried some what the voters would think, but somethin' musta convinced him to go against his political instincts this one time.

Didn't do much good in the long run. Jesus got arrested for a capital crime and wound up gettin' executed. I thought after that that Mr. Nick would lay low, but no siree. Some friend of his went down to the execution site big as you please askin' for Jesus' body. Mr. Nick and this other feller had already made the funeral arrangements.

I never asked him, but I figure he must've done some real thinkin' about what Jesus said about gettin' born and God lovin' the whole world. I have just about decided it wasn't no midlife crisis after all. No, it was just that after Jesus, life for Mr. Nick was never as simple again. *(Michael E. Williams)*

# The Samaritan Woman

*The Samaritan woman encounters Jesus at the well and becomes an exemplary disciple.*

### The Story

NEWS now reached the Pharisees that Jesus was winning and baptizing more disciples than John; although, in fact, it was his disciples who were baptizing, not Jesus himself. When Jesus heard this, he left Judaea and set out once more for Galilee. He had to pass through Samaria, and on his way came to a Samaritan town called Sychar, near the plot of ground which Jacob gave to his son Joseph; Jacob's well was there. It was about noon, and Jesus, tired after his journey, was sitting by the well.

His disciples had gone into the town to buy food. Meanwhile a Samaritan woman came to draw water, and Jesus said to her, 'Give me a drink.' The woman said, 'What! You, a Jew, ask for a drink from a Samaritan woman?' (Jews do not share drinking vessels with Samaritans.) Jesus replied, 'If only you knew what God gives, and who it is that is asking you for a drink, you would have asked him and he would have given you living water.' 'Sir,' the woman said, 'you have no bucket and the well is deep, so where can you get "living water"? Are you greater than Jacob our ancestor who gave us the well and drank from it himself, he and his sons and his cattle too?' Jesus answered,

'Everyone who drinks this water will be thirsty again; but whoever drinks the water I shall give will never again be thirsty. The water that I shall give will be a spring of water within him, welling up and bringing eternal life.' 'Sir,' said the woman, 'give me this water, and then I shall not be thirsty, nor have to come all this way to draw water.'

'Go and call your husband,' said Jesus, 'and come back here.' She answered, 'I have no husband.' Jesus said, 'You are right in saying that you have no husband, for though you have had five husbands, the man you are living with now is not your husband. You have spoken the truth!' 'Sir,' replied the woman, 'I can see you are a prophet. Our fathers worshipped on this mountain, but you Jews say that the place where God must be worshipped is in Jerusalem.' 'Believe me,' said Jesus, 'the time is coming when you will worship the Father neither on this mountain nor in Jerusalem. You Samaritans worship you know not what; we worship what we know. It is from the Jews that salvation comes. But the time is coming, indeed it is already here, when true worshippers will worship the Father in spirit and in truth. These are the worshippers the Father wants. God is spirit, and those who worship him must worship in spirit and in truth.' The woman answered, 'I know that Messiah' (that is, Christ) 'is coming. When he comes he will make everything clear to us.' Jesus said to her, 'I am he, I who am speaking to you.'

At that moment his disciples returned, and were astonished to find him talking with a woman; but none of them said, 'What do you want?' or, 'Why are you talking with her?' The woman left her water-jar and went off to the town, where she said to the people, 'Come and see a man who has told me everything I ever did. Could this be the Messiah?' They left the town and made their way towards him.

Meanwhile the disciples were urging him, 'Rabbi, have something to eat.' But he said, 'I have food to eat of which you know nothing.' At this the disciples said to one another, 'Can someone have brought him food?' But Jesus said, 'For me it is meat and drink to do the will of him who sent me until I have finished his work.

'Do you not say, "Four months more and then comes harvest"? But look, I tell you, look around at the fields: they are already white, ripe for harvesting. The reaper is drawing his pay and harvesting a crop for eternal life, so that sower and reaper may rejoice together. That is how the saying comes true: "One sows, another reaps." I sent you to reap a crop for which you have not laboured. Others laboured and you have come in for the harvest of their labour.'

Many Samaritans of that town came to believe in him because of the woman's testimony: 'He told me everything I every did.' So when these Samaritans came to him they pressed him to stay with them; and he stayed there two days. Many more became believers because of what they heard from his own lips. They told the woman, 'It is no longer because of what you said that we believe, for we have heard him ourselves; and we are convinced that he is the Saviour of the world.'

## Comments on the Story

The story of the Samaritan woman is one of the most elaborate stories of discipleship in John. Like other such stories, it is constructed to present in symbolic terms the process of true discipleship. Here, as elsewhere in John, this process centers on Christology, on the theme of the identity of Jesus. Jesus is the Divine Word, and it is those who "see his glory" (see 1:14) who are the ones of true faith. Thus Jesus speaks as if in riddles, and through the process of interpreting what Jesus is saying, the woman is led on a path toward true faith.

The story begins in a setting that reflects biblical traditions. Jesus is at a place identified by local tradition as Jacob's well, presumably the well where the biblical patriarch met Rachel (Gen. 29:1-12). Thus, Jesus, like many patriarchs in the Bible, pauses on a journey through a foreign land to stop and converse with a woman at a well. In those other stories, the meeting at the well has a romantic theme, for it is by means of the meeting that the patriarch finds his wife (compare also the stories of Isaac and Rebekah [Gen. 24:10-27] and

58

Moses and Zipporah [Exod. 2:15-22]). In this story, the woman finds not a husband but a savior.

Jesus initiates the conversation with the traditional request, "Give me a drink" (as in Gen. 24:17). The woman responds in shock and indignation that he would talk to her, a Samaritan. But Jesus immediately moves the conversation to a higher level, noting that he is not like normal people, he is the one who brings "living water." In this way, he implicitly responds to her retort by implying that the one who brings "living water" is not constrained by human barriers.

The woman continues the conversation on a mundane, almost humorous level, opposing his elevated, esoteric speech with pragmatic realism: "You have no bucket, how can you get water?" But she also takes a step toward faith by inquiring, "Are you greater than Jacob who gave us this well?" Jesus responds with a statement at the highest level of theological discourse, presented in the enigmatic, symbolic form that is typical of John: "Everyone who drinks of this water will be thirsty again, but those who drink of the water that I will give them will never be thirsty." It is like a test, to see if the woman, unlike Nicodemus, is able to see the light. She does: "Sir, give me this water."

Now she is ready for the next level of discipleship—she must acknowledge who she is before God. Jesus introduces this theme with a request that sounds patently conventional, "Go, call your husband, and come back." According to convention, Jesus should be talking to the husband rather than the wife anyway. But Jesus has an ulterior motive here. When she responds that she has no husband, he reveals his knowledge that she has in fact had five husbands, and is not legally married to the man with whom she currently lives. Here, in a move typical of John's Gospel, Jesus reveals a divine knowledge of the inner thoughts of people (compare John 2:24-25). The woman responds with a statement of dry humor: "Sir, I see you are a prophet." Yet in John, to confess Jesus as a prophet is to be on the way toward true faith, though not yet there (compare John 6:14). Convention (and the immediate turmoil in John's community) requires a test for this presumed prophet, so the woman asks him to resolve an age-old religious controversy. "Who is right, the Samaritans or the Jews?" But Jesus speaks instead of a new order that renders all religious controversies obsolete: "The time is coming, indeed it is already here, when true worshippers will worship the Father in spirit and in truth." The woman correctly surmises that such an "hour" can only mean that the Messiah has come. Can Jesus be the Messiah? He responds, "I am he."

But her story is not over yet. She now must follow up on her insight into Jesus' true identity with a radical action of discipleship. This she does by preaching to the villagers. Meanwhile, the disciples appear on the scene to take on the role of those who are caught in the middle, those who have faith, but who lack the insight to see its true meaning and implications. Thus they fail to see beyond their stereotypical views of the woman. While Jesus has been pushing the borders of the faith, they have been resisting and have lingered behind, still trapped in the presuppositions of their culture. Now they must listen as Jesus informs them of their status, how it is that they will, in fact, reap what another has sown. While they have been idling away their time, the woman has been carrying out the mission of a true disciple, outshining the very disciples of Jesus' inner circle. Now they see the results of her work as the villagers arrive to see Jesus for themselves. The church of John must have been challenged to see themselves mirrored in the response of the disciples in this story. Like the disciples, they too must recognize the challenges of their mission with new vision. It is a message for the church of every generation.

The woman is a symbol, but not a stereotype that is easily reduced, for the storyteller has many opportunities to explore her character. As a Samaritan she offers us an opportunity to overcome our prejudices about ethnic identity and religious intolerance. The story of Jesus' response to her at the well would resonate with John's community of disciples who are seeking a new identity apart from their former ethnic context. That new identity must also include an openness to those whom they used to despise, yet whom God has now called. This is a message with timeless meaning for the church in any generation, but especially for today's church as it responds to the new reality of a global community.

The woman is also a symbol for women in general. Here she takes on several stereotypical personas: woman as householder (the one who collects water at the well), woman as wife, and fallen woman (she is not even married to the man with whom she lives). Yet Jesus seeks her out by entering into the world of women, which is what the location at the well represents, and by bringing her through the process of faith. Even his retort to get her husband does not end the conversation; he continues to talk to her and thus affirms her as one who is to respond to God as an individual in her own right, not simply as a wife. With the insight of the Divine Word, Jesus identifies her as a "fallen woman." Yet he does not dwell on that point, relishing her sin. Rather his insight serves to move her to a higher level of faith. It is the point in the story of faith in which the individual knows there are no secrets before God, that one comes to God warts and all.

What Jesus offers is "living water," a term that echoes other symbolic references in John to such entities as "bread from heaven" (6:25-51) and "water . . . turned into wine" (2:1-11). Since the symbol is of drinking water, it almost sounds sacramental, except that wine, rather than water, is the usual counterpart to bread at the sacrament. The reference therefore must be seen as one of many that refer to the higher level of faith to which disciples are being called throughout John. Like the woman in this story, readers of John's Gospel are being challenged to go beyond the normal understanding of reality, to "see the glory," to see things not as they are but as they can be.

Does this story suggest that women were functioning in leadership roles in John's church? Jesus seems to affirm the woman in all respects, but neither the disciples nor the villagers follow his lead. The disciples don't ask and don't tell (v. 27), and the villagers' response is condescending (in v. 42). Since the story maintains a tension between Jesus' understanding and that of the disciples in regard to the place of women in the church, it suggests that the issue was under debate in John's church. And each time the story is told, in every generation of the church, it turns out the same—Jesus' vision for the church is always one step ahead of that of his disciples.

## Retelling the Story

At that moment his disciples returned. and were astonished to find him talking with a woman. (John 4:27)

Gathering water from the well. Can you imagine what that must have been like? First of all, you had no other water available in the house except what you brought from the well. Second, the well was not exactly next door, but was quite a walk away. Third, it was the women who had the job of bringing the water. The men had more important things to do: They had to get together with all the other men in the village square.

Now as far as the men were concerned, everything important took place in their part of the world. They discussed world events, crops, and even religion—what the law really means and how important it was to know why the Samaritans are right and the Jews are wrong. They rarely discussed these things with the women—after all, what did they know? Everything important belonged to the world of the men. If anyone important ever came to their village, you can bet he would show up at the village square—that's where the action was.

It was not uncommon for Jewish pilgrims from Galilee to pass through Samaria on their way to Jerusalem at festival time. Such occasions often led to unexpected encounters, such as the occasion when a group of pilgrims was ambushed by Samaritan brigands. Josephus lists this as just one more reason why there was hatred between Samaritans and Jews. (*Antiquities* 20.118 [ca. 90 C.E.])

Meanwhile, back at the house, the women went about their tasks. One such woman is the "she-ro" of our story. She had been the first one out of bed that morning. She lit the fire, began breakfast, waked the kids, roused her husband, finished breakfast, broke up a fight among the two brothers, served breakfast, cleaned up a mess made by the youngest, cleaned the table, washed the dishes, entertained the kids for an hour, sent them out to play, and finally had sat down to rest briefly before going about her next task. Meanwhile, her husband went out to do man's work—he went to the village square to talk over important events with the "boys."

Now it was time to get water for the evening. She got the huge water jar and swung it up to her head. It was easy to carry now—it was empty—but it would be quite a load when she returned.

As she walked out to the well, her mind began to wander as it often did on this regular walk to the well. She passed other women returning from the well, and she saw herself reflected in their images. Women walking carefully and skillfully along the uneven ground, balancing a heavy water jar on their heads, moving along as if the jar were a fancy hat. But of course, it wasn't—it was a heavy weight that could give you a neck ache for weeks if you so much as slipped on a pebble and lost your balance.

Women had been carrying water this way for generations—ever since Rachel, and before that. In fact, it was at this very well that Rachel had met her future husband, Jacob. She thought of that story as she walked to the well. Maybe this would be her lucky day as well! Maybe she would meet a man who would take her away from all this! Yeah, right!

When she arrived at the well, someone was already there. He was a traveler who was passing through and had stopped to rest. She could tell by his dress that he was not from Samaria—he was a Jew. She shuddered, hoping she would not have to talk to him. Jews could be such difficult people to get along with. She walked to the part of the well that was farthest away from him and set down her jug so she could lower it down to draw water.

Then he spoke to her. The nerve! "I want a drink," he said. Typical of a man not to be able to get a drink for himself without the help of a woman! But why would a Jew be speaking to her anyway, even if he was thirsty?

"You know, it's not polite for a Jew to talk that way to a Samaritan, especially when you are here in my country. You want to withdraw that question? We can pretend it never happened."

Then he got even more weird. Didn't she know who he was? Why, if he wanted to, he could get even better water than this. He knew where he could get spring water, the purest kind, and it would come direct from God. Then he said, "Everyone who drinks of this well water will be thirsty again, but those who drink of the water that I will give them will never be thirsty."

She took a closer look at him. Why, he must be some kind of holy man, she thought, one of those crazy people who walk through the countryside talking to themselves. She decided to test him. "Sir," she said, "give me this water, so that I may never be thirsty or have to keep coming here to draw water."

Then he made a typical good ole boy move. "Go get your husband," he said. "I will talk to him." Of course—if there was something important to talk about, he would have to talk with the man of the house. She began to lose interest in the entire conversation. If he wanted to talk to the men, he could find them himself! She was not about to leave her water jug and go running off to find some buddies for him to jaw with!

"I don't have a husband," she blurted. She hoped this would put him off so she could be on her way.

"That's right," he said. "You don't have a husband—you have had five husbands. That means you can't even call the man you are living with now a husband!"

What a low blow! How did he know so much about her? And what did he know about how hard it was to be a woman in this world? She had mouths to feed—and she did it the only way she could. After all, a woman could not make it on her own in this world. She always had to depend on a man—even if some men were just not dependable.

And besides, it was a man's world anyway. A woman could not always control what happened to her—she had to get by the best she could. How could he have the nerve to blame her? If he was so knowledgeable about her, surely he knew why she did what she did.

"Sir, I perceive that you are a prophet," she said. "If you are a prophet, then answer this question. We Samaritans have always worshiped at this mountain. But you Jews say that people can only worship God in Jerusalem. Which is right?"

"Neither," he said. "A new day is coming when we will all worship together. It won't be at this place or that, but it will be wherever we are. Because it will be a new kind of worship."

She paused and stared intently at him. She knew exactly what he was saying. He might be surprised to know it, but she was a fair scholar of the Bible.

"I know that such things will happen when the Messiah comes," she said.

"That is who I am," he said.

> To Chrysostom, the Samaritan woman was an example of faith: "Let us, then, imitate the Samaritan woman; let us converse with Christ. For even now He has taken up His stand in the midst of us, speaking to us through the Prophets and the disciples. Therefore, let us listen and obey." (Chrysostom, *Homilies on John* 31 [late-fourth century C.E.])

She was stunned. This was almost too much to take in. Could it be? Could he be the one? Then it came to her. Of course, who else but the Messiah could have known so much about her? And who else but the Messiah would have spent so much time talking with a woman and overturned generations of tradition in the process?

As she stood there dazed, they were suddenly interrupted by the arrival of his companions. They brushed past her and looked at her as if she did not belong there. They could not understand why Jesus had spent so much time with a woman. They had their own ideas about the priorities of his mission.

The woman left her water jug, ran back to the village, and did something she had never done before. She burst into the village square, right in the midst of the men, and told them the news. At first they were startled that she had the nerve to speak out so boldly in the presence of men. But when they heard what she had to say, that she had met the Messiah, they decided that this was too important to ignore, so they followed her to meet this strange person.

And Jesus began to teach his disciples with a story. "It is like a harvest," he said. "You will find yourselves harvesting what others have planted."

Then he asked those men from the village how they had known where to find him. "Well, we heard from the woman, but we don't put any credence in what a woman says, so we had to come and see for ourselves."

He sighed and looked at the woman, and maybe he smiled. They just didn't get it—but he did. *(Dennis E. Smith and Barbara McBride-Smith)*

# The Royal Officer from Capernaum

*Jesus performs his second sign in Cana by healing the officers' son from afar.*

### The Story

ONCE again he visited Cana-in-Galilee, where he had turned the water into wine. An officer in the royal service was there, whose son was lying ill at Capernaum. When he heard that Jesus had come from Judaea into Galilee, he went to him and begged him to go down and cure his son, who was at the point of death. Jesus said to him, 'Will none of you ever believe without seeing signs and portents?' The officer pleaded with him, 'Sir, come down before my boy dies.' 'Return home,' said Jesus; 'your son will live.' The man believed what Jesus said and started for home. While he was on his way down his servants met him with the news that his child was going to live. So he asked them at what time he had begun to recover, and they told him, 'It was at one o'clock yesterday afternoon that the fever left him.' The father realized that this was the time at which Jesus had said to him, 'Your son will live,' and he and all his household became believers.

This was the second sign which Jesus performed after coming from Judaea into Galilee.

### Comments on the Story

In this story Jesus returns to the scene of the sign, to Cana where he did his first sign. Clearly this sign is meant to be compared with the miracle at the wedding feast (2:1-11). On the surface, the two stories seem unconnected, since one is about miraculous wine and the other is a healing miracle. In our minds, healing would outweigh in importance the provision of wine for a party. But that is not how John sees the miracles. As signs, they all carry equal weight as symbolic events, and all are meant to point to the same theme, the "glory" or divinity of Jesus.

The similarities between the two stories begins with the location at Cana where both signs take place. There is another, more subtle similarity as well. In both stories, the recipient(s) of the miracle do not themselves respond to Jesus. Rather, at the wedding feast it is the disciples who respond, and here it is the officer. This story, then, is clearly the officer's story of faith, and it serves as a model for how faith is to operate in the Christian community in every generation.

65

The man is identified as a *basilikos*, a term designating him as a royal officer who presumably served under Herod Antipas, tetrarch of Galilee. This story is one of the few in John that is also found in the synoptic Gospels. There the story speaks of a Roman centurion from Capernaum who meets Jesus while in Capernaum and expresses his faith that Jesus can heal his slave from afar (Matt. 8:5-13; Luke 7:1-10). John has taken the story and adapted it to his interests. It is still a story of a Capernaum officer who has a son who is healed from afar; but in John, to connect this with Jesus' first sign, the encounter takes place in Cana. John and the synoptics also differ in the manner in which they describe the coming to faith of the officer.

In its context, this story follows on a rather enigmatic section in which Jesus, after leaving Samaria, goes to Galilee specifically because "he himself had declared that a prophet is without honour in his own country." Yet the next verse declares, "On his arrival the Galileans made him welcome, because they had seen all he did at the festival in Jerusalem" (4:43-45). These seemingly contradictory verses can be reconciled if we compare them with 2:23-25. There, also, many were believing in Jesus because of his signs, but Jesus knew better, "for he himself could tell what was in people." Those verses introduce the Nicodemus story. Here, in a similar context, we have another faith story like that of Nicodemus, except where Nicodemus the religious leader failed, the officer succeeds, once again illustrating how true faith can come from unexpected sources, despite our presuppositions about ethnic, social, or religious priority.

Initially, however, it appears that his story will be like that of Nicodemus. For when the officer makes his request of Jesus that he "go down and cure his son, who was at the point of death," Jesus replies angrily, "Will none of you ever believe without seeing signs and portents?" (4:47-48). Once more we come up against John's enigmatic language. Faith in signs is both the proper and the improper means to faith. That equivocation in John's language arose out of the crisis that had engulfed his Christian community. A "signs and wonders" faith was supposed to be correct faith, but when it failed, the whole issue had to be looked at again, and this is one of those instances.

The story has subtleties that must be carefully delineated. First Jesus complains about the request for signs, then he goes ahead and does a sign. What gives? Notice that the original request was that Jesus go down to Capernaum and heal the officer's son. What Jesus says in response is that the man should return home for his son will live. The officer, then, believes the word of Jesus and acts on it, returning home to find his son well. The text then says that "he and all his household became believers" (4:53).

The officer presents a model for faith because (1) he believed in the sign first on the basis of the word alone, and (2) because he acted on his belief by undertaking a journey on the basis of his faith. In the same way, the community of John must believe in the sign, in the glory, of Jesus, but they will have to do so on the basis of the word, for Jesus was no longer present with them to provide signs directly. Like the officer, their faith would need to be expressed by actions, by an uncertain journey toward a distant goal. And, like the officer, they will find life at the end of their journey, but only if they undertake the journey in the first place.

This miracle, like all the miracles in John, is best understood on a symbolic level. When Jesus complains about those who only seek signs, he is rejecting a form of faith that demands miracles in one's individual life, as if to tempt God. What true signs faith is, then, is a faith that sees beyond the miracle to focus on the one who himself is the true miracle. The healing of the officer's son does not provide assurance that Jesus will heal physical illnesses; rather it proclaims that Jesus is the one who brings life, or spiritual healing. Those who miss this point, and still long for the spectacular—in distrust of the Word—will find their faith inadequate when life takes unexpected turns, especially during times of cultural upheaval.

### Retelling the Story

'Return home,' said Jesus; 'your son will live.' The man believed what Jesus said and started for home. (John 4:50)

The general, as he was called, had always been a careful person. He never made rash judgments. It was a characteristic of his profession. He had been a soldier, after all, before he became an officer of the royal court. It was his job to make wise decisions, and he never acted without thoroughly considering all the consequences.

Marcus was the general's only son and he was his pride and joy. When Marcus became ill, the general had begun to search frantically far and wide for a cure, but to no avail. Then he heard about Jesus, and, as a last resort, he decided to look him up.

Now the servants had begun to worry. It was unlike the general to place any credence in magicians. They suspected he had been flimflammed. After all, he had requested that Jesus return with him to Capernaum. That way Jesus would be there to be held accountable if his healing arts did not work. But that Galilean was too slick. He convinced the general to return home without him, on the flimsy claim that he could heal the boy from a distance. Now, here they were, traveling back home on a journey sure to end in disappointment.

"I wonder how much money that shyster got out of the general," Rufus said to the other servants. He decided to try to find out. He strolled over to where his master rode astride his horse and walked beside him.

"General, sir," he said.

A similar story of a healing from afar is told about Rabbi Hanina ben Dosa: "There was the case in which the son of Rabban Gamaliel fell ill. He sent two disciples of sages to Rabbi Hanina ben Dosa to pray for mercy for him. When he saw them, he went up to his upper room and prayed for mercy for him. When he came down, he said to them, 'Go, for his fever has left him.' They said to him, 'Are you a prophet?' He said to them, 'I am not a prophet nor a disciple of a prophet, but this is what I have received as a tradition: If my prayer is fluent, then I know that he [for whom I pray] is accepted, and if not, then I know that he is rejected.' They sat down and wrote down the hour, and when they came back to Rabban Gamaliel, he said to them 'By the Temple service! You were neither early nor late, but that is just how it happened. At that very moment, his fever left him and he asked us for water to drink.' " (*Babylonian Talmud Berakoth* 34B; from Boring, p. 266, no. 404)

"Yes, Rufus, what is it?" the general replied.

"Do you remember when we were stationed on the eastern frontier and met up with that magician?" Rufus asked.

"Yes, I remember it well," said the general. "He was a strange one. But as I recall he had just about everybody convinced that he had special powers."

"Everybody except you," said Rufus. "You were the only one who saw through him. We begged you to pay him off so he would not curse us and cause us bad luck against the enemy. But you didn't. And our victory that day was glorious. You convinced everyone that you have a sixth sense for charlatans."

"So now you're wondering what happened to that sixth sense?" replied the general. "Is that it? You're wondering why I put so much trust in this Galilean peasant that I was willing to set out on this journey without a shred of proof that any good was going to come of it? Is that what's bothering you?"

"Well . . . yes," said Rufus.

"I thought as much," said the general. "Don't think I haven't been asking myself those same questions. Normally, I don't make impulsive decisions. In fact, I am downright skittish about taking any action without considering all the options and looking at all the evidence. How else could I have survived as a soldier for so long?"

"Yes, sir," replied Rufus.

"So what was different about this man? Why did I have such a strong gut feeling to trust him? Well, he was different from any man I have ever met before. You see, one way to identify a charlatan is by the fact that he always wants something from you. But this man asked for nothing in return. In fact, his eyes spoke of such a deep compassion and spiritual wisdom that I could not imagine him doing anything false or hurtful to others. So when he told me to go ahead home because my son would live, I just had to believe him."

"But sir," said Rufus, "the journey is long, and Marcus was already near death when we left. What if Jesus was wrong? We will have lost valuable time—it will be hard to find another healer in time to help Marcus."

"Yes, I've thought of that," said the general. "But Rufus," he said, bending down to look him straight in the eyes, "when I saw what kind of man this Jesus was, I knew he could be trusted. So I intend to do exactly as he told me. Because I believe that at the end of the journey I will find exactly what he said I would find." *(Dennis E. Smith)*

# The Cripple at Bethesda

*Jesus heals a cripple at the Bethesda pool but is accused of disobeying sabbath law.*

## The Story

SOME time later, Jesus went up to Jerusalem for one of the Jewish festivals. Now at the Sheep Gate in Jerusalem there is a pool whose Hebrew name is Bethesda. It has five colonnades and in them lay a great number of sick people, blind, lame, and paralysed. Among them was a man who had been crippled for thirty-eight years. Jesus saw him lying there, and knowing that he had been ill a long time he asked him, 'Do you want to get well?' 'Sir,' he replied, 'I have no one to put me in the pool when the water is disturbed; while I am getting there, someone else steps into the pool before me.' Jesus answered, 'Stand up, take your bed and walk.' The man recovered instantly; he took up his bed, and began to walk.

That day was a sabbath. So the Jews said to the man who had been cured, 'It is the sabbath. It is against the law for you to carry your bed.' He answered, 'The man who cured me, he told me, "Take up your bed and walk." ' They asked him, 'Who is this man who told you to take it up and walk?' But the man who had been cured did not know who it was; for the place was crowded and Jesus had slipped away. A little later Jesus found him in the temple and said to him, 'Now that you are well, give up your sinful ways, or something worse may happen to you.' The man went off and told the Jews that it was Jesus who had cured him.

It was for doing such things on the sabbath that the Jews began to take action against Jesus. He defended himself by saying, 'My Father continues to work, and I must work too.' This made the Jews all the more determined to kill him, because not only was he breaking the sabbath but, by calling God his own Father, he was claiming equality with God.

## Comments on the Story

Signs and wonders do not always work. Sometimes instead of faith they produce indifference or even hostility. Take the story of the cripple at Bethesda, for example. At first, this story proceeds just like the story of the blind man that will follow later (John 9). In both cases, an individual is healed and then is left to deal with the Jewish authorities afterward. The blind man will triumph in that encounter and will come to authentic faith. The cripple in this story does not; his is a story of indifference or perhaps even failure.

But this is not only a story about the cripple. It also includes "the Jews." This term in John does not refer to the nation of Israel, since John's own community is also Jewish. Rather it is used in this Gospel as a symbolic term for the enemies of Jesus in general. They also view the sign, but see something entirely different in it. Rather than a manifestation of God's glory, they see a manifestation of religious heresy. How can the same sign produce such different responses?

Bethesda, the place where Jesus and the cripple met, was famous in antiquity as a pool of healing. A later insertion into John's text, verse 4 in the REB footnote, provides a popular explanation of the day for how the healing took place: "for from time to time an angel came down into the pool and stirred up the water. The first to plunge in after this disturbance recovered from whatever disease had afflicted him." Though this verse was not in the earliest manuscripts of John, it provides missing data that helps the text make more sense. The pool itself continued to be a famous healing site for several centuries and has been identified in archaeological excavations in Jerusalem.

Jesus takes the initiative here, and asks the question that sets the tone for this story, "Do you want to get well?" That question leaps off the page and becomes a question for every reader of John. The cripple replies in what seems like a weak excuse, "I have no one to help me into the water at the right time, so I have not been able to be healed." And this has gone on for thirty-eight years? we think incredulously. Yet in John's telling of the story the man's explanation seems acceptable, for Jesus makes no further comment; he merely tells the man, "Stand up, take your bed and walk." We miss the point of the story if we interpret it to mean that the cripple could have done this all along if he had only taken the initiative. For John, the healing can take place only through the power of the word of Jesus.

There is an important interaction here between the question of Jesus, the excuse of the man, and the subsequent healing command of Jesus. The question, "Do you want to get well?" is a question addressed not just to the cripple, but to any person who seeks spiritual healing. The choice that is offered is whether one will continue to chase popular remedies or whether one will respond to the word of Jesus. The cripple makes his choice, responds in faith, and experiences healing as a result.

Yet he has only just begun his faith journey, and now he must deal with the implications of his decision. For with the same command with which he secured healing, he also, by taking up his bed, disobeyed the sabbath law. So Jesus' directive to step out in faith included a step into a more radical religious identity. That is what it means to be made "well"; it means to boldly step out along a new religious path.

71

But such actions can get you into trouble. No sooner had the former crip-ple stepped out with his bed than he was accosted by "the Jews" and told he was engaging in an illegal religious act. But the man who cured him told him to do this, he says. They then demand that he find out who it was. When he meets up with Jesus later, Jesus tells him, "Now that you are well, give up your sinful ways, or something worse may happen to you." The category of "sinful ways" presumably refers to the previous condition of the man, both physically and spiritually. Now, however, he has been made well, or, in the language from the Nicodemus story, he has been "born again." His act of carrying his bed on the sabbath was meant to proclaim his new identity. But he has not caught on. For him, to be "made well" means no more than to solve his problem of the moment. It does not mean following a new life. So he does, in fact, revert to his "sinful ways"—he turns Jesus in to the authorities.

The breaking of the sabbath law becomes the straw that broke the camel's back for Jesus' enemies, for it provides a pretext for them to seek his death. It represents a rejection of religious law, and Jesus' explanation does not help, for he claims to do so in imitation of God his "Father." This com-pounds his crime for it leads to the conclusion that he is claiming equality with God. In the following verses, Jesus explains what he means. "The Son," he says, "does only what he sees the Father doing . . . as the Father raises the dead and gives them life, so the Son gives life as he chooses" (5:19-21). In a marvelous domestic image, we are reminded how a son learns by observing what a father does. So Jesus' action here is deemed appropriate because, as Son, he has observed his "Father" give life. The healing of the cripple is therefore interpreted as a sign of the life-giving power of the Son. Consequently, "the Jews" represent those who reject "life" in favor of rules.

This story contrasts three religious paths. The path of the cripple is a short-sighted one; he willingly accepts the healing of the moment, but shrinks from the commitment it takes to continue in a life of wholeness. The path of the ene-mies of Jesus is one that is bound by rules and restrictions, so much so that they no longer have access to "life." The path of Jesus is a path of wholeness and life. It is not an easy path—the cripple quickly found that this new life brought conflict. But it is a new quality of life, so rich and rewarding that those who pursue it can be said to possess "eternal life" now (5:24).

## Retelling the Story

The Jews said to the man who had been cured, 'It is the sabbath. It is against the law for you to carry your bed.' He answered, 'The man who cured me, he told me, "Take up your bed and walk." ' (John 5:10-11)

Back in old Jerusalem, down by the Sheep Gate, there was a pool that was called Bethesda. Now this was no ordinary pool. Folks used to say that from time to time an angel of the Lord came down and turned it into a health spa.

A lot of sick and hurting people came to this pool, because it was said that if you were the first one in when the water got stirred up, you would be healed of whatever ailed you. It got to be something like a first-century "run for the roses" with everyone dashing for the pool as soon as the celestial lifeguard blew his whistle. But in this case, it was not "last one in is a rotten egg" but "first one in gets the heavenly prize." Needless to say, that pool was more crowded than the seashore on a Memorial Day weekend.

> The Greeks told similar stories about the healing power of a well at the Temple of Asclepius, a Greek deity. "For many by bathing in it have recovered their sight, and many by drinking it have been cured of chest trouble and have regained the breath of life. It has cured one man's feet and another part of the body for someone else. Once someone drank it and spoke after being mute . . . thus to the sick it is an antidote and a cure." (*Aelius Aristides* 39:15; from Boring, p. 266, no. 405 [second century C.E.])

Now there was a man named Ephraim who had been sick for thirty-eight years. As Jesus was passing by the pool, he noticed the man and knew that he had been here for a long time. He knew he shouldn't heal the man—it was the Sabbath after all, and it would be against all those blue laws. But he did decide to pay a pastoral call on the man, so he went over to say hi.

Except Jesus was never one to make small talk. The first thing he said was, "Do you want to be made well?"

The man didn't know who Jesus was, but he was happy for the company. He told Jesus he wanted to be made whole, but had discovered he couldn't do it on his own. He kind of hoped someone would come along and intercede for him.

Now, Ephraim was sure that this nice man was going to stick around and help him when the water got all stirred up. But Jesus surprised him by passing up the race for the pool altogether. Instead he gave him a simple command.

"Pick up your bed and walk, then," he said.

And the man did!

But there was a problem. It was the Sabbath and there was to be no carrying-on on holidays. In fact, there was not to be any carrying of anything. There were some folks there who let it be known that they were not pleased.

"You're carrying things too far," these people said.

"The healing?" the man replied.

"No. The pallet. Who told you to do that?"

"It's not my fault. He told me to."

Well, it wasn't long before the healed man met up with Jesus again—in the

Chrysostom saw the cripple as a model example of the virtue of persistence: "Let us, then, be ashamed; let us be ashamed, beloved, and let us bewail our great sluggishness. He spent thirty-eight years lying there, and did not obtain what he wished, yet did not give up. Besides, he had failed to obtain help, not through his own carelessness, but because he was pushed aside by others and given harsh treatment; yet, even though treated this way, he did not lose heart." (Chrysostom, *Homilies on John* 36 [late-fourth century C.E.])

temple. Jesus said, "You really showed your new character when you carried that bed, but remember—getting rid of your sinful ways doesn't just stop with getting rid of the pallet."

But Ephraim did not understand. He kept the healing, but turned in the healer. He didn't know there was more to being well than walking.

*(Phyllis Williams Provost)*

# The Miracle of the Loaves

*Jesus feeds five thousand with five loaves and two fish and walks on water.*

### The Story

SOME time later Jesus withdrew to the farther shore of the sea of Galilee (or Tiberias), and a large crowd of people followed him because they had seen the signs he performed in healing the sick. Jesus went up the hillside and sat down with his disciples. It was near the time of Passover, the great Jewish festival. Looking up and seeing a large crowd coming towards him, Jesus said to Philip, 'Where are we to buy bread to feed these people?' He said this to test him; Jesus himself knew what he meant to do. Philip replied, 'We would need two hundred denarii to buy enough bread for each of them to have a little.' One of his disciples, Andrew, the brother of Simon Peter, said to him, 'There is a boy here who has five barley loaves and two fish; but what is that among so many?' Jesus said, 'Make the people sit down.' There was plenty of grass there, so the men sat down, about five thousand of them. Then Jesus took the loaves, gave thanks, and distributed them to the people as they sat there. He did the same with the fish, and they had as much as they wanted.

When everyone had had enough, he said to his disciples, 'Gather up the pieces left over, so that nothing is wasted.' They gathered them up, and filled twelve baskets with the pieces of the five barley loaves that were left uneaten.

When the people saw the sign Jesus had performed, the word went round, 'Surely this must be the Prophet who was to come into the world.' Jesus, realizing that they meant to come and seize him to proclaim him king, withdrew again to the hills by himself.

At nightfall his disciples went down to the sea, and set off by boat to cross to Capernaum. Though darkness had fallen, Jesus had not yet joined them; a strong wind was blowing and the sea grew rough. When they had rowed about three or four miles they saw Jesus walking on the sea and approaching the boat. They were terrified, but he called out, 'It is I; do not be afraid.' With that they were ready to take him on board, and immediately the boat reached the land they were making for.

### Comments on the Story

This story begins with Jesus' multiplication of the loaves and fish and walking on the water and ends with the discourse on the bread of life. The two mir-

75

acles will be discussed in this chapter. The next chapter will take up the continuation of the story with the discourse.

The structure is a classic one for John: miracle followed by discourse. The miracle includes the miraculous provision of bread; the discourse focuses on the identity of Jesus as "bread of life." "Sign" leads to faith, but inadequate faith, because it sees only the fact that a miracle was done. Jesus follows with a discourse that challenges that faith to a higher level.

The two miracles that are combined here, multiplication of the loaves followed by the walking on the water, are closely patterned after the stories in the synoptic tradition, one of the few times John reflects usage of the synoptic tradition. Here the match is remarkably close, including not only the combination of the two miracles together, but even some of the dialogue. Where John got this story is debated; he does not seem to be familiar with Mark in most other respects, so the usual suggestion is that he did not use Mark, but drew on a source also used by Mark. Even so, John gives this story his own twist.

There are three points where John's emphasis in these stories in comparison with the synoptic versions is especially clear (not counting his addition of the discourse on the bread of life). First, he adds the notation that these miracles are taking place in Passover season (6:4). Since Passover is also known as the feast of unleavened bread, it forms an important backdrop to Jesus' miraculous provision of bread. As elsewhere in John, so also here, Jesus' ministry presents a critique and renewal of Jewish traditions.

Second, John adds the notation that Jesus is in charge of the events of this story. This is found in the comment of the narrator, "He said this to test him; Jesus himself knew what he meant to do" (6:6). This is a common motif in John and refers to the emphasis in this Gospel on Jesus' divinity. This emphasis is what allows Jesus to read people's minds and manipulate events so as to bring about the results he has already planned. Because of this twist in the plot, it is no longer a story in which Jesus shows compassion on the crowd, unlike the parallel stories in the synoptics. Indeed, there is very little difference between the provision of miraculous bread on this occasion and the provision of miraculous wine on the occasion of the wedding feast at Cana. In both cases, the point is not to fill basic human needs. Rather the focus is on the symbolism of the banquet.

The actual miracle of the loaves and fish begins with Jesus' leading question, "Where are we to buy bread to feed these people?" The emphasis from the outset is on bread and on the tremendous amount that would be necessary to feed everyone, as is seen by Philip's comment. Peter then takes the lead and mentions a boy with three barley loaves and two fish, but expresses his doubt that this will help. With the scene thus set, contrasting the amount needed in real figures to feed the crowd with the meager amount actually available, Jesus has the people prepare themselves by taking the reclining posture, a posture normally reserved for the most lavish and celebrative of feasts. He then proceeds to feed the entire crowd as much as any could want, truly a feast without parallel. Indeed, the amount he has provided is so great that leftovers remain.

What Jesus does in providing abundant bread and fish on this occasion is to symbolize the messianic banquet, a banquet that only the Messiah can provide. The messianic banquet is described in Isa. 25:6-8 as a great feast when God will feed all nations. It is equated with the coming of the Messiah and the blessings of the messianic age. Here Jesus has the people "recline," for that is what the Greek word translated here as "sit down" really means (6:10-11). In the world of Jesus, reclining is the posture taken at a festive banquet. And at the banquet Jesus provides, everyone eats their fill ("they had as much as they wanted," 6:11). The unending table is one of the images connected with the messianic banquet and made it a powerful symbol for the joys of heaven for a people who were acquainted with the reality of famine and the rarity of a lavish feast.

The third way in which John puts his imprint on the story is in the response of the people. They conclude, "Surely this must be the Prophet who was to come into the world" (6:14). The confession that Jesus is the Prophet is an important one in John, for it represents a first step toward true faith, as is seen, for example, in the questions asked of John the Baptist (1:21, 24) and in the response of the Samaritan woman (4:19). At this point the crowd is on track. And according to the logic of the story, what they have responded to is the way in which Jesus, through the provision of the bread, has duplicated an action connected either with the prophet Elijah or with the idea of a prophet like Moses. Elijah was believed to return someday (Mal. 4:5-6) and his successor, Elisha, once multiplied loaves of barley in a similar miracle (2 Kings 4:42-44). More likely, however, the identification is with Moses, who provided the manna in the wilderness. The Moses story actually forms the backdrop for the discourse that follows.

They have identified Jesus with a messianic figure; the question yet to be determined is how deep their faith will be. Already they seem to have stopped short of full awareness of Jesus' identity, for they attempt to crown him king. They do not yet understand the meaning of his messiahship. His kingdom is not of this world (18:36).

The segue to walking on the water at first glance seems to add little to the story. It is true that it is here apparently because John's source placed it after the loaves miracle. But John has still worked it into his story. It forms the transition between the miracle of loaves and the discourse. The crowd will notice that he could not have arrived at the other shore by normal means, and in a statement full of irony, will ask him, "Rabbi, when did you come here?" The miraculous way in which Jesus arrived at the other shore is not commented on, but is certainly known to us, the readers.

How would this story have been heard in John's community? For a community of God's people in an uncertain time, it is a message, a sign, that counsels looking beyond the everyday needs for daily bread. Instead, the community of faith will recognize the presence of the living Lord who provides spiritual nourishment far exceeding their wildest dreams. There are also overtones of the eucharist, since the ceremonial way in which Jesus gives thanks and distributes the bread reflects traditional eucharistic liturgies, although John does not include such a text in his last supper account. For the community, the text provides affirmation that the community meal that they partake together is understood on the spiritual level to be a lavish banquet in the presence of the Lord.

## Retelling the Story

'There is a boy here who has five barley loaves and two fish; but what is that among so many?' (John 6:9)

It was a miracle if Josh ever made it to dinner on time. For him, life was an adventure. His grandmother used to say that boy was "always at one end of trouble—either going in or coming out." But he was a good boy—a curious ten-year-old who loved to go exploring in the hills near his home. He'd gone out exploring that very day and had himself an adventure! He couldn't wait to get home to tell his mother about it. She met him as he rushed in the door.

"Josh!" she scolded. "Where have you been all day? I was worried sick about you! Do you know what time it is? And just look at you! You're all dusty and dirty! *And* you're an hour late for supper! Where were you?"

"Mom," he said, his eyes shining, "you'll never believe it! I've got to tell you about it!"

"After supper. I've saved you a plate."

"No, Mom, *now*," he said. "Besides I'm not hungry."

"Well, I guess it was a good thing I packed you a large lunch, wasn't it?" she said. "Did you finish it all off?"

"*No!* I shared it! That's what I was trying to tell you about," the little boy replied.

"You shared it!" said his mother. "Who'd you share it with? That Samuelson boy down the road?"

"Yes! And Matthew, and John and his mom and . . . "

"You shared five barley loaves and two small fish with all those people?" she asked.

"Yeah! And a whole lot more!"

"Were you trying to get out of eating those fish?" she asked suspiciously. "I told you! They're good for you!"

"Mother!"

"Okay, so how many people did you share your lunch with?"

"About five thousand," he replied.

"Five thousand! Do you expect me to believe a story like that?" she asked.

"Yep," he said solemnly. "This man, Jesus, and his friends came up to Herod Hill where I was jumping frogs, and even though his friends seemed to be wanting to move on, he just stopped right there and sat down with me! A grown-up *man*, Mom! And he sat down there and jumped frogs with me!

"So then his friends—there were about a dozen of them—*they* all sat down, too. But we didn't get to play for very long. Pretty soon, this whole crowd of people started arriving and wanting Jesus to talk to them.

"He looked kind of sad, so I asked him what was wrong. . . ."

"You asked Jesus?"

"Well, sure. Anyway, he said they were all hungry for what God had for them. So then I knew why he was sad— because if they were all hungry, I didn't see where he and his friends had any food there to give them. So I asked him if he wanted me to go buy some bread for him."

John tells the feeding story like a midrash on the Old Testament manna story (see next chapter) and on stories in the Elijah/Elisha tradition. When the people conclude that Jesus must be "the Prophet who was to come into the world," they provide an explicit reference to John's allusions. The story of Elisha's miracle is in 2 Kings 4:42-44. Here a man has twenty barley loaves, comparable to the five barley loaves in John's story. Elisha says, "Give this to the people to eat," to which his attendant protests, "I cannot set this before a hundred people." In John's story, Andrew also protests that the bread and fish are not enough for so many. And, just like the Elisha story, not only are all of the people fed, but there is food left over.

"What did he say?" asked his mother.

"He looked at me kind of funny, and then turned to his friend, Philip, and said, 'Where are we going to buy bread for these people?' "

"And then I felt bad 'cause this was my hill, and I hadn't offered them anything even though I had my lunch bag right there. Then I was embarrassed to say anything to Jesus, but I told his friend, Andrew, who was sitting beside me, that they could have what I had with me.

"Well, he just laughed and looked at all those people who kept coming up the hill. He told Jesus like it was some kind of a joke, and then I felt really dumb. But Jesus didn't make me feel dumb. He put his hand right here on my shoulder and thanked me, and then said we could be hosts together. Then he took my lunch and fed everybody with it. Me and Jesus—we fed five thousand people today," he finished.

"Who is this Jesus?" she wondered aloud. "You make him sound like he can walk on water." *(Phyllis Williams Provost)*

John has correlated the miracle of the loaves and the walking on the water stories with the Passover setting (6:4). He therefore reflects a long midrashic tradition that is still preserved in the Passover Haggadah (or liturgy), in which the accounts of God's miracles of deliverance include the crossing of the Red Sea and the giving of the manna. This tradition is also reflected in the litany of the acts of deliverance of God in Psalm 78 where reference to the parting of the waters is soon followed by reference to the manna ("he divided the sea and brought them through . . . he rained down manna for them to eat," [78:13, 24]). These themes are echoed in Psalm 107. There the people cry out in hunger as they wander in a desert land (107:4-6) and God responds: "he has satisfied the thirsty and filled the hungry with good things" (107:9). Some then take to the sea in ships, God raises a storm, they cry out in distress, and "the waves of the sea were stilled" (107:23-29). In another reference to the miraculous crossing of the sea, it is God who guides the people across: "Your path was through the sea, your way through mighty waters, and none could mark your footsteps. You guided your people like a flock shepherded by Moses and Aaron" (Ps. 77:19-20). In the Septuagint version (Greek translation) of Job 9:8, the Lord "walks on the sea as on firm ground." (Brown, *The Gospel According to John*, 1.255; Haenchen, 1.280)

# The Bread of Life Discourse

*Jesus proclaims himself to be the bread of life with the result that some are scandalized while others believe.*

### The Story

NEXT morning the crowd was still on the opposite shore. They had seen only one boat there, and Jesus, they knew, had not embarked with his disciples, who had set off by themselves. Boats from Tiberias, however, had come ashore near the place where the people had eaten the bread over which the Lord gave thanks. When the crowd saw that Jesus had gone as well as his disciples, they went on board these boats and made for Capernaum in search of him. They found him on the other side. 'Rabbi,' they asked, 'when did you come here?' Jesus replied, 'In very truth I tell you, it is not because you saw signs that you came looking for me, but because you ate the bread and your hunger was satisfied. You should work, not for this perishable food, but for the food that lasts, the food of eternal life.

'This food the Son of Man will give you, for on him God the Father has set the seal of his authority.' 'Then what must we do', they asked him, 'if our work is to be the work of God?' Jesus replied, 'This is the work that God requires: to believe in the one whom he has sent.'

They asked, 'What sign can you give us, so that we may see it and believe you? What is the work you are doing? Our ancestors had manna to eat in the desert; as scripture says, "He gave them bread from heaven to eat." ' Jesus answered, 'In very truth I tell you, it was not Moses who gave you the bread from heaven; it is my Father who gives you the true bread from heaven. The bread that God gives comes down from heaven and brings life to the world.' 'Sir,' they said to him, 'give us this bread now and always.' Jesus said to them, 'I am the bread of life. Whoever comes to me will never be hungry, and whoever believes in me will never be thirsty. But you, as I said, have seen and yet you do not believe. All that the Father gives me will come to me, and anyone who comes to me I will never turn away. I have come down from heaven, to do not my own will, but the will of him who sent me. It is his will that I should not lose even one of those he has given me, but should raise them all up on the last day. For it is my Father's will that everyone who sees the Son and has faith in him should have eternal life; and I will raise them up on the last day.'

At this the Jews began to grumble because he said, 'I am the bread which came down from heaven.' They said, 'Surely this is Jesus, Joseph's son! We know his father and mother. How can he say, "I have come down from heaven"?' 'Stop complaining among yourselves,' Jesus told them. 'No one can come to me unless he is drawn by the Father who sent me; and I will raise him up on the last day. It is written in the prophets: "They will all be taught by God." Everyone who has listened to the Father and learned from him comes to me.

'I do not mean that anyone has seen the Father; he who has come from God has seen the Father, and he alone. In very truth I tell you, whoever believes has eternal life. I am the bread of life. Your ancestors ate manna in the wilderness, yet they are dead. I am speaking of the bread that comes down from heaven; whoever eats it will never die. I am the living bread that has come down from heaven; if anyone eats this bread, he will live for ever. The bread which I shall give is my own flesh, given for the life of the world.'

This led to a fierce dispute among the Jews. 'How can this man give us his flesh to eat?' they protested. Jesus answered them, 'In very truth I tell you, unless you eat the flesh of the Son of Man and drink his blood you can have no life in you. Whoever eats my flesh and drinks my blood has eternal life, and I will raise him up on the last day. My flesh is real food; my blood is real drink. Whoever eats my flesh and drinks my blood dwells in me and I in him. As the living Father sent me, and I live because of the

Father, so whoever eats me will live because of me. This is the bread which came down from heaven; it is not like the bread which our fathers ate; they are dead, but whoever eats this bread will live for ever.'

Jesus said these things in the synagogue as he taught in Capernaum. On hearing them, many of his disciples exclaimed, 'This is more than we can stand! How can anyone listen to such talk?' Jesus was aware that his disciples were grumbling about it and asked them, 'Does this shock you? Then what if you see the Son of Man ascending to where he was before? It is the spirit that gives life; the flesh can achieve nothing; the words I have spoken to you are both spirit and life. Yet there are some of you who have no faith.' For Jesus knew from the outset who were without faith and who was to betray him. So he said, 'This is why I told you that no one can come to me unless it has been granted to him by the Father.'

From that moment many of his disciples drew back and no longer went about with him. So Jesus asked the Twelve, 'Do you also want to leave?' Simon Peter answered him, 'Lord, to whom shall we go? Your words are words of eternal life. We believe and know that you are God's Holy One.' Jesus answered, 'Have I not chosen the twelve of you? Yet one of you is a devil.' He meant Judas son of Simon Iscariot. It was he who would betray him, and he was one of the Twelve.

## Comments on the Story

This section presents the discourse that is a commentary on the miracle of the loaves, which was previously described. Although loaves and fish are both included in the miracle, and though there is a walking on the water, nevertheless it is the bread that receives the emphasis in the discourse. This is indicated by Jesus' words, which introduce the miracle, "Where are we going to buy bread for these people to eat?" (6:5). It is further emphasized by the identification of the crowd on the other side as those who "had eaten the bread after the Lord had given thanks" (6:23). The bread is carrying multiple symbolic meanings. It is the counterpart to the Passover bread, since the Passover is mentioned in 6:4. It carries overtones of eucharistic bread, since it is connected with a ceremony of thanksgiving and distributing (6:11). This is probably true even though John does not have a Lord's Supper liturgy in his Gospel. The bread also carries the primary symbol for the discourse, in which Jesus comes to be proclaimed as the "bread of life" (6:35).

There are three divisions in the discourse proper, characterized by the responses of three different sets of characters: the crowd, the "Jews," and the disciples.

The crowd represents the world to whom God sent the son (3:16). They are somewhat neutral in their portrayal by John, open to belief, but not yet there. They came to Jesus because of his signs (6:2), he fed them (6:11-13), they proclaimed him to be the prophet, thus taking the first step of faith (6:14), and now they have followed him to the other side.

Their first question is full of irony: "Rabbi, when did you come here?" In actuality, the "how" of his coming was a miracle as well, a fact alluded to, but not remarked on, by the people. Jesus responds by pointing them not to the fact that bread was provided for their hunger, but to the meaning underlying the sign, that "the food of eternal life" is available from the Son of Man. They then raise a biblical question, comparing Jesus' sign to that of Moses who gave manna in the wilderness. Jesus reinterprets the text to point out that it was not Moses who gave the bread but God; therefore it was a bread that came down from heaven, a kind of bread that God continues to give. It is at this point that the crowd makes an important advance in their faith. "Sir, give us this bread now and always," they say, in a request that can be compared with the request of the Samaritan woman for the "living water" (4:15).

At this point Jesus presents the heart of his message. "I am the bread of life. Whoever comes to me will never be hungry, and whoever believes in me will never be thirsty. . . . I have come down from heaven." It is one of the characteristic "I am" sayings in John that express the high Christology of this Gospel. It has two parts. First there is the "I am" statement proper, in which the symbolism of the sign is reused as a metaphor for the life-giving power of the Christ. Second, John also emphasizes another christological theme, that Jesus is the one who came down from heaven. This theme provides assurance to a community in conflict that their source of power is greater than what they confront in their daily world. But if they follow the journey of the crowd, they must be willing to look beyond the desire to "expect a miracle" and recognize instead the true miracle that is the spiritual nourishment that comes from the living Lord.

"The Jews" are the archetypical enemies of Jesus in John, and they appear next on the scene as detractors. At this point the text begins to read like a midrash, for their response mirrors that of the children of Israel in the wilderness who "grumbled" against Moses and who then received manna. Their gripe is about Jesus' origin. How can he say that he came from heaven since they know he came from Joseph? Interestingly, John refers to a family legacy of Jesus that is nowhere recounted in his Gospel. "The Jews" complain about the fleshly reality of Jesus; what they fail to see is the glorious (divine) identity of Jesus.

The dialogue then takes an unusual turn. Up to this point Jesus as bread of life is seen as an analogy for faith; the believer receives the spiritual sustenance through faith. Now the text moves to a different type of language, in which Jesus says that it is the flesh of the Son of Man that must be eaten and his blood that must be drunk. This no longer seems to be a metaphor for faith but rather a reference to the sacramental sense of the eucharist. The distinction seems to be drawn between those who share in the ritual world of the Christian community and those who don't. "The Jews," as the archetypes of the enemies of the community, reject this teaching. Here, and throughout John, it is not Jews as a nation that is John's emphasis but "Jews" as a stereotype for unbelief. (See comments on this term in the introduction, p. 15.)

The third category of respondents to Jesus are the disciples. They, too, find the saying about the flesh to be hard to take. Perhaps their hesitation reflects the realities of the worship life of the Johannine community. Those who participated in the ritual life of this community in effect cut themselves off from their Jewish heritage. To do so was to cut oneself adrift from all that had given one comfort and self-identity. It is indeed hard to take, to say that belief will require cutting the ties to roots that one holds dear. No wonder so many of the disciples leave him at this point. And no wonder that even among those who stay, one will betray him. The call to discipleship is a demanding call—it demands all or nothing. Yet the words of Peter are true to the experience of those who believe: "Lord, to whom shall we go? Your words are words of eternal life." No other words, no other message, offer what this message offers.

## Retelling the Story

*Jesus said to them, "I am the bread of life." (John 6:35a)*

Angels do not usually take part in ordinary jobs like humans do. The word *angel* means messenger, so most of the time an angel will have something important to tell a person, if the person has ears to listen. During times of crisis, though, the angels get assigned tasks according to the way God has chosen to respond to that particular crisis. After all, messages can come in different and surprising forms.

The most memorable time when the angels were mobilized to help in a tough time was long ago when God's people were brought out of slavery in Egypt. I say a long time ago knowing full well that for an angel time doesn't exist as it does for us. When an angel remembers something it is as if the event were happening at that very moment.

When the people were running from Pharaoh's army and approached the Sea of Reeds, they were forced to stop, as you surely recall. Moses raised his staff, and the waters parted so that the people could cross the sea between two walls of water. I don't know how Cecil B. DeMille did it on film, but originally it was angels holding that water back. There they were, creatures who don't ordinarily like water, flapping and splashing, spewing and huffing, holding back millions of gallons of water. You've never heard such sighs of relief as the angels let out when God told them they could let go of the water. The angels let go of the water when the Egyptian army was in the middle of the sea, the wheels of their chariots mired in the mud. When the angels saw the drops creeping down God's face they thought they had splashed a little too much. Angels have never shown the compassion one might expect, being as close to God as they are.

The next problem was feeding the people who came out of Egypt. I'm sure you know about manna but I would wager you don't have any idea

John's story of the miracle of the loaves and the dialogue that follows is told largely as a midrash on the story of the manna found in Exodus 16, Numbers 11, and Ps. 78:17-31, which is itself a midrash on the manna story. Jesus' discourse begins with this reference at 6:31, "He gave them bread from heaven to eat," a text that derives from Exod. 16:4 ("The Lord said to Moses, 'I shall rain down bread from heaven for you.'") and Ps. 78:24 ("He rained down manna for them to eat and gave them the grain of heaven"). Earlier in the story, Jesus' question to Philip, "where are we to buy bread to feed these people?" is reminiscent of Moses' question to God "Where am I to find meat to give them all?" (Num. 11:13). In Num. 11:1, the people grumble, much like they do in John 6:41 and 43. The request for "meat" or flesh by the people of Israel (Num. 11:13) is paralleled by Jesus' identification of the bread with his flesh (John 6:51). The identification of the miracle and the discourse with Passover (6:4) correlates with the emphasis on the manna story in the Jewish Passover liturgy.

how the manna got to the people. No one sees what goes on behind the scenes, except the ones doing the work—the angels. God would speak and round, flat pieces of dough would appear before each angel. It was the angel's task to

85

knead the dough, take a quick run over to the fires of Gehenna to bake it, then crumble it up all over the ground to be found the next morning. Thursdays were the worst since they had to double production to allow for Shabbat, since no manna could be collected after sundown Friday. In fact, the angels used to say that making manna on Thursdays was pure Gehenna. But they never said it when God was around.

After a time, though, people forgot about all that God had done for them and went chasing after other garden variety deities like sex, money, fame, and a whole host of others. Eventually, a crisis would come along and the people would come dragging back making pitiful noises and begging God to take them back. God always did take them back, and even managed to seem genuinely pleased that they were around again. This generosity of spirit made the angels more than a little nervous. After all, if blatant ingratitude wasn't enough to get on God's bad side, what would it take? The angels grumbled but they always came through in a pinch, completing in a timely fashion whatever job they were assigned.

One day word went around the angelic grapevine that one of them would be chosen for a big assignment, a starring role you might say. The rest would be called on to provide the backup singing for the big event that God had planned. After extensive auditioning, Gabriel was chosen for the solo part. You could hear the would-be star practicing lines, "Hail Mary full of grace. . . . "

The other angels took a crash course in Latin. Of course they preferred their assignments to be in Hebrew, but most angels were quick studies and had a great facility for language. *"Gloria in excelsis deo"* went their part.

> Jesus' reference to the manna tradition would call to mind the messianic banquet at the end of time, a popular Jewish belief in which manna would once more be provided by the Messiah. A representative text is 2 Bar. 29:1-8: "It will happen that when all that which should come to pass in these parts has been accomplished, the Anointed One will begin to be revealed. . . . And it will happen at that time that the treasury of manna will come down again from on high, and they will eat of it in those years because these are they who will have arrived at the consummation of time." Other Jewish midrash traditions make similar references: "You will not find it [manna] in this age, but you shall find it in the age that is coming" (Midrash *Mekilta on Exodus* 16:25). "As the first redeemer caused manna to descend, as it is stated, 'Behold, I will cause to rain bread from heaven for you' (Exod. 16:4), so will the latter redeemer cause manna to descend" (Midrash *Rabbah on Ecclesiastes* 1:9). (Boring, pp. 249-50, no. 375; Brown, *The Gospel According to John*, 1.265)

Well, the big day came. The angels waited to see if making public appearances would make the people more grateful to God or help them remember God's goodness longer. Then the rumor went around that the people would have to be fed again. The angels remembered the hard work manna took, especially on Thursdays and were about to go to God in protest. Then, they heard that they were not going to be involved this time, that God would take care of all the details of the project. They were greatly relieved but questioned how God was going to feed this generation and all future generations without their help.

Their questions were answered when one day they heard a familiar voice drifting up from an unexpected place. There on the earth they heard the voice of God in the language of humans. The voice said, "I am the bread of life."

Then they knew. *(Michael E. Williams)*

## JOHN 7:1-18, 24-32, 37-52

# The Fickle Crowd

*Jesus meets with controversy in Jerusalem.*

### The Story

AFTER that Jesus travelled around within Galilee; he decided to avoid Judaea because the Jews were looking for a chance to kill him. But when the Jewish feast of Tabernacles was close at hand, his brothers said to him, 'You should leave here and go into Judaea, so that your disciples may see the great things you are doing. No one can hope for recognition if he works in obscurity. If you can really do such things as these, show yourself to the world.' For even his brothers had no faith in him. Jesus answered: 'The right time for me has not yet come, but any time is right for you. The world cannot hate you; but it hates me for exposing the wickedness of its ways. Go up to the festival yourselves. I am not going to this festival, because the right time for me has not yet come.' So saying he stayed behind in Galilee.

Later, when his brothers had gone to the festival, he went up too, not openly, but in secret. At the festival the Jews were looking for him and asking where he was, and there was much murmuring about him in the crowds. 'He is a good man,' said some. 'No,' said others, 'he is leading the people astray.' No one talked freely about him, however, for fear of the Jews.

When the festival was already half over, Jesus went up to the temple and began to teach. The Jews were astonished: 'How is it', they said, 'that this untrained man has such learning?' Jesus replied, 'My teaching is not my own but his who sent me. Whoever chooses to do the will of God will know whether my teaching comes from him or is merely my own. Anyone whose teaching is merely his own seeks his own glory; but if anyone seeks the glory of him who sent him, he is sincere and there is nothing false in him.'

. . . . . . . . . . . . . . . . . . . . . . . . . . . .

'Stop judging by appearances; be just in your judgements.'

This prompted some of the people of Jerusalem to say, 'Is not this the man they want to put to death? Yet here he is, speaking in public, and they say not one word to him. Can it be that our rulers have decided that this is the Messiah? Yet we know where this man comes from; when the Messiah appears no one is to know where he comes from.' Jesus responded to this as he taught in the temple: 'Certainly you know me,' he declared, 'and you know where I come from. Yet I have not come of my own accord; I was sent by one who is true, and him you do not know. I know him because I come from him, and he it is who sent me.' At this they tried to seize him, but no one could lay hands on him because his appointed hour had not yet come. Among the people many believed in him. 'When the Messiah comes,' they said, 'is it likely that he will perform more signs than this man?'

The Pharisees overheard these mutterings about him among the people, so the chief priests and the Pharisees sent temple police to arrest him.

. . . . . . . . . . . . . . . . . . . . . . . . . . . .

ON the last and greatest day of the festival Jesus stood and declared, 'If anyone is thirsty, let him come to me and drink. Whoever believes in me, as scripture says, "Streams of living water shall flow from within him." ' He was speaking of the Spirit which believers in him would later receive; for the Spirit had not yet been given, because Jesus had not yet been glorified.

On hearing his words some of the crowd said, 'This must certainly be the Prophet.' Others said, 'This is the Messiah.' But others argued, 'Surely

the Messiah is not to come from Galilee? Does not scripture say that the Messiah is to be of the family of David, from David's village of Bethlehem?' Thus he was the cause of a division among the people. Some were for arresting him, but no one laid hands on him.

The temple police went back to the chief priests and Pharisees, who asked them, 'Why have you not brought him?' 'No one ever spoke as this man speaks,' they replied. The Pharisees retorted, 'Have you too been misled? Has a single one of our rulers believed in him, or any of the Pharisees? As for his rabble, which cares nothing for the law, a curse is on them.' Then one of their number, Nicodemus (the man who once visited Jesus), intervened. 'Does our law', he asked them, 'permit us to pass judgement on someone without first giving him a hearing and learning the facts?' 'Are you a Galilean too?' they retorted. 'Study the scriptures and you will find that the Prophet does not come from Galilee.'

## Comments on the Story

This chapter of John reads like a week in the life of the Messiah. It is full of controversy, plots, intrigue, and public debate, and introduces a host of characters who confront Jesus and respond in a variety of ways.

It begins with the notation that Jesus has chosen to avoid Judea because "the Jews were looking for a chance to kill him" (7:1). But it is festival time, and his brothers feel he should go to Jerusalem when there will be big crowds and he can make a big impact. The author explains that their request was not based on faith, and Jesus refuses to take their suggestion. They depart for the feast, while Jesus stays behind in Galilee. Yet after they have left, he then decides to go secretly. Why this change of heart? Apparently it is important for Jesus to establish that his actions are not in response to worldly considerations. His brothers represent a group who, because of their closeness to him, should have known better about what he was doing. Yet they are more intent on fame than mission. As Jesus explains, they operate on "world standard time" ("any time is right for you"), while he operates on God's time ("the right time for me has not yet come" [7:6]).

This pattern defines the course of his life throughout John as well as the manner of his death. For when he dies, no one will take his life from him; rather he will choose the time and place for his death (10:18). Thus in this story, though he initially avoids Jerusalem because his life would be in danger there, he eventually elects to go on his own terms. Jesus sets in motion the events that will lead to his death. But the choice was his. And the manner of death will be his as well. That is why he also rejects the opportunity to take the path of fame and fortune that his brothers promote.

The trip to Jerusalem plunges Jesus into an encounter once more with "the Jews" and "the crowd." The twin terms "the Jews" and "the Pharisees" are obviously catchall terms for his enemies; that is the usage of these terms throughout John. Similarly "the crowd" plays a consistent role in John. They are first introduced in 6:2 as those who followed Jesus because of the sign he did. They manifest faith in the sign, which is an appropriate first step, but they still tend to vacillate. That is clearly their role here in chapter 7. In fact, the crowd maintains a position throughout John as a group of people on the margins, people who debate the pros and cons of Jesus but never fully commit one way or another.

The people first begin to murmur when news about Jesus' arrival in Jerusalem begins to spread. Typically they are of two minds: some say "He is a good man" while others say "he is leading the people astray" (7:12). They remain of two minds throughout the story.

Halfway through the festival celebration, Jesus finally makes his appearance in the temple and begins to teach there. The crowd begins to debate whether he is the Messiah. The issue finally turns on a key argument: where does scripture say the Messiah should hail from? Jesus is known to be from Galilee. Yet this does not agree with scripture. Some argue that the Messiah is supposed to be from an unknown origin, others that the Messiah is supposed to be from Bethlehem. But in either case he cannot be from Galilee (7:27, 41-42). However, the irony of this debate is clear, for in John it is exactly Jesus' true origin, from heaven, that establishes his identity. Jesus even says as much: "I was sent by one who is true, . . . I know him . . . and he it is who sent me" (7:28-29). Jesus argues that they do "know where I come from" (7:28), as if to say they know more than they are admitting. Perhaps that is why they respond so decisively to him, some attempting to seize him, while others believe in him (7:30-31).

Meanwhile, his enemies are responding to him in their own way. At first, when he begins to teach in the temple, they raise the objection, "How is it that this untrained man has such learning?" (v. 15). It is another slap at Jesus' humble origins. Later, when they learn that some in the crowd are believing in him, they seem to conclude that this has gone on long enough. They then send the temple police to arrest him (7:32).

The temple police are presumably present when Jesus declares, "if anyone is thirsty, let him come to me and drink" (7:37). When they return to their bosses, they are empty-handed. "Why have you not brought him?" they are asked. "No one ever spoke as this man speaks," they reply. Here the temple police show themselves to be one with "the crowd" in their positive response to Jesus. Even Nicodemus, that archetypal example of the fence-sitter, shows up in this scene and argues on Jesus' behalf.

There is much good will for Jesus throughout chapter 7. The problem is that no one is really acting on it in a decisive way.

The Pharisees get the last word. They declare, "Study the scriptures and you will find that the Prophet does not come from Galilee" (7:52). Theologically, they have hit the nail on the head, though not in the way that they think. In one sense, they are right, since this Messiah did not come from Galilee; he came from heaven. In another sense, they are wrong, for the Galilean identity of the early Jesus turns out to be central to his messianic identity.

To be from Galilee identifies Jesus as one who has the wrong pedigree and who therefore is unworthy of the notice of those who rule. They consider him unlearned (7:15) and a member of the "rabble, which cares nothing for the law" (7:49). By definition those who rule know what is best for the people (7:48), and that theme is ripe for political storytelling in our time. The stereotypical type of ruler pictured here, one who despises the common people, the very people for whose well-being he has oversight, is not unknown to us today. When such individuals are measured against the Jesus story, as John does here, they always come up short.

Though the rulers despise the people, they still maintain profound influence over them. The people tend to follow their lead and look for one who has the "proper" credentials to be their leader (7:13, 26). They have learned to check the prevailing winds and go with the trends. Like the brothers of Jesus who urged that he seek popular recognition, these people tend to look at appearances rather than character in their leadership (7:24). They have been so blinded that they fail to recognize one of their own. For to be from Galilee makes Jesus a Messiah who is one of the people. It makes him one with "the world" that God loved so much that he gave his only Son (3:16).

## Retelling the Story

On hearing his words some of the crowd said, 'This must certainly be the Prophet.' Others said, 'This is the Messiah.' But others argued, 'Surely the Messiah is not to come from Galilee?' (John 7:40-41)

Why would Jesus avoid Judaea at one point because of the danger it presented to him, and then go to Judaea later and yet still evade danger? Chrysostom's answer to this dilemma was developed out of fourth-century Christian theology, but it still makes sense of John's style today. "It was not in order that he might obtain the reputation of speaking in riddles that John spoke in this way. Perish the thought! On the contrary, he did this to make it clear that at one time Christ's divinity was being attested; at another, his humanity. When he said 'He could not [go to Judaea]' (7:1) he was speaking of him as a man who did many things even in a human way; but when he asserted that he stood in their midst and they did not seize him (7:25-26), he was, of course, proving the power of his Godhead. And this is so for in fleeing Christ was acting as a man, and in making his appearance he was acting as God; in both cases, genuinely." (Chrysostom, *Homilies on John* 48 [late-fourth century C.E.])

It had been an unusual day. Events were being rehashed by groups of men and women in the marketplace.

"I say he is a fraud," said Ephraim. Ephraim was a leading figure in the community with ties to the chief priests and Pharisees. His opinion was widely respected. "If he were a real religious leader," Ephraim continued, "he would look and speak like one. That Galilean accent is a dead giveaway. This man speaks no better than a common peasant."

"But how can a common peasant have such learning?" said Ruth, the shopkeeper's wife. "I heard him explain the law as though he were a graduate of the Jerusalem Academy for Rabbinical Training. But he claimed his learning had come direct from God."

"You see, just like I said," exclaimed Joshua the rag-picker. "He is the Messiah."

Just then one of the temple policemen came into view. The crowd quickly gathered around him.

"Tell us what happened, Eli. We heard you were sent to arrest him. Is he in prison now?"

"No, he's not," said Eli.

"What happened? Was there a fight? Were his disciples too much for you?"

Eli swaggered a bit as he spoke, "No, of course not. We could have easily handled them if they had tried anything. We . . . well, we just decided not to go through with it."

"Why not? Did he buy you off or something? Or have you decided to become his disciple also?"

Eli laughed. "That is what the Pharisees wanted to know. It's hard to explain really. There was something about the way he spoke—with such insight on the law and such knowledge of the scriptures! I have never heard anything like it! Somehow, when push came to shove, we just couldn't do it."

"Just like I said, he's the Messiah," Joshua the rag-picker insisted once more. This time others joined him in that judgment.

"No, no, no," said Ephraim, "he cannot be the Messiah. Look, the measure of a leader is determined by the kinds of people he attracts. This man has been exposed as a fraud by our own religious scholars. If he were the Messiah, our leaders would have certified him as such. If he does not have their respect, he does not deserve ours."

There was a hushed silence as the people considered this argument. It was true; the Messiah would surely stand out as a respected leader—he would not be a pariah like this man. They began to waver to Ephraim's side of the debate.

Meanwhile, Eli looked at Ephraim thoughtfully for a moment, then surveyed the listening crowd. They were a motley group of shopkeepers and servants, representative of the common people of the land. He smiled ruefully, then said, "You know, Ephraim, the Pharisees said the same thing. 'You can judge a leader by the people he attracts,' they said. And I guess they are right. After all, it is only people like yourselves who have paid any attention to him. Since this Galilean has only managed to attract 'common rabble' like yourselves, as the Pharisees put it, it is obvious he has his priorities all wrong, isn't it?"

At this, Eli turned away sadly and walked on, leaving the people to wonder at his words. *(Dennis E. Smith)*

The Feast of Tabernacles was celebrated over an eight-day period during which the Jews would live in makeshift huts or "booths" to commemorate the tents where the Israelites lived during their time in the wilderness (Lev. 23:39-43). As one of the three major pilgrimage festivals in Judaism, it attracted large crowds to Jerusalem, and, especially to the temple where a number of ritual activities were carried out (*Mishnah Sukkah* 5:2-5). This correlates with Jesus' choice to go to the temple and teach. According to the Mishnah (*Sukkah* 4:9), there was a water libation included in the festival rituals in which a "golden flagon" was filled with water from the pool of Siloam and used in a ritual libation in the temple. John probably intends an intentional contrast between the water of the festival and the "living water" of Jesus when he provides the setting of "the last and greatest day of the festival" for Jesus' saying, "If anyone is thirsty, let him come to me and drink" (7:37). It is also likely that the tradition that the future gathering of all nations to Jerusalem to worship God at the Feast of Tabernacles (Zech. 14:16) provided a backdrop for John's presentation of Jesus' teachings on this occasion.

# The Blind Man

*After being healed by Jesus, the former blind man must undergo a trial before the Jewish officials.*

## The Story

**[SCENE ONE]** As HE went on his way Jesus saw a man who had been blind from birth. His disciples asked him, 'Rabbi, why was this man born blind? Who sinned, this man or his parents?' 'It is not that he or his parents sinned,' Jesus answered; 'he was born blind so that God's power might be displayed in curing him. While daylight lasts we must carry on the work of him who sent me; night is coming, when no one can work. While I am in the world I am the light of the world.'

With these words he spat on the ground and made a paste with the spittle; he spread it on the man's eyes, and said to him, 'Go and wash in the pool of Siloam.' (The name means 'Sent'.) The man went off and washed, and came back able to see.

**[SCENE TWO]** His neighbours and those who were accustomed to see him begging said, 'Is not this the man who used to sit and beg?' Some said, 'Yes, it is.'

Others said, 'No, but it is someone like him.' He himself said, 'I am the man.' They asked him, 'How were your eyes opened?' He replied, 'The man called Jesus made a paste and smeared my eyes with it, and told me to go to Siloam and wash. So I went and washed, and found I could see.'

'Where is he?' they asked. 'I do not know,' he said.

**[SCENE THREE]** The man who had been blind was brought before the Pharisees. As it was a sabbath day when Jesus made the paste and opened his eyes, the Pharisees too asked him how he had gained his sight. The man told them, 'He spread a paste on my eyes; then I washed, and now I can see.' Some of the Pharisees said, 'This man cannot be from God; he does not keep the sabbath.' Others said, 'How could such signs come from a sinful man?' So they took different sides. Then they continued to question him: 'What have you to say about him? It was your eyes he opened.' He answered, 'He is a prophet.'

**[SCENE FOUR]** The Jews would not believe that the man had been blind and had gained his sight, until they had summoned his parents and questioned them: 'Is this your son? Do you say that he was born blind? How is it that he can see now?' The parents replied, 'We know that he is our son, and that he was born blind. But how it is that he can now see, or who opened his eyes, we do not know. Ask him; he is of age; let him speak for himself.'

94

His parents gave this answer because they were afraid of the Jews; for the Jewish authorities had already agreed that anyone who acknowledged Jesus as Messiah should be banned from the synagogue. That is why the parents said, 'He is of age; ask him.'

[SCENE FIVE]    So for the second time they summoned the man who had been blind, and said, 'Speak the truth before God. We know that this man is a sinner.' 'Whether or not he is a sinner, I do not know,' the man replied. 'All I know is this: I was blind and now I can see.' 'What did he do to you?' they asked. 'How did he open your eyes?' 'I have told you already,' he retorted, 'but you took no notice. Why do you want to hear it again? Do you also want to become his disciples?' Then they became abusive. 'You are that man's disciple,' they said, 'but we are disciples of Moses. We know that God spoke to Moses, but as for this man, we do not know where he comes from.'

The man replied, 'How extraordinary! Here is a man who has opened my eyes, yet you do not know where he comes from! We know that God does not listen to sinners; he listens to anyone who is devout and obeys his will. To open the eyes of a man born blind—that is unheard of since time began. If this man was not from God he could do nothing.' 'Who are you to lecture us?' they retorted. 'You were born and bred in sin.' Then they turned him out.

[SCENE SIX]    Hearing that they had turned him out, Jesus found him and asked, 'Have you faith in the Son of Man?' The man answered, 'Tell me who he is, sir, that I may put my faith in him.' 'You have seen him,' said Jesus; 'indeed, it is he who is speaking to you.' 'Lord, I believe,' he said, and fell on his knees before him.

[SCENE SEVEN]    Jesus said, 'It is for judgement that I have come into this world—to give sight to the sightless and to make blind those who see.' Some Pharisees who were present asked, 'Do you mean that we are blind?' 'If you were blind,' said Jesus, 'you would not be guilty, but because you claim to see, your guilt remains.'

## Comments on the Story

This is one of the most highly structured stories in John. It divides easily into dramatic scenes, and follows conventional patterns of ancient drama. There are seven scenes in all. In each scene, only two characters or groups of characters have speaking roles, a common convention. Furthermore, the scenes are arranged in a structured order that the ancients called *chiasm*. That is, scenes one and seven, two and six, and three and five are related thematically. This arrangement places the emphasis on scene four as central to the overall meaning of the story.

Scenes one and seven concern Jesus and significant observers of the action; scene one presents Jesus and the disciples (believers) while scene seven presents Jesus and the Pharisees (nonbelievers). Scenes two and six concern the blind man's encounters at the early and late stages of his story. In scene two, he encounters the neighbors and expresses his initial analysis of the event of his healing, while in scene six, he encounters Jesus and confesses his faith. Scenes three and five present early and late stages of his trial before the Pharisees. In scene three, he makes his initial response to the Pharisees, judging Jesus to be a prophet. In scene five, he has moved so far in his evaluation of Jesus that they cast him out.

Scene four has no counterparts in the structure, and presents a set of characters that only enter the story here: the parents. The episode with the parents presents an important focus to the story because it makes an explicit connection with the world of John's community. J. L. Martyn has made the point that the period in which believers were being cast out of the synagogue, as is mentioned here, could only have happened in the latter decades of the first century. Neither in Jesus' day nor in the earliest years of the church was there any official action within Judaism in which Christians as a group would be cast out of the synagogue. In Jesus' day, the Christian movement had not yet developed such a sectarian identity. In the earliest years of the church, the church started out as a Jewish sect with only sporadic tension developing with Judaism at large. Only in the period after the destruction of the temple (70 C.E.), when Judaism began to centralize and defend its identity around the traditions of the rabbis (collected in the Mishnah), could such an official action be envisioned. Martyn identifies the action of official expulsion from the synagogue with the period of ca. 80–85 C.E. when the so-called council of Jamnia began to exert influence over the remnants of Judaism and centralize Jewish beliefs. Connected with this were the benedictions that developed at this time in which those who confessed Christ were to be cursed. This seems best to fit the situation reflected in John.

This is not the first time John's story has reflected issues of the time of John, but this is one of the most blatant of such instances. Thus the story of the blind man presents a model for discipleship that reflects the story of the church.

It was clearly a church in conflict. The church's members began in Judaism, and now were faced with the severe crisis of being cast out of the only church home they had ever known. How were they to understand their faith in this new circumstance?

The symbolic overtones of the story are indicated in the preceding context when Jesus proclaims, "I am the light of the world." The healing of the blind man will be a story of bringing light to one in darkness. Yet when the man receives light, he still must go through a pilgrimage of faith. Like other stories of discipleship in John, the process to true faith starts with the sign, but then must proceed to higher levels of understanding about the identity of Jesus before true faith is arrived at.

The pilgrimage of the blind man proceeds in a context of conflict. In scene one, when he receives his sight, the conversation between Jesus and the disciples places a theological interpretation on the event, and in doing so alerts us that it is the symbolism of the story that we should be noticing. For Jesus says, "While I am in the world I am the light of the world." It is not the healing of physical blindness that is at issue here, but the healing of spiritual blindness. Now the blind man has received that healing, that spiritual insight. But his faith is still at an early stage. It is the conflict that spurs his faith to grow.

First it is the neighbors, in scene two, who challenge the blind man, and elicit his testimony that Jesus is the one responsible for his healing. At this point, he has not yet begun to form conclusions about Jesus. Then the trial scene begins. It is not described as a formal trial, but it does proceed like a trial. What we are to picture is the real event of trials that John's church was experiencing before the synagogue officials of the day. In scene three, the challenge of his interlocutors at the trial produces the former blind man's first step of faith when he says of Jesus, "he is a prophet." To pronounce Jesus as a prophet is an appropriate early stage of faith in John. It means he is on the right track, but he still has a way to go.

The parents in scene four apparently represent one of the factions in John's community. They are those who are secret believers but will not confess their belief publicly out of fear of being cast out of the synagogue. Such "fence-sitting" is obviously not acceptable. Instead, the path of faith must inevitably lead to conflict.

The conflict of the path of faith comes to a head in scene five, when the former blind man mocks the Pharisees and is cast out. The phrase "turned him out" has a specific meaning, namely that he has been cast out of the synagogue.

His faith journey has brought him to this point. He is now, and only now, ready to be encountered by Jesus once more. In this final encounter, Jesus asks if he believes. The man is now ready to confess Jesus as the Messiah. But he could not have done so sooner. The lesson would not have been lost on John's community. True faith can only be realized when one is willing to take a "leap of faith" into a radical and frightening new world of religious reality.

The final scene provides the epilogue with the Pharisees. Now judgment is pronounced on them. They are the ones who are blind—it is the community of faith that sees. And their new sight, their new faith, has been confirmed by their experience of estrangement from the synagogue. That is how this story worked for them. For us today the story still presents a definition of faith in which a radical change of life is presupposed.

## Retelling the Story

The parents replied, 'We know that he is our son, and that he was born blind. But how it is that he can now see, or who opened his eyes, we

97

Stories of healings of blind men were not uncommon in the ancient world. Such stories could be found engraved on stones at sanctuary sites, functioning as a form of propaganda, such as this inscription from a temple of the healing god Asclepius in Rome: "To the blind soldier Valerius Aprus the god commanded by an oracle to come and take the blood of a white rooster, to mix it with honey and eye salve and to spread it on his eyes for three days. And he recovered his sight, and came and presented an offering of thanksgiving to the god." (*SIG* 1173, 138 C.E.; Boring, p. 284, no. 434)

do not know. Ask him; he is of age; let him speak for himself.' His parents gave this answer because they were afraid of the Jews.

(John 9:20-22)

"Samuel, I'm telling you! If I hear one more person ask what I did to cause my son's blindness, I'm going to hit him with my cookpot!"

The elderly Jew reached out to stroke his wife's shoulders. "Sarah, Sarah. Enough," he said. "We've been through all this a hundred times."

Benjamin was the light of their lives, the child for whom they had hoped for so long. But light was something that had no meaning for him. Benjamin had been born blind. Every day they had watched him struggle. Every day they had listened to the townspeople ask: "What did you do to cause his blindness?" Samuel and Sarah had searched their minds, their very souls, and still they did not know. It couldn't have been Benjamin's fault. He'd never had a chance to offend anyone. So it must be theirs. But what had they done that was so horrible that their child deserved to suffer?

No one ever asked how they could help Benjamin, only what his parents had done wrong. Even today it had happened again. That group of men from out of town had seen her son begging by the side of the road and she had heard one ask their leader the old question. All afternoon she had been pondering the answer she'd overheard. He had said, "It's not anyone's fault. It's so God's work can be shown through this man's life." What had he meant by that? And who was he?

In the middle of her reverie the door burst open and a disheveled man plunged through. He was dripping wet and grasping wildly at everything. At first she did not recognize him. Then he turned toward her. She heard herself gasp as she gazed into the familiar eyes of her son—eyes that now returned her gaze. "Benjamin? Benjamin!"

He whooped as he swung his mother high above him and then gently set her down and held her close. He was like a child again. The world was brand new to him—wonderful and bright.

His father and mother knelt beside him, their hands exploring his face.

Legends of healings commonly grew up about powerful figures in antiquity. One such popular tale told about the healing powers of the Emperor Vespasian. "During the months while Vespasian was waiting at Alexandria for the regular season of the summer winds and a settled sea, many marvels occurred to mark the favor of heaven and a certain partiality of the gods toward him. One of the common people of Alexandria, well known for his loss of sight, threw himself before Vespasian's knees, praying him with groans to cure his blindness, being so directed by the God Serapis, whom this most superstitious of nations worships before all others; and he besought the emperor to deign to moisten his cheeks and eyes with his spittle. . . . So Vespasian, believing that his good fortune was capable of anything and that nothing was any longer incredible, with a smiling countenance and amid intense excitement on the part of the bystanders, did as he was asked to do. . . . and the day again shone for the blind man. [This fact is] told by eyewitnesses even now when falsehood brings no reward." (Tacitus, *Histories* 4.89; from Boring, p. 285, no. 436 [ca. 110 C.E.])

"Benjamin! What happened? Can you really see?"

He looked up and for the first time in his life, they saw tears in his eyes. "I don't really know how it happened. A man, the one they call Jesus, knelt beside me on the road today. He asked me if I wanted to see. Then I felt something cool on my eyelids—it turned out to be mud. He told me to go wash in the pool of Siloam, so I did. Then when I pulled my head out of the water it was as if scales were falling from my eyes, and the light—I finally know what you mean by *light*—it was pouring in!

"I began running wildly, touching everything I could—*seeing* it for the first time! It was incredible! But then people started crowding around me, shouting questions at me. They took me before the Pharisees who started interrogating me. It was as though I were on trial! Question after question!"

The sound of an angry fist on the open door interrupted their reunion. Irate voices from outside called for Sarah and Samuel. They were ordered to appear before the Pharisees.

Amazed and confused, they could scarcely keep their minds on what they were being asked. It seemed so impossible, such a miracle. All they wanted to do was to sit with their son—look at him and rejoice that, for the first time, he could look back at them.

"Yes, he is our son," they said. "Yes, he was born blind." Questions and more questions. What did they want? Sarah struggled, her anger flushing her cheeks. Samuel laid a restraining hand on her arm. She knew. He didn't have to tell her. They had spent most of their lives trying to find out what they had done to cause their son's blindness; they were not going to speak now and risk angering God's representatives. "Ask him yourselves," was Samuel's wry comment as they left.

Sarah leaned heavily on her husband's arm as they left the crowd behind. "Did we do the right thing?" she said. "What should we have said, Samuel?"

Samuel sighed and turned to his wife. "For thirty years we have asked that," he said, "but only now do I feel that we have truly done something wrong. We both know what the man, Jesus, did for Benjamin. Why couldn't I *say* it?"

"You know why, Samuel," said Sarah. "You heard their threats. It has been hard for us to fight back the rumors all these years that we were at fault for what happened to Benjamin. But now, we would have really ended up being outcasts."

Between clenched teeth Samuel barely whispered. "Is that all we've learned—only to fear the God who would grant us such a precious gift, but not to honor his prophet? All this time I was sure we had not failed our son. Now I am not so sure anymore." *(Phyllis Williams Provost)*

# The Good Shepherd

*Jesus summarizes his mission and the nature of discipleship with the parable of the good shepherd.*

### The Story

I N very truth I tell you, the man who does not enter the sheepfold by the door, but climbs in some other way, is nothing but a thief and a robber. He who enters by the door is the shepherd in charge of the sheep. The doorkeeper admits him, and the sheep hear his voice; he calls his own sheep by name, and leads them out. When he has brought them all out, he goes ahead of them and the sheep follow, because they know his voice. They will not follow a stranger; they will run away from him, because they do not recognize the voice of strangers.'

This was a parable that Jesus told them, but they did not understand what he meant by it.

So Jesus spoke again: 'In very truth I tell you, I am the door of the sheepfold. The sheep paid no heed to any who came before me, for they were all thieves and robbers. I am the door; anyone who comes into the fold through me will be safe. He will go in and out and find pasture.

'A thief comes only to steal, kill, and destroy; I have come that they may have life, and may have it in all its fullness. I am the good shepherd; the good shepherd lays down his life for the sheep. The hired man, when he sees the wolf coming, abandons the sheep and runs away, because he is not the shepherd and the sheep are not his. Then the wolf harries the flock and scatters the sheep. The man runs away because he is a hired man and cares nothing for the sheep.

'I am the good shepherd; I know my own and my own know me, as the Father knows me and I know the Father; and I lay down my life for the sheep. But there are other sheep of mine, not belonging to this fold; I must lead them as well, and they too will listen to my voice. There will then be one flock, one shepherd. The Father loves me because I lay down my life, to receive it back again. No one takes it away from me; I am laying it down of my own free will. I have the right to lay it down, and I have the right to receive it back again; this charge I have received from my Father.'

These words once again caused a division among the Jews. Many of them said, 'He is possessed, he is out of his mind. Why listen to him?' Others said, 'No one possessed by a demon could speak like this. Could a demon open the eyes of the blind?'

## Comments on the Story

Whereas in the other Gospels Jesus often uses parables in his teaching, he rarely speaks in parables in John. This is one of those rare instances. This parable is actually a collection of several metaphorical expressions all of which relate to the central image of the shepherd and his sheep. In addition, there are explanations of Jesus attached. What we have here is not a traditional parable at all, but a collection of allegories in story form that provide interpretations of central themes in John's Gospel. The shepherd theme is borrowed by John from the Old Testament, where God and God's chosen leaders are often compared to shepherds who tend the flock that is Israel.

The parable proper is in verses 1-5, the first paragraph of the story. It tells a story in which the true shepherd comes in the proper way, by the door, to lead the sheep out of the sheepfold into a new pasture. The way he does this is to call them by name, then lead them out. They recognize his voice and follow only him. They will not follow a stranger "because they do not recognize the voice of strangers" (v. 5).

The immediate context for this parable is the story of the blind man that precedes it, which is mentioned again afterward (10:21). The blind man's pilgrimage of faith, which mirrors that of John's community, requires that he be "turned out" of his former place of safety, the synagogue, and move to a new place (9:34). The term translated "turned out" is used in the parable at 10:4, although there it is translated "when he has brought them all out." A similar term is used in 10:3 and is translated "lead out" (see 10:3). When the two stories are placed side by side, they describe the same experience from two different perspectives. The pilgrimage of the community of John out of the synagogue is not only a "turning out," but also a calling out. By taking this step into the religious unknown, a step that is being forced on them, they are at the same time responding to the call of Jesus to follow wherever he leads. In both stories, it should be noted, the path of true faith requires movement into an unknown future. The Christian can no more remain complacently in a place of safety than the sheep can remain in the fold and not respond to the call of the shepherd to new pasture.

But if Jesus is the shepherd who calls to a new pasture, who are the other characters mentioned here? They apparently refer to various figures in John's story and their counterparts in the experience of John's community.

First there is the "thief and robber" who does not enter by the door but tries to climb in by another way to steal the sheep. Then there is the stranger who calls the sheep but whose voice they recognize as not that of the true shepherd. These characters seem to represent other voices and pressures that attempt to turn the people of faith away from their calling. Both are evasive and slippery characters. They might even be persuasive. But in the final analysis, their aim

102

is to destroy the flock for their own self-interest, rather than lead it along the true path. The same may be said for the wolf, who represents a particularly dangerous, demonic force that is capable of devouring the flock. As long as the sheep respond to the voice of the good shepherd, they will be protected from these forces.

Other characters help to facilitate the work of the good shepherd. The door-keeper, for example, recognizes the true shepherd and lets him in. He is the one who prepares for the arrival of the shepherd when he comes to claim his sheep. John the Baptist is such a character in John's story. In the life of the church, the doorkeeper would seem to be the paraclete, or Spirit of Truth, who testifies to the identity and future coming of the Christ (16:13-14); that testimony, inci-dentally, is known to the community through the Gospel itself (20:31).

The hired hand is an ambivalent character. He is not the enemy of the sheep; in fact, he has been entrusted with their keeping. Yet the sheep are not really his, and when danger threatens, he runs away. There are many such characters in John's story, people like the parents of the blind man (9:22), who have the potential to be leaders in the community but who shrink back for fear of the consequences. The cowardice of such leaders functions as a betrayal of the church.

The imagery then shifts. Jesus is not the shepherd but the door to the sheep-fold. The door protects from the thieves and robbers; it is an image of safety. The sheep can go in and out and find pasture and know they are safe as long as they go by way of the door. This image may be compared with the saying of Jesus elsewhere in John, "I am the way, the truth, and the life; no one comes to the Father except by me" (14:6).

In the most powerful imagery drawn from this text, however, Jesus identifies himself as "the good shepherd." This term refers to the shepherd in the role of protector and martyr for the sheep. This is one of the most direct and profound of John's images for the meaning of Jesus' death. The good shepherd lays down his life for the sheep as an act of his own will. The point is strongly made that no one can take his life from him. He lays it down on his own.

This is, in fact, the primary imagery for Jesus' death throughout John's pas-sion narrative. In contrast with the story in the synoptic Gospels, in which there is more emphasis on Jesus' suffering, in John, the story is told in such a way that it is clear that Jesus is in charge. He directs his own arrest; he proclaims to Pilate that he can do nothing unless God allows it; he carries his own cross; he decides when it is time to die and then "gives up his spirit."

For John, it is the self-sacrifice of the Word become flesh that provides one of the most profound definitions of the meaning of Jesus' death. It is an act undertaken in obedience to God's plan, as seen in its fulfillment of a divinely ordained pattern. Yet it is also an act of compassion, exhibiting the love of God for the entire world (3:16). It expresses love of the highest order, such as when "someone should lay down his life for his friends" (15:13) or when a shepherd lays down his life for the sheep.

## Retelling the Story

> God is often referred to as a shepherd, as in the well-known Ps. 23:1, "The LORD is my shepherd." But the text that is most reflected here is Ezekiel 34. Here the leaders of Israel are cast as shepherds who have not properly cared for the sheep: "Woe betide Israel's shepherds who care only for themselves! Should not the shepherd care for the flock? . . . You do not feed the sheep. You have not restored the weak, tended the sick, bandaged the injured, recovered the straggler, or searched for the lost; you have driven them with ruthless severity. They are scattered abroad for want of a shepherd, and have become the prey of every wild beast. . . . Therefore, you shepherds, hear the word of the Lord. . . . I shall dismiss those shepherds from tending my flock: no longer will they care only for themselves; I shall rescue my sheep from their mouths, and they will feed on them no more . . . I myself shall tend my flock, and find them a place to rest, says the Lord God. . . . I shall set over them one shepherd to take care of them, my servant David." (Ezek. 34:1-23)

'The sheep paid no heed to any who came before me, for they were all thieves and robbers.'

(John 10:8)

"What was that? . . . Someone's out there!" The girl turned to her brother in fear. His eyes widened but he remained motionless, too frightened to respond.

A shadow slowly brushed across the doorway. Someone was stealthily entering the place where they had lain sleeping. Silence. The intruder had paused there.

What would he do? Would he hurt them? Would he take them away? Leah moved closer to her younger brother.

The trespasser must have seen the movement for with sinewy steps he began moving closer to where they lay. And then an outstretched bony hand reached toward them. It was motioning for them to come to him!

"You!" he hissed softly. "Come with me. No need to fear," he whispered. "I'll . . . take care of you."

The two remained where they were, huddled together, trembling in fear at this unfamiliar figure.

Again he started toward them, but was stopped short by a blinding light that cut across the yard. It startled the man and he hesitated. For an eternal moment, he looked back at the young innocents and then turned and disappeared into the night. The two siblings clung tightly to each other, their bodies flooded with relief.

Suddenly a shadow again filled the doorway. Had the intruder returned? Perhaps with a weapon? They shut their eyes tight. Nothing would deter him this time.

Then a voice spoke softly.

"Leah. Avram. It's all right. I'm here."

"Father!" They rushed toward the one they loved. They were safe!

Softly the shepherd turned, motioned to them, and led the willing lambs out of their pen and into the light.

*(Phyllis Williams Provost)*

For Chrysostom, the "door" represents scripture: "With good reason did he call scripture a 'door.' For it leads us to God and opens to us the knowledge of God; it makes us his sheep; it guards us; and it does not permit the wolves to enter. Indeed, just as a door provides security, so scripture prevents the entrance of heretics, places us in safety with regard to all our desires, and does not permit us to go astray. If we do not remove it, we shall not easily be overcome by our enemies. By means of it we shall be able to discriminate between all men: both the true shepherds and those who are not." (Chrysostom, *Homilies on John,* 59 [late-fourth century C.E.])

# The Raising of Lazarus

*Jesus raises Lazarus from the dead with the result that Mary and Martha believe in him but his enemies seek to kill him.*

**The Story**

**[SCENE ONE]**     There was a man named Lazarus who had fallen ill. His home was at Bethany, the village of Mary and her sister Martha. This Mary, whose brother Lazarus had fallen ill, was the woman who anointed the Lord with ointment and wiped his feet with her hair. The sisters sent a message to him: 'Sir, you should know that your friend lies ill.' When Jesus heard this he said, 'This illness is not to end in death; through it God's glory is to be revealed and the Son of God glorified.' Therefore, though he loved Martha and her sister and Lazarus, he stayed where he was for two days after hearing of Lazarus's illness.

He then said to his disciples, 'Let us go back to Judaea.' 'Rabbi,' his disciples said, 'it is not long since the Jews there were wanting to stone you. Are you going there again?' Jesus replied, 'Are there not twelve hours of daylight? Anyone can walk in the daylight without stumbling, because he has this world's light to see by. But if he walks after nightfall he stumbles, because the light fails him.'

After saying this he added, 'Our friend Lazarus has fallen asleep, but I shall go and wake him.' The disciples said, 'Master, if he is sleeping he will recover.' Jesus had been speaking of Lazarus's death, but they thought that he meant natural sleep. Then Jesus told them plainly: 'Lazarus is dead. I am glad for your sake that I was not there; for it will lead you to believe. But let us go to him.' Thomas, called 'the Twin', said to his fellow-disciples, 'Let us also go and die with him.'

**[SCENE TWO]**     On his arrival Jesus found that Lazarus had already been four days in the tomb. Bethany was just under two miles from Jerusalem, and many of the Jews had come from the city to visit Martha and Mary and condole with them about their brother. As soon as Martha heard that Jesus was on his way, she went to meet him, and left Mary sitting at home.

Martha said to Jesus, 'Lord, if you had been here my brother would not have died. Even now I know that God will grant you whatever you ask of him.' Jesus said, 'Your brother will rise again.' 'I know that he will rise again', said Martha, 'at the resurrection on the last day.' Jesus said, 'I am the resurrection and the life. Whoever has faith in me shall live, even though he dies; and no one who lives and has faith in me shall ever die. Do you believe this?' 'I do, Lord,' she answered; 'I believe that you are the

Messiah, the Son of God who was to come into the world.'

So saying she went to call her sister Mary and, taking her aside, she said, 'The Master is here and is asking for you.' As soon as Mary heard this she rose and went to him. Jesus had not yet entered the village, but was still at the place where Martha had met him. When the Jews who were in the house condoling with Mary saw her hurry out, they went after her, assuming that she was going to the tomb to weep there.

Mary came to the place where Jesus was, and as soon as she saw him she fell at his feet and said, 'Lord, if you had been here my brother would not have died.' When Jesus saw her weeping and the Jews who had come with her weeping, he was moved with indignation and deeply distressed. 'Where have you laid him?' he asked. They replied, 'Come and see.' Jesus wept. The Jews said, 'How dearly he must have loved him!' But some of them said, 'Could not this man, who opened the blind man's eyes, have done something to keep Lazarus from dying?'

**[SCENE THREE]**   Jesus, again deeply moved, went to the tomb. It was a cave, with a stone placed against it. Jesus said, 'Take away the stone.' Martha, the dead man's sister, said to him, 'Sir, by now there will be a stench; he has been there four days.' Jesus said, 'Did I not tell you that if you have faith you will see the glory of God?' Then they removed the stone.

Jesus looked upwards and said, 'Father, I thank you for hearing me. I know that you always hear me, but I have spoken for the sake of the people standing round, that they may believe it was you who sent me.'

Then he raised his voice in a great cry: 'Lazarus, come out.' The dead man came out, his hands and feet bound with linen bandages, his face wrapped in a cloth. Jesus said, 'Loose him; let him go.'

Many of the Jews who had come to visit Mary, and had seen what Jesus did, put their faith in him. But some of them went off to the Pharisees and reported what he had done.

**[SCENE FOUR]**   Thereupon the chief priests and the Pharisees convened a meeting of the Council. 'This man is performing many signs,' they said, 'and what action are we taking? If we let him go on like this the whole populace will believe in him, and then the Romans will come and sweep away our temple and our nation.' But one of them, Caiaphas, who was high priest that year, said, 'You have no grasp of the situation at all; you do not realize that it is more to your interest that one man should die for the people, than that the whole nation should be destroyed.' He did not say this of his own accord, but as the high priest that year he was prophesying that Jesus would die for the nation, and not for the nation alone but to gather together the scattered children of God. So from that day on they plotted his death.

Accordingly Jesus no longer went about openly among the Jews, but withdrew to a town called Ephraim, in the country bordering on the desert, and stayed there with his disciples.

## Comments on the Story

This story is the climactic event of Jesus' public ministry in the Gospel of John. It becomes the evidence that leads to the decision of the Jewish leadership that Jesus must die. Yet it is a story found only in John; the other Gospels connect other events with the decision that Jesus must die. It is a story like others in John, in which the sign mirrors the theological truth it teaches. Here Jesus gives life to a dead man, and within the dialogue that accompanies the sign, he identifies himself as "the resurrection and the life." The Jewish leaders then decide he must die because his signs are attracting crowds and therefore threatening the Jewish nation with retribution from the Romans. But there is great irony in their decision. The giver of life must die, and, in an ironic reversal, it is the death itself that will be the means of life.

The story is divided into four scenes. Scene one takes place across the Jordan, where Jesus first baptized. Here Jesus hears about Lazarus's death and discusses its significance for his ministry with his disciples. Scene two takes place on the road to Bethany, a village near Jerusalem. Here Martha meets him and responds in faith even before the sign is done. Scene three takes place at the tomb of Lazarus where Jesus calls him forth from the tomb. Scene four takes us back to Jerusalem at the council of the Pharisees where the significance of Jesus' deeds are being discussed and the decision is made that he must die. At the conclusion of this story, a turning point in Jesus' ministry is indicated. From this point on "Jesus no longer went about openly among the Jews." His ministry to "his own" (1:11) was over.

Jesus is brought word that Lazarus is sick. He immediately responds on two levels. On the one hand, he loved the sisters and Lazarus deeply. On the other hand, he recognized that this is to be the opportunity for a sign, and that this sign will be a revelation of his glory (v. 4). It is an enigmatic scene, for Jesus intentionally delays until Lazarus is thoroughly dead (vv. 5-6, 15), and in so doing seems to confuse his disciples. Yet his actions are not to be analyzed on a human level; he is simply following through with his role in the divine drama. The author emphasizes the fact that Jesus' actions are deliberate, almost as if he is carrying out a role that is already scripted.

The disciples here, as elsewhere in John, do not understand clearly what Jesus' actions mean. We, the hearers of the story, are informed of their confusion. Thus we are able to recognize the irony in their concern that Jesus, in returning to the vicinity of Jerusalem, will be returning to a place where he could be stoned. They recognize the danger but do not understand its significance.

Normally in John the sign is performed first, then the dialogue explaining what it means occurs; this pattern is followed in John 6, for example. Here that pattern is reversed. The dialogue comes first and the sign comes after. This allows the action to move swiftly from the raising of Lazarus to the plotting of Jesus' enemies against him. It also functions to give emphasis to the pilgrimage of faith recorded in the scene on the road to Bethany, for Martha is seen to arrive at a level of saving faith in anticipation of the sign—not after having experienced it. Her faith therefore emerges as more profound than that of many others in John's Gospel. In fact, her faith is the closest model throughout John for the kind of faith that the Christian community is to have, for theirs, too, must be a faith without physical evidence of the signs (20:29).

Martha is given the role of the exemplary disciple in the story. It is she who comes to meet Jesus first. Jesus chooses this occasion to question her directly about her faith, to which she responds, "I know that he will rise again at the resurrection of the just." To this Jesus responds with one of the "I am" sayings in John, those sayings that represent the highest level of christological statement. "I am the resurrection and the life," he says. "Do you believe this?" She responds without wavering, "I believe that you are the Messiah, the Son of God who was to come into the world." In the synoptic Gospels, the closest parallel to this story is the confession of Peter (as in Mark 8:27-29). At a climactic point in Jesus' ministry, he finally asks the disciples who they think he is. Peter responds with the exemplary statement of faith, "you are the Messiah." That story is not found in John, though there is a similar confession of Peter in John 6. But it is this story that forms the closest parallel to the confession of Peter. The story of Peter's confession in the synoptics comes to be interpreted as the point at which Peter's leadership among the disciples and within the church is affirmed (as in Matt. 16:13-19). By paralleling that story with this one, John once more surprises us by placing a woman in the leadership role of exemplary disciple instead of Peter.

After Martha leaves and informs Mary of Jesus' arrival, Mary rushes out to the road to meet him as well. In response to the weeping of Mary and of those around her, Jesus is "moved with indignation and deeply distressed." Eventually, he himself weeps. And when he arrives at the tomb, he is said to be "deeply moved." What are we to make of these references to the emotional response of Jesus? They seem odd in many respects. After all, he intentionally delayed his arrival so as to make the miracle even more spectacular, or so it would seem. He knows Lazarus will be raised, so he should not be sad. And up to this time he has seemed calm and collected, knowing all along where the events are heading. Furthermore, the terms used here are puzzling, suggesting a sort of groaning and distressed feeling. It is not completely clear what the narrator wants to convey. Readers of John will often point to this text as one that shows us better than any others the humanity of Jesus. Yet that seems far from the author's intention, for the entire story has been set up as a divine sign, not an act of compassion. It seems more likely that the narrator sees some connection between the emotional response of Jesus and his divine character. Some have suggested that Jesus groans with emotion because of the weakness of the faith of those around him. But this does not explain the reference to his weeping, for in the context he is pictured as joining the others in their weeping at that point. Perhaps we are to see here a divine compassion for the human condition in general, as if to say that God weeps with us when we weep. In this way, though the story overcomes death for one person, Lazarus, and thereby prefigures the overcoming of death for all believers, it does not deny the reality of death and the sorrow it brings.

The miracle at the tomb itself is rather stark and brief. The meaning has already been explicated in the preceding events. Jesus adds one last interpretation with his prayer, which we are allowed to overhear, in which he thanks God for the fact that the sign will produce faith. Then he simply says, "Lazarus, come out," and he does, wrapped in his burial clothes. Jesus' final words are, "Loose him; let him go." No further response of the crowd is indicated.

Rather, the response to the miracle that immediately follows is that which takes place in the council of Pharisees in Jerusalem. Here Caiaphas makes a statement of high and memorable irony: "It is more to your interest that one man should die for the people, than that the whole nation should be destroyed." In the immediate story, he intends his statement to be referring to the threat that Jesus' popularity may bring about Roman oppression. But in the larger story, he has, unknowingly, interpreted the events exactly right.

The raising of Lazarus becomes the primary event on which the decision to kill Jesus comes to be founded. This motif is found only in John, and it is heavy with irony. Supposedly the Jewish leaders worry most about the fact that crowds keep following him because of this sign (11:48; 12:9-11, 17-19). Yet its meaning lies at another level. The raising of Lazarus is a sign that Jesus is the one who gives life. It is precisely because of that that the powers of darkness are arrayed against him. It is not because of the popularity it brings about but because of the inherent meaning of the miracle that Jesus must die. But as the final ironic twist, it will be through that death that he will bring life.

## Retelling the Story

The sisters sent a message to him: 'Sir, you should know that your friend lies ill.' When Jesus heard this he said, 'This illness is not to end in death; through it God's glory is to be revealed and the Son of God glorified.' (John 11:3-4)

Getting stoned is something you never want to do—especially if you're on the wrong end of the stones. Well, there were some folks in Judea who wanted Jesus to be on the wrong end of those stones. Word was going around that he had said, "The Father and I are one." Now someone could have called him a magician, a mystic, or even a demon, and someone in the crowd would have slapped someone else on the back and said, "See there, Harvey, I told you so! You owe me five bucks." But calling himself *God*! This was *blasphemy*!

The people had all been pestering him to tell them who he was—"Come on, Jesus! Who are you really? Are you like David Copperfield or something? I bet you're the Messiah! Tell us you're the Messiah! Come on! Admit it! You're the Messiah, aren't you? Who are you?"

"I'm the Messiah."

"Are not!" "I can't believe he said that!" "The nerve of him!" "What made him say that?"

And Jesus went on an instant retreat—to the other side of the Jordan—just before they got out the tar, feathers, and rocks.

They had been in Perea only a short while when the message came from Bethany. His friend, Lazarus, was sick—really sick—and Lazarus's sisters, Mary and Martha, had sent for Jesus.

When he heard the message, Jesus sat down on the sand, his head in his hands. Finally, he said, "He won't die. We stay here." And so they did. The disciples thought that was the end of the matter. But then, two days later at breakfast, Jesus announced, "We're going to Judea."

"Uh, excuse me," Peter interrupted. "Do the words, 'Stone the blasphemer' mean anything to you? Don't you remember what happened the last time we were in Judea? Wouldn't a trip to the Mediterranean work just as well?"

Jesus explained. "We're going back because Lazarus is asleep."

"Right. Jesus, a lot of people are asleep at this hour."

Sometimes Jesus must have felt like his disciples had all the insight of a rutabaga, but he tried again.

"Lazarus is dead."

They got it.

"And so now we've got to go there."

They didn't get it. Maybe Jesus needed to do the funeral.

The silence was broken by Thomas. "Let's go die with Jesus when he goes!"

You can't say that he was lacking for support.

When they arrived in Bethany, they found that Lazarus had been in the tomb for about four days, and all his

It was widely believed in the ancient world that the soul hovered near the body for up to three days before departing. "When a human being dies, the soul remains two days without being judged, and it travels around with an angel wherever it wants to go. . . . And on the third day the angel takes the soul to heaven." According to the ancient view, then, Jesus waited until the soul had finally departed. (Addition to the *Life of Adam and Eve;* from Boring, p. 290, no. 444 [ca. 800-900 C.E.])

Chrysostom, who like most preachers, tends to interpret the text with a view to his own social context, notes that by ending their grieving when Jesus arrived, Martha and Mary gave a good example of women with "virtuous minds." He contrasts this with customs in his day. "At present, on the contrary, along with the rest of our vices there is one disorder especially prevalent among women. They make a show of their mourning and lamentation: baring their arms, tearing their hair, making scratches down their cheeks. Moreover, some do this because of grief, others for show and vain display. Still others through depravity both bare their arms and do these other things to attract the gaze of men. . . . Will not the heathen ridicule you? Will they not think our teachings are myths? For they will say: 'There is no resurrection; the Christian teachings are jokes, lies, and tricks. The women among them, in fact, lament as if no one exists after this life." (Chrysostom, *Homilies on John* 62 [late-fourth century C.E.])

friends and kinfolk were really upset. Martha met him at the gate. "Where *were* you?" She demanded. "If you'd have been here, he wouldn't have died."

Jesus said to her, "I was with you—and I am with you now."

And then . . . Jesus wept.

They went to the tomb together.

Now, tombs in those days were usually caves cut into the limestone hillside. And this particular cave already had several people placed in it. A big rock had been rolled in place in front to seal it.

When they got there, Jesus stood right in front of the tomb. He drew himself up to full height and commanded, "Remove the stone!"

What was he going to do? Was Jesus planning on going inside? Two of the disciples moved the rock—and held their breath in anticipation.

Jesus raised his arms toward heaven . . . and prayed. And then, in a loud voice, he commanded, "Come *out*!" Who or what did he think was going to emerge from that tomb? A skeleton? A ghost?

The dank air of the tomb slowly hissed from the hillside. The breeze suddenly stilled as a form walked from the dark cave. Jesus turned to them and said, "Go unbind him!" It was Lazarus! He was alive!

From that point on, people began to recognize that Jesus was more than a holy man—he could give life to *everyone*!

But some were more attuned to death than life, and from that moment on, they began to plot the death of Jesus. *(Phyllis Williams Provost)*

# The Anointing at Bethany

*Mary anoints Jesus' feet at a banquet in Bethany.*

### The Story

Six days before the Passover festival Jesus came to Bethany, the home of Lazarus whom he had raised from the dead. They gave a supper in his honour, at which Martha served, and Lazarus was among the guests with Jesus. Then Mary brought a pound of very costly perfume, pure oil of nard, and anointed Jesus's feet and wiped them with her hair, till the house was filled with the fragrance. At this, Judas Iscariot, one of his disciples—the one who was to betray him—protested, 'Could not this perfume have been sold for three hundred denarii and the money given to the poor?' He said this, not out of any concern for the poor, but because he was a thief; he had charge of the common purse and used to pilfer the money kept in it. 'Leave her alone,' said Jesus. 'Let her keep it for the day of my burial. The poor you have always among you, but you will not always have me.'

### Comments on the Story

This story takes place "six days before the Passover" in John's narrative. Jesus is on his way to Jerusalem and passes through Bethany once more. He had just been in Bethany when he raised Lazarus, but had then withdrawn to Ephraim to escape from the crowds (11:54). This trip to Bethany is therefore the first event of the passion narrative. If the Passover is six days away, then Jesus' death is five days away, since, in John, he dies at the same time the Passover lambs are slain. This is the beginning of his journey to his death.

The story seems to collect details from a variety of traditions. All four Gospels have anointing stories, but they differ. Mark's basic story, which is followed by Matthew, tells of an unnamed woman who anoints Jesus' head with expensive ointment. That story takes place in the home of Simon the Leper two days before the Passover, yet the event is basically the same, since it takes place in Bethany during the passion narrative, and since it leads to a controversy about the expensive ointment and how the money could have been given to the poor (Mark 14:3-9; Matt. 26:6-13). Luke omits that story, but has another anointing story earlier in his narrative in which a woman who is a sinner approaches Jesus while he dines at the home of a Pharisee. She has ointment but does not anoint his head. Instead, she washes his feet with her tears and dries them with her hair and then anoints his feet with the ointment (Luke 7:36-50). John's story is unusual because it seems to draw on both of these traditions. On the one hand, Mary, according to John, has expensive ointment. But instead of anointing his head, she anoints his feet. Then she wipes the ointment off with her hair. The story also shares details with another story about Mary and Martha from Luke, in which Martha serves at a meal while Mary joins Jesus at the table to listen to his teachings (10:40). In that story in Luke, however, there is no anointing and there is no mention of a brother named Lazarus.

Proper etiquette at ancient banquets would call for the guests' feet to be washed, as Jesus does later at the Last Supper, according to John's account. It was also a common custom to provide perfumes to anoint the head. But to anoint the feet, then wipe it off with one's hair, seems to be an unparalleled practice, and makes sense only as a literary sign. John is clearly focusing on the symbolism of the event. The act of foot washing is made into a symbol for the death of Jesus at the Last Supper (13:6-10). Apparently that text has influenced this one, so that the anointing with ointment in preparation for burial is done in the form of a foot washing, thus connecting with the later foot washing as a symbol for Jesus' death.

Mary, Martha, and Lazarus have given a banquet in Jesus' honor. Lazarus dines with Jesus, Martha serves, and Mary anoints him. Judas, who is identified as the one who was to betray him, raises the question about how the money for the perfume could have been given to the poor. The narrator tells us that this did not represent a concern for the poor on Judas's part, but rather that Judas kept the common purse and used to steal from it. That comment gives a certain slant to Jesus' reply. Since Judas's concern for the poor was not genuine, then Jesus' response is not a rejection of giving to the poor but rather is a rejection of Judas's embezzling of community funds.

The words of Jesus provide the interpretation of the event. The first statement, "let her keep it for the day of my burial," connects this event with Jesus' impending death. Even though John's Gospel does have an anointing of Jesus' body before burial (unlike the other Gospels), this story nevertheless allows Mary to participate in that anointing in advance.

The next statement of Jesus is unusual. Jesus seems to be opposing charity for the poor: "The poor you have always among you, but you will not always have me." However, in this case, charity for the poor has been overridden by the profound nature of Jesus' impending death. His death will do more for the poor and for all people than any single act of charity.

It is not unusual for a meal to be connected with death. According to ancient custom, a banquet, known as a funerary banquet, was commonly held in honor of the deceased. That imagery may be present here. Furthermore, since it is the Son of God himself who is being honored, this meal is also to be connected with the imagery of the messianic banquet, that is, the abundant banquet in heaven at the end of time.

The act of Mary is an act of exemplary faith. Like Martha in the previous story, Mary has insights into the meaning of Jesus' ministry prior to the sign itself, which, in this case, would be his death. This is the highest level of faith. Her faith is further signified by her role as servant. She has performed a supreme act of servanthood for the Messiah.

Every religious community has its Mary and its Judas. The Mary of a community is one who has insights that go very deep, but whose witness to those insights are expressed through symbolic acts of love and charity. Her opposite is the Judas character. This is an individual whose words are loud, forceful, and theologically impressive. But his true intentions are vain and selfish.

### Retelling the Story

Then Mary brought a pound of very costly perfume, pure oil of nard, and anointed Jesus's feet and wiped them with her hair, till the house was filled with the fragrance. (John 12:3)

Judas was furious at the woman who knelt at Jesus' feet. "Why wasn't that perfume sold and the money given to the poor?"

Jesus closed his eyes, savoring the fragrant aroma that filled the room.

This is a family meal in a Jewish household; consequently, it would not be unusual for women to be present. Nevertheless, ancient sensibilities suggested that women could compromise themselves by their behavior at a reclining banquet, since prostitutes were the kind of women often associated with banquets. This story may be trying to avoid that stigma by noting that Lazarus "was among the guests (Greek: reclined) with Jesus" while Martha served, and by placing Mary at the feet of Jesus in the role of a servant rather than as a reclining participant at the meal along with the men. Jewish sensibilities are expressed in Ecclus. 9:9 [ca. 180 B.C.E.]: "Never sit down (Greek: recline) with another man's wife or join her in a drinking party, for fear of succumbing to her charms and slipping into fatal disaster." Christian sensibilities are expressed by Clement of Alexandria [late second century C.E.]: "But if any necessity arises, commanding the presence of married women (at a banquet), let them be well clothed—without by raiment, within by modesty. But as for such as are unmarried, it is the extremest scandal for them to be present at a banquet of men, especially men under the influence of wine" (*Paedagogos* 2.54). (adapted from Corley, 70, 76, 102-6)

Anointing the head with perfumes at a banquet was a common custom in the ancient world. This description of a Greek banquet, which describes activities at the beginning of the symposium, notes that the servants provide perfume for the guests. "Now, at last, the floor is swept, and clean are the hands of all the guests, and their cups as well; one slave puts plaited wreaths on their heads, another offers sweet-smelling perfume in a saucer; the mixing-bowl stands full of good cheer; and another wine is ready, which promises never to give out" (Athenaeus 11.462c-d). Josephus refers to an incident once when Agrippa wanted to convince the senate that he had been engaged in innocuous activities: "On being summoned by the senate, he anointed his head with unguents as if he had arrived from a banquet that had just broken up." (*Antiquities* 19.239)

Somehow it reminded him of another place. It was a scent reminiscent of both life and death.

"Leave her alone," he sighed. "She has prepared me for my burial."

How had she known? Why had she done that? Anointing one's guest was common—but the head, not the feet. No one anointed the feet. It was a grimy and distasteful job to wash the feet of guests who had walked through the dirt and muck and mire of the open road, and especially the slop and refuse of the city streets. Not even all servants could be required to do that job. Yet this woman not only washed his feet, she anointed them—as one would anoint feet that would walk no more—and with pure and costly nard. The fragrance must have saturated the room!

How did she know? How could she have known he was about to die? Surely she was aware that anointing the body of one who had died was a symbol of love for that person—a way one demonstrated tenderly placing a person in the hands of God. Did she even know that was what she was doing?

She looked up into his eyes. What was he thinking? She could never tell. Did he know that this was the only way she could express her feelings? Gently, lovingly, she wiped the oil away with her hair. She knew the fragrance, the scent of her gift would stay with him for days.

The next day, when all of Jerusalem was at his feet as he entered the city in a triumphal parade of palms, the fragrance, indeed, surrounded him—reminding him of why he had come and where this road would lead.

Later that day the people heard him preach. He heard them murmur among themselves about blasphemy. He closed his eyes and was strengthened by the memories the fragrance evoked.

In a few days, he, too, knelt to wash the feet of those whom he loved—the twelve who followed him. And as he leaned down and assumed the role of servant, again, just faintly, he smelled the fragrance.

It was later that evening and the soldiers came to take him away. Was that something more than merely the fragrance of the olive tree in the air, reminding him he had already been lovingly placed in God's hands?

Then came countless hours of interrogation, flogging, and pain. But when he closed his eyes and was still, the barest hint of the fragrance remained with him—and it sustained him.

He was led to Golgotha and remained there in agony—with a sign above his head and a crowd below. Yet as he hung there alone, mixed with sweat and blood from his brow was . . . the fragrance.

It was two days later and another Mary had discovered that Jesus was gone. Weakly, she sat in the empty tomb in the place where his body had lain, and closed her eyes.

"Woman, why are you crying?" asked a gentle voice. She didn't even look up.

"They have taken my Lord away and I don't know where they have put him."

A sweet fragrance wafted toward her, startled her, seemed to surround her, to somehow penetrate her very soul and fill her with hope.

"Mary."

She opened her eyes and saw the figure—and moved toward the fragrance.

*(Phyllis Williams Provost)*

# Jesus Enters Jerusalem

*Jesus is greeted as a king when he enters Jerusalem on a donkey.*

## The Story

THE next day the great crowd of pilgrims who had come for the festival, hearing that Jesus was on the way to Jerusalem, went out to meet him with palm branches in their hands, shouting, 'Hosanna! Blessed is he who comes in the name of the Lord! Blessed is the king of Israel!' Jesus found a donkey and mounted it, in accordance with the words of scripture: 'Fear no more, daughter of Zion; see, your king is coming, mounted on a donkey's colt.' At the time his disciples did not understand this, but after Jesus had been glorified they remembered that this had been written about him, and that it had happened to him.

The people who were present when he called Lazarus out of the tomb and raised him from the dead kept telling what they had seen and heard. That is why the crowd went to meet him: they had heard of this sign that he had performed. The Pharisees said to one another, 'You can see we are getting nowhere; all the world has gone after him!'

## Comments on the Story

The entry into Jerusalem is the keynote event for the passion narrative in all four Gospels. They share the same basic structure of the story as well, suggesting that they all draw from a common tradition. John has in common with the other Gospels the entry by Jesus on a donkey, the acclamation of the crowd with the accompaniment of waving palm branches, and implicit or explicit reference to fulfillment of scripture regarding the entry of a king into Jerusalem. Like the other Gospels, John has modified this basic story to fit his own plot.

John has earlier noted that the decision that Jesus must die develops in response to the raising of Lazarus. Reminders of that event bracket this story. Immediately prior to this story there is the reference that crowds have gathered around Jesus because of the Lazarus miracle. Therefore "the chief priests then resolved to do away with Lazarus as well, since on his account many Jews were going over to Jesus and putting their faith in him" (vv. 10-11). When the entry story itself is related, the crowd that meets Jesus is identified as "pilgrims who had come for the [Passover] festival" (v. 12). Later, however, the narrator will include the additional detail: "that is why the crowd went to meet him:

they had heard of this sign [the raising of Lazarus] that he had performed"
(v. 18). And once more the Pharisees will conclude that the crowds are a problem: "You can see we are getting nowhere; all the world has gone after him!"
(v. 19).

Jerusalem at Passover season would have been a center of pilgrimage for
Jews from all parts of the world, for it was only in Jerusalem that the Passover
meal could be properly celebrated, since only in the temple in Jerusalem could
the lambs be sacrificed for the meal. Passover was a festive celebration com-
memorating God's deliverance of the Israelites from Egyptian bondage. Many
Jews under Roman rule longed for another deliverance from bondage; it would
be just thirty years later that a full-fledged war of the Jews against Rome
would erupt. During such a season, therefore, longing for the Messiah-King
was rampant.

This event takes place "the next day" (v. 12) after the event at Bethany,
which was "six days before the Passover festival" (v. 1). That would place this
event on a Sunday, since the Passover meal would be eaten on Friday night
(which was actually Saturday night according to Jewish reckoning, since each
new day began at six in the evening rather than midnight). The use of the palm
branches gives us the background for the Christian festival Palm Sunday. Palm
branches were normally associated with the Feast of Tabernacles rather than
Passover. Their use here seems to be derived from the connection of the palm
with celebrations of the nationhood of Israel. Thus the palms derive not from
the festival but are related directly to the proclamation of Jesus as king: this is
how a king is to be welcomed.

John's version of the entry story has an interesting twist at this point. Unlike
the other Gospels, here when Jesus mounts the donkey, it is in response to the
crowd's acclamation, almost as if Jesus is trying to escape them. Raymond
Brown has proposed that what Jesus is doing is opposing their interpretation
with another one. Whereas the crowd proclaims him as king of Israel, Jesus
takes on the posture of the king described in Zech. 9:9, which John paraphrases
in this way: "Fear no more, daughter of Zion; see, your king is coming, mounted on a donkey's colt." This text lies behind the narrating of this story in all the
Gospel traditions. Matthew also quotes the verse and uses it to stress the
humility of Jesus. But John seems to have a different purpose. For the very
next verse in Zechariah stresses that this king "will proclaim peace to the
nations . . . his rule shall extend from sea to sea" (Zech. 9:10). Jesus' symbolic
action connects him, therefore, not with a nationalistic king but with a universal king, one whose realm includes the entire world, not just the Jews. The
scene is correctly, and ironically, interpreted by the Pharisees: "all the world
has gone after him" (12:19).

In John, "the crowd" is usually a neutral character. Once before they followed Jesus in response to the signs and were fed by him, but when they tried

to make him king, he withdrew from them (6:1-15). They represent those who respond, but who misinterpret what Jesus is all about. They want an all-powerful king and try to make Jesus into that image. They cannot accept him as he is, as a servant-king. Though they represent a great mass of those who confess Jesus, their mistake is in trying to make Jesus fit the image they want.

The disciples, on the other hand, are on a faith journey filled with equal measures of doubt and certainty. Though they experience the glory of Jesus, they do not always understand its true meaning. They often find themselves following even though they continue to doubt. Later experience will teach them what they cannot now understand; then they will develop the insight to see clearly that which remains hidden to them now.

## Retelling the Story

> Jesus found a donkey and mounted it, in accordance with the words of scripture: "Fear no more, daughter of Zion; see, your king is coming, mounted on a donkey's colt." (John 12:14-15)

While she was doing her graduate work in theater at Northwestern, Susan had never thought that the only job she could land upon graduation would be in an outdoor drama, a Passion play at that. No, she had visions of going to New York, at least in an off-Broadway role. Or maybe she would wind up in Hollywood making connections with Garry Marshall or another powerful and well-placed NU theater alum. Instead, she was in some godforsaken frontier outpost of the arts performing on the concrete stage of a half-completed outdoor theater with a strange assortment of misfits who, like her, could find no other work for the summer. She really didn't like to think of herself as one of them.

Every evening about 5:30 she would show up for makeup. When they had started the production there hadn't even been dressing rooms finished for costume changes or lighted mirrors for makeup. The Passion play was the lifelong dream of a retired pastor who had little knowledge of the requirements of a theatrical production, and it really showed. The director of the Institute for Outdoor Drama came to look at the production and facilities and said he didn't know why the cast didn't revolt. Susan wasn't too sure either, except the one hundred dollars each week came in handy, and it was too late in the summer to get a job at Sears. In fact, the cast had make a pact that if anyone ever asked what they did this summer, they would say that they had worked at Sears. As the summer progressed, even that lame joke lost most of its humor.

Some of the other players were talented, though none had worked in any big-time productions. Some had worked in small, unheard of regional theaters in Dallas or Louisville. Most were local residents, some even recent graduates of the nearby high school on whose football field the actors had most of their rehearsal season. At first she had been pleased that she was cast in the lead female role, that of Mary Magdalene. The first flush of pleasure soon faded under the rigors of the scorching noonday sun on the football field or during the necessity of making costume changes in the scenery shed "right out in front of God and everybody." Such phrases were as close as most of the cast got to even pretending to be religious. The pastor/founder/director of the Passion play seemed to view his play as a holy calling but few, if any, of the others found anything spiritually uplifting about the work.

In fact, after a while the actors began to play tricks on one another just to combat the boredom that inevitably sets in during a show's long run. The disciples would come backstage after the Last Supper scene to tell her what gross and objectionable objects had been placed in the wine cup that evening. They ranged from cigarette butts to things too disgusting to mention. One of the temple functionaries whose line read, "the fraud continues even now" changed it to "the frog continues even now." This seemed especially appropriate since there were frogs in the woods nearby who would sometimes seek to drown out the actors with their croaking. The audience never saw what went on behind the scenes, or sometimes even right on stage. Many assumed that the players were in a kind of spiritual reverie throughout the performance. Part of the performance was in not letting the audience know otherwise.

Behind the stage area there was a hill that was crossed by a fairly steep path. This served various purposes during the show, one of which was the entryway for Jesus when he rode his donkey into Jerusalem. The donkey was named Jack, of course, and was probably the most reliable and arguably the most religious of the cast. He certainly was the most sensible. Like Balaam's donkey in the Bible who refused to pass by the angel blocking the way, Jack refused to maneuver the path down the hill after it had rained. If rain was not the worst enemy of outdoor drama, it was certainly a complicating factor.

Palm branches symbolize victory in Jewish tradition, as seen in this text from 1 Maccabees: "It was on the twenty-third day of the second month in the year 171 that the Jews entered the city amid a chorus of praise and the waving of palm branches, with lutes, cymbals, and zithers, with hymns and songs, to celebrate Israel's final riddance of a formidable enemy." (1 Macc. 13:51)

Not only did rain and mud make the actors' jobs more difficult, in this case it presented a theological problem in their telling the story of the triumphal entry. It was of vital importance that Jesus make his entrance riding a donkey. The prophetic tradition called for it. Besides, the lines wouldn't make sense otherwise. The problem was that Jack, the sensible donkey, absolutely refused to move toward the hill path. Finally, at the risk of changing several thousand years of tradition, the actor playing Jesus walked along the muddy, slippery path. About one third of the way down he slipped and fell. One of the actors near Susan quoted, under his breath, the line about Jesus entering Jerusalem on his ass. Susan didn't laugh, though. Instead she felt the embarrassment that the actor playing Jesus must have felt, and she got an immediate and painful sense of his vulnerability—and her own.

According to a fourth-century C.E. rabbinic source, the entry into Jerusalem on an ass was one of three signs of the Messiah as a new Moses. All three signs are found in John. "Rabbi Berekiah said in the name of Rabbi Isaac: 'As the first redeemer was so shall the latter Redeemer be. What is stated of the former redeemer? "And Moses took his wife and his sons, and set them upon an ass" (Exod. 4:20). Similarly will it be with the latter Redeemer, as it is stated, "Lowly and riding upon an ass" (Zech. 9:9). As the former redeemer caused manna to descend, as it is stated, "Behold, I will cause to rain bread from heaven for you" (Exod. 16:4), so will the latter Redeemer cause manna to descend, as it is stated, "May he be as a rich cornfield in the land" (Ps. 72:16). As the former redeemer made a well to rise, so will the latter Redeemer bring up water, as it is stated, "And a fountain shall come forth of the house of the Lord, and shall water the valley of Shittim" (Joel 4:18). (*Midrash Rabbah* on Ecclesiastes 1.9; from Martyn, 109-10)

At that moment the story came together for her in a way it never had before. She felt Jesus' vulnerability as he moved (in whatever fashion) toward his cruel death. For a moment she knew why Mary Magdalene and the others would have followed him, why they could have loved him. A line from a children's song passed through her memory. "They are weak but he is strong," the song went. It was not his strength but his weakness that attracted her now. The God who could incorporate such helplessness into some divine yearning might even use a ragtag band of irreverent actors rewriting the story of Jesus on a muddy hillside as well.

Jesus made it down the hill, after two more falls and, finally, to the cross. As Mary Magdalene stood at the foot of the cross watching for the umpteenth time this pretended crucifixion, it was as if she felt every fall of every child who had ever come running to its mother in its weakness and pain showing bloody knees. Tears welled in her eyes and slipped quietly down her cheeks. In the silence and darkness she could almost hear her heart break.

*(Michael E. Williams)*

# The Foot Washing at the Last Supper

*At the last supper before his death, Jesus washes the disciples' feet.*

## The Story

IT was before the Passover festival, and Jesus knew that his hour had come and that he must leave this world and go to the Father. He had always loved his own who were in the world, and he loved them to the end.

The devil had already put it into the mind of Judas son of Simon Iscariot to betray him. During supper, Jesus, well aware that the Father had entrusted everything to him, and that he had come from God and was going back to God, rose from the supper table, took off his outer garment and, taking a towel, tied it round him. Then he poured water into a basin, and began to wash his disciples' feet and to wipe them with the towel.

When he came to Simon Peter, Peter said to him, 'You, Lord, washing my feet?' Jesus replied, 'You do not understand now what I am doing, but one day you will.' Peter said, 'I will never let you wash my feet.' 'If I do not wash you,' Jesus replied, 'you have no part with me.' 'Then, Lord,' said Simon Peter, 'not my feet only; wash my hands and head as well!'

Jesus said to him, 'Anyone who has bathed needs no further washing; he is clean all over; and you are clean, though not every one of you.' He added the words 'not every one of you' because he knew who was going to betray him.

After washing their feet he put on his garment and sat down again. 'Do you understand what I have done for you?' he asked. 'You call me Teacher and Lord, and rightly so, for that is what I am. Then if I, your Lord and Teacher, have washed your feet, you also ought to wash one another's feet. I have set you an example: you are to do as I have done for you. In very truth I tell you, a servant is not greater than his master, nor a messenger than the one who sent him. If you know this, happy are you if you act upon it.

'I am not speaking about all of you; I know whom I have chosen. But there is a text of scripture to be fulfilled: "He who eats bread with me has turned against me." I tell you this now, before the event, so that when it happens you may believe that I am what I am. In very truth I tell you, whoever receives any messenger of mine receives me; and receiving me, he receives the One who sent me.'

After saying this, Jesus exclaimed in deep distress, 'In very truth I tell you, one of you is going to betray me.' The disciples looked at one another in bewilderment: which of them could he mean? One of them, the disciple he loved, was reclining close beside Jesus. Simon Peter signalled to him to find out which one he meant. That disciple leaned back close to Jesus and asked, 'Lord, who is it?' Jesus replied, 'It is the one to whom I give this piece of bread when I have dipped it in the dish.' Then he took it, dipped it in the dish, and gave it to Judas son of Simon Iscariot. As soon as Judas had received it Satan entered him. Jesus said to him, 'Do quickly what you have to do.' No one at the table understood what he meant by this. Some supposed that, as Judas was in charge of the common purse, Jesus was telling him to buy what was needed for the festival, or to make some gift to the poor. As soon as Judas had received the bread he went out. It was night.

## Comments on the Story

This is John's version of the Last Supper, yet it is a radical departure from the depiction of that event in the other Gospels and in 1 Cor. 11:23-26. The story begins with a long preliminary statement giving the basis for what Jesus will do (vv. 1-3). This complex section sets the stage and gives a definitive interpretation to Jesus' action: what he does is in response to all of these points.

First, the meal is taking place before the Passover festival. This is a detail of John's story alone; in the synoptic Gospels, the Last Supper is a Passover meal. Here the Passover meal will be on the next night after this one because, in John, Jesus dies on the afternoon before the Passover meal at the same time the lambs are being sacrificed for the meal (18:28, 19:14). This correlates with Jesus' identity as "the Lamb of God who takes away the sin of the world" (1:29). In John, the continual references to Passover season in the passion narrative represent references to Jesus' death.

"Jesus knew that his hour had come." Throughout John, it is the coming of the "hour" that the story is heading toward. Now that hour has arrived; it is, of course, the hour of his death. In John's language, it is the hour when "he must leave this world and go to the Father." Now he is in the last phase of his ministry tending to last minute details, as it were. Now it is time to respond to those who are "his own" and who must remain "in the world" though he will depart. Events are drawing to a climax, for "the devil" is already at work in the mind of Judas to betray him.

Knowing all of this, Jesus carries out a deliberate symbolic act. He removes himself from his position as host of the meal and instead takes on the role of one who is not even a guest at the meal. He takes on the dress and the role of the servant—the one who, according to custom, would greet the guests as they arrive and wash their feet before they take their positions reclining on couches at the table. This role for Jesus is hinted at in other Gospels where Jesus speaks of taking the role of servant. In Mark, it represents an interpretation of his death as "suffering servant" (10:45). In Luke, it is at the Last Supper that Jesus speaks of himself as taking the role of servant as an example for how the disciples should model their lives (22:27). Only in John does he actually act out that role. Both interpretations are also utilized here in John.

The first interpretation of the action comes in response to Peter's objection that Jesus should not abase himself in this way. The essence of Jesus' response to Peter is contained in verse 8: "If I do not wash you, you have no part with me." The action is intended to symbolize the efficacy of Jesus' death. There are also overtones here, especially in verse 10, of the sacrament of baptism.

The second interpretation of the action is in verses 12-16. Here Jesus enjoins the disciples to follow his example and wash one another's feet. It is an example of humility expressed in graphic terms. Christian interpretations over the centuries agree that the example refers to the choice of a lifestyle of humility that all Christians are to follow. Sometimes the ritual itself is followed as an affirmation of that lifestyle, though this is not universal in Christian practice, since foot washing has never been widely accepted as a sacrament.

The story now moves to the prediction of the betrayal, an event at the Last Supper that is found in all of the Gospels. Jesus first makes reference to the scripture from Ps. 41:9, "He who eats bread with me has turned against me," and interprets this by saying, "one of you will betray me" (13:18, 21). There then follows a peculiar story in which Peter motions to the Beloved Disciple, who was reclining next to Jesus, to find out who he means. The Beloved Disciple asks Jesus, who indicates, apparently to him alone, that it is the one with whom he will share the bread. Jesus then dips bread and gives it to Judas and says, "Do quickly what you have to do." Judas then rushes out. The narrator tells us that no one at the table knew what Jesus meant by this statement, evidently including the Beloved Disciple. They all thought it had something to do with Judas's duties as treasurer for the group. Once more we as hearers of the story are privy to information that the characters in the story do not have. We know what Jesus means. In fact, Jesus' words follow a theme that dominates John's telling of the passion narrative: throughout this narrative, it is Jesus who is in charge of events. It is told in a form that proves true the interpretation presented in John 10:18: "No one takes it [my life] away from me; I am laying it down of my own free will."

All of the Gospels connect the betrayal by Judas with the Last Supper. This gives particular power to the event, and John, like all of the Gospel writers, plays off of this. The Greek term for "betray" literally means "hand over." The Greek word does not carry the same pejorative overtones as the English term "betray." It is the context that gives it this meaning. What makes Judas a betrayer is the fact that he was one of them, as close to Jesus as any disciple could be. Thus Jesus notes the fact that though all have had their feet washed, including Judas, not all are clean, indicating that he knew who would betray him (vv. 10-11). The symbolism of sharing bread continues this theme, for the sharing of bread was a primary symbol for the sharing of meal fellowship. Such meal fellowship was seen as a bonding of a group into a community; that is the point Paul makes about the Christian act of sharing bread in 1 Cor. 10:16-17. Judas thus partakes of the most solemn act of communal bonding with Jesus by sharing bread with him. And it is at that moment that Satan enters his heart. That is why he was a betrayer—because he was, in fact, as close to Jesus as any disciple could be.

Peter is his usual impetuous self in this story, and as such is a mouthpiece for all disciples. He speaks for all of us when he attempts to reject Jesus' washing of his feet. The self-giving of Jesus in his death can be hard to accept fully. We want to be self-sufficient and not dependent on others. Yet Jesus' words strike right to the core: "if I do not wash you, you have no part with me."

The Beloved Disciple appears here for the first time in John. He is a character unique to John, and he is never named; he is only identified as "the disciple whom Jesus loved." Many suggestions have been made about his identity. A traditional suggestion is that he was the apostle John. Others have suggested that he was Lazarus, since Lazarus is consistently identified as one whom Jesus especially loved. The author is enigmatic here, however, for he steadfastly refuses to name the Beloved Disciple yet seems to imply that the reader should know him. The answer to the riddle of this disciple's identity seems to have been known only to John's community. It is most likely he was a figure who is not named in John and who was not famous except within this community. As a character in this Gospel, the Beloved Disciple often functions as a stand-in for the community itself.

In this story, the Beloved Disciple is given prominence not only by the designation that he was the one Jesus loved; he is also made prominent by his place at the table. To be at the position next to Jesus would be in a position of honor. This position allowed him to receive special insight into the events. It is this insight into the true meaning of the events of Jesus' life that is the legacy of the Beloved Disciple to the Johannine community. His place in the story operates to remind them of the authority that lies behind the interpretation of Jesus that they profess in this Gospel and that sustains them even in the face of the persecution that surrounds them. For the rest of us, those who share the legacy of that first-century community through the Gospel story they left behind, the Beloved Disciple functions in a similar way. He forms a bridge between the events in the story and the insights into their meaning to which we are led with the guidance of the author. In that sense, the author speaks with the voice of the Beloved Disciple, not only to the first-century church but to us as well.

## Retelling the Story

> [Jesus] rose from the supper table, took off his outer garment and, taking a towel, tied it round him. Then he poured water into a basin, and began to wash his disciples' feet and to wipe them with the towel. (John 13:4-5)

"Excuse me. I need your assistance."

The servant regarded his questioner suspiciously. He had the lowliest of duties and people tended to try avoiding so much as eye contact with him. It was rare someone spoke to him—and it generally meant trouble.

This guest, however, seemed—well—somehow different. His voice was pleasant; his eyes were kind. The servant stopped nervously shifting from foot to foot.

"I want to show them something," the stranger was saying, "but I'll need to borrow your equipment." The man picked up the servant's wash basin and towel from beside his feet.

The servant was confused. "Forgive me, sir, but I'll be needing that shortly. You see, the feet of the guests have to be washed."

"Yes, I know," the man replied. "That's what I intend to do."

"But, sir!" The servant was getting flustered. "You can't do that!"

The guest's face registered concern. "I hadn't thought of that," he said. "It must take quite a bit of practice to do this correctly."

"Well," mumbled the servant, "actually there is something of a knack to it." He was warming up to this guest who had taken an interest in his work. "A lot of people don't appreciate everything that goes into being a servant. Doing a good foot washing is really an art. When you do it right, you make people feel good about themselves. You can see it in their faces. They sit up a little taller; they're more relaxed. When you wash their feet, you really make them feel *welcome*."

"Then you enjoy your work," the stranger commented.

"Enjoy it! No way!" the servant blurted out. "You wouldn't believe the things I have to put up with around here!" The servant put his foot up on the stool in front of him and leaned, conspiratorially, toward the guest.

"Mister, you wouldn't believe the things I go through in a day's work! First you've got your smelly feet. Some

Washing the feet of the guests before a meal was an ancient custom of hospitality, as evidenced in Gen. 18:3-5, where Abraham tells the three divine visitors: "Sirs, if I have deserved your favour, do not go past your servant without a visit. Let me send for some water so that you may bathe your feet; and rest under this tree, while I fetch a little food so that you may refresh yourselves." It was also a standard custom at banquets in the Greco-Roman world. Since the guests were reclining, it made sense to have their feet washed from the dust of the road before they stretched them out on the couch. It was generally the duty of a servant to do this, as is described in Plato's *Symposium*: "So the attendant washed him and made him ready for reclining" (175A). Jewish tradition prescribed that a Jewish slave could not be required to wash the master's feet, as opposed to slaves of other nationalities (*Midrash Mekhilta* on Exod. 21:2). Disciples might be expected to wash the feet of their rabbi, however.

of those little puppies'll knock you right over with their stink if they don't just knock you over first with a well-placed punt to the head for sport. Some folks get a kick out of harassing the servants, you know—if you'll pardon the pun.

"Then you have your folks with an attitude. Most of them try to have as little contact as they can with people they consider beneath them. You get the feeling they're afraid that, if they make any contact with you, they're in danger of being seen as equal with you. There seems to be a real fear of that—and I guess you can't blame them. Who'd want to be seen as a servant if they didn't have to?

"On the other hand," he continued thoughtfully, "they're really missing out on some things. You see, when you wash someone's feet, they almost have to look right at you. And for a brief moment they know *you* know about all their warts and calluses but that you're willing to hold their feet anyway. And then you have a chance to treat some of the cuts and bruises life has given them. That's why you need to know what you're doing. When you're around people's tender spots, you can either help heal them or really hurt them more. They're vulnerable then, and they know it. That's why most folks are pretty uncomfortable at first. But a good servant knows how to put them at ease, how to use the skill he has right then to help renew them.

"It can go either way, you know," he continued. "That's why, when people get this attitude toward you that makes you feel like, because you're serving them, you're some kind of nonperson, you want to just grab those bunions and . . ." the servant stopped. "But you don't. Because it's not their attitude that matters, but yours, and nine out of ten times, if you work it right, you can make a difference with their attitude."

The servant lowered his eyes apologetically. "Hey. I didn't mean to go on and on about this. You just wanted to borrow the bowl, didn't you?"

The man smiled back at him. "No. You've been very helpful. But please do one more favor for me if you would."

"Well, sure, but I didn't do anything for you yet."

"Oh, but you did. I tell people why to serve; you told me *how*. Now please, would you allow me the honor of washing your feet?"

And Jesus knelt before him.

*(Phyllis Williams Provost)*

> Foot washing as a religious ritual of servanthood evidently existed in certain communities of early Christianity. In 1 Tim. 5:10, those who served the community as widows took on the responsibility of "showing hospitality" and "washing the feet of God's people." This was evidently an actual practice in which servanthood would be exemplified. The occasion may have simply been the community meals, which were occasions for "showing hospitality." There is no indication that this practice was seen at the time to be related to the example of Jesus, but later Christian tradition would connect the two.

128

# The Last Discourse

*Jesus answers concerns of his disciples about his imminent departure in a discourse following the Last Supper.*

### The Story

WHEN he [Judas] had gone out, Jesus said, 'Now the Son of Man is glorified, and in him God is glorified. If God is glorified in him, God will also glorify him in himself; and he will glorify him now. My children, I am to be with you for a little longer; then you will look for me, and, as I told the Jews, I tell you now: where I am going you cannot come. I give you a new commandment: love one another; as I have loved you, so you are to love one another. If there is this love among you, then everyone will know that you are my disciples.'

Simon Peter said to him, 'Lord, where are you going?' Jesus replied, 'I am going where you cannot follow me now, but one day you will.' Peter said, 'Lord, why cannot I follow you now? I will lay down my life for you.' Jesus answered, 'Will you really lay down your life for me? In very truth I tell you, before the cock crows you will have denied me three times.

'Set your troubled hearts at rest. Trust in God always; trust also in me. There are many dwelling-places in my Father's house; if it were not so I should have told you; for I am going to prepare a place for you. And if I go and prepare a place for you, I shall come again and take you to myself, so that where I am you may be also; and you know the way I am taking.' Thomas said, 'Lord, we do not know where you are going, so how can we know the way?' Jesus replied, 'I am the way, the truth, and the life; no one comes to the Father except by me.

'If you knew me you would know my Father too. From now on you do know him; you have seen him.' Philip said to him, 'Lord, show us the Father; we ask no more.' Jesus answered, 'Have I been all this time with you, Philip, and still you do not know me? Anyone who has seen me has seen the Father. Then how can you say, "Show us the Father"? Do you not believe that I am in the Father and the Father in me? I am not myself the source of the words I speak to you: it is the Father who dwells in me doing his own work. Believe me when I say that I am in the Father and the Father in me; or else accept the evidence of the deeds themselves. In very truth I tell you, whoever has faith in me will do what I am doing; indeed he will do greater things still because I am going to the Father. Anything you ask in my name I will do, so that the Father may be glorified in the Son. If you ask anything in my name I will do it.

129

'If you love me you will obey my commands; and I will ask the Father, and he will give you another to be your advocate, who will be with you for ever—the Spirit of truth. The world cannot accept him, because the world neither sees nor knows him; but you know him, because he dwells with you and will be in you. I will not leave you bereft; I am coming back to you. In a little while the world will see me no longer, but you will see me; because I live, you too will live. When that day comes you will know that I am in my Father, and you in me and I in you. Anyone who has received my commands and obeys them—he it is who loves me; and he who loves me will be loved by my Father; and I will love him and disclose myself to him.'

Judas said—the other Judas, not Iscariot—'Lord, how has it come about that you mean to disclose yourself to us and not to the world?' Jesus replied, 'Anyone who loves me will heed what I say; then my Father will love him, and we will come to him and make our dwelling will him; but whoever does not love me does not heed what I say. And the word you hear is not my own: it is the word of the Father who sent me. I have told you these things while I am still with you; but the advocate, the Holy Spirit whom the Father will send in my name, will teach you everything and remind you of all that I have told you.

'Peace is my parting gift to you, my own peace, such as the world cannot give. Set your troubled hearts at rest, and banish your fears. You heard me say, "I am going away, and I am coming back to you." If you loved me you would be glad that I am going to the Father; for the Father is greater than I am. I have told you now, before it happens, so that when it does happen you may have faith.

'I shall not talk much longer with you, for the prince of this world approaches. He has no rights over me; but the world must be shown that I love the Father and am doing what he commands; come, let us go!'

· · · · · · · · · · · · · · · · · · · · · · · · · · ·

THEN Jesus looked up to heaven and said:

'Father, the hour has come. Glorify your Son, that the Son may glorify you.'

· · · · · · · · · · · · · · · · · · · · · · · · · · ·

'I am no longer in the world; they are still in the world, but I am coming to you. Holy Father, protect them by the power of your name, the name you have given me, that they may be one, as we are one. While I was with them, I protected them by the power of your name which you gave me, and kept them safe. Not one of them is lost except the man doomed to be lost, for scripture has to be fulfilled.

'Now I am coming to you; but while I am still in the world I speak these words, so that they may have my joy within them in full measure. I have delivered your word to them, and the world hates them because they are strangers in the world, as I am. I do not pray you to take them out of the world, but to keep them from the evil one. They are strangers in the world, as I am. Consecrate them by the truth; your word is truth. As you sent me into the world, I have sent them into the world, and for their sake I consecrate myself, that they too may be consecrated by the truth.

'It is not for these alone that I pray, but for those also who through their words put their faith in me. May they all be one; as you, Father, are in me, and I in you, so also may they be in us, that the world may believe that you sent me.'

## Comments on the Story

If Jesus had left a last will and testament, what would he have said? This text in John attempts to provide an answer to that question. The entire discourse extends from 13:31–17:26; we have provided a representative section of passages that best guide a storyteller. The concerns here are not so much those of the disciples at this moment in Jesus' life, for little is said about what they are to do when he is tried and arrested, for example. Rather the concerns expressed here are for the Christian community as it faces a future without Jesus. Therefore Jesus' last will is addressed to the church in John's day, and, by extension, to the church today as well.

The story follows Judas's departure from the supper table. Thus we are to imagine Jesus and the disciples still reclining at the table. The conversation continues at the table for most if not all of the discourse, for even though Jesus proclaims at 14:31, "come, let us go!," they do not seem to go anywhere until after he finishes his prayer at 17:26. Only then do we get the next change of setting at 18:1, "After this prayer, Jesus went out with his disciples across the Kedron ravine. There was a garden there, and he and his disciples went into it."

The setting at table gives a particular form to this story. Ancient meals had two main courses, the *deipnon*, or supper proper, when the meal was actually eaten, and the *symposium* during which there was an extended period of wine drinking accompanied by conversation or other entertainment. The Greek philosophers preferred conversation at their symposia, as is attested in Plato's *Symposium*. Jewish sages also did the same, as is attested in the aprocryphal writing Ecclus. 32:1-13, where appropriate conversation, especially in praise to God, is enjoined along with musical entertainment. The synoptic Gospels often picture Jesus teaching his disciples at table, during the symposia. John has taken this well-known format and applied it to the Last Supper, providing an occasion for Jesus to present his last discourse to the inner circle of his disciples.

The philosophical symposium was conducted in a semiconversational form, with individuals at the table taking turns discoursing on the specified topic. Here Jesus is the only one speaking, with his disciples breaking in from time to time with questions, as was appropriate to the setting. The setting in a symposium contributes to the conversation in other ways, for when Jesus presents the metaphor of the vine and the branches (15:1-6), we can appreciate its

131

appropriateness to the moment when they are engaged in drinking from the wine cup.

The primary concerns of this last will of Jesus are nicely summarized in his opening statement. He speaks of (a) his imminent departure ("now the Son of Man is glorified" [13:31]) (b) the effect his absence will have on them ("where I am going you cannot come" [13:33]), and (c) what their response should be in his absence ("love one another" [13:34]). Later in the discourse, another theme will be introduced: (d) to compensate for the absence of Jesus, the disciples will be given the presence of the Spirit ("I will ask the Father, and he will give you another to be your advocate, who will be with you for ever—the Spirit of truth" [14:16-17]).

These issues make sense in the thought world of John. John draws on a dualistic form of religious speculation and casts the story of Jesus within that framework. Thus the coming of the Messiah is described as the descent of the "Word" from heaven to earth. The death of Jesus will then be the ascent of the "Word" back to heaven. These two realms, heaven and earth, are conceived as opposites, so much so that Jesus, in effect, is an "alien" in a world that rejects him. The same is true of those he leaves behind, who, like Jesus, must contend with the experience that "the world hates them because they are strangers in the world, as I am," as Jesus says in his final prayer (17:14).

This point of view helps us to understand better the subject matter of the discourse. With such a gulf between the human and divine worlds, it is no wonder that the disciples feel so bereft at the departure of Jesus. They have been left behind in an alien world, and they must wait until it is their time to depart before they can enjoy the "many dwelling-places" that await them.

Thus their questions to Jesus represent generic misunderstandings of the person of faith. "Where are you going?" and "Why cannot I follow you now?" asks Peter. He represents a longing for escape, yet, as Jesus points out, he has missed the point. He is so intent on defining his place in heaven that he misses out on his calling on earth. "Before the cock crows you will have denied me three times," Jesus must point out to him.

Thomas, Philip, and Judas also have their heads in the clouds. "Lord, we do not know where you are going, so how can we know the way?" says Thomas. "Lord, show us the Father" is Philip's request. Judas inquires, "Lord, how has it come about that you mean to disclose yourself to us and not to the world?"

How could they have been so dense? Here we can recognize a variation on the issue of signs faith that one finds throughout John. These questions come from people of faith, but somehow they have been looking for Jesus to be something other than what he is. What Jesus is saying to these disciples, as well as to later generations of Christians, in effect, is, "Pay attention to the story; there you will find 'the way' and there you will find 'the Father.' "

The description of the disciples as aliens in a hostile world fit the situation of John's community in which they had been made aliens in their own community and culture. For they had been expelled from the only "church" home they had ever known, the synagogue. They no longer had a "home" on this earth. In such a situation, it was comforting for them to be told of their "home" in heaven. But what is the modern Christian to make of this? After all, most of us do not live in a situation in which we face an alien world outside our control. But there is a sense in which the church is called at every time and every place never to be completely comfortable with the world as it is. There is always more to be done to bring about the kind of world where people "love one another" or experience the kind of unity for which Jesus prays here. Those virtues are to define the community of God on earth, and to the extent that they are absent in the world, to that extent will the church experience itself as a stranger in its midst. But to be a stranger is not an excuse for withdrawing from the world, for we have been "sent into the world" just as he was "sent into the world" (17:18).

### Retelling the Story

"[Jesus said], 'My children, I am to be with you for a little longer; then you will look for me, . . . [but] where I am going you cannot come.'" (John 13:33)

Sometimes Jesus could be so darn obscure, and a party pooper besides!

Ironically, Jesus was the one who usually enjoyed parties the most, beginning with that marvelous wedding feast at Cana. What a party that was! What wonderful wine! And so much of it! Why, they had partied like there would be no end to it. And they paid for it the day after, too!

Then there had been that picnic in the park, when they had had a feast unlike any they had ever experienced. And it all started with a few fish and

The last will and testament of a great man before he dies is a standard theme in the Bible and related literature. Jacob gives his last testament in Genesis 48–49; Moses gives his in Deuteronomy 33; David gives his in 2 Samuel 23. A genre of literature grew up around this motif, with the best examples being the Testaments of the Twelve Patriarchs, which are found among the Old Testament pseudepigrapha. They were written in the second century B.C.E. and purport to present the last testaments of the sons of Jacob. The common form is for the patriarch to address his sons and daughters in his farewell speech: "My children, behold I am dying, and I am going the way of my fathers" (*Testament of Reuben,* 1:3). Jesus addressed his disciples in a similar form: "my children, I am to be with you for a little longer" (13:33). (adapted from Brown, *The Gospel According to John,* 2.611)

The concept of "dwelling-places" in heaven derives from Jewish apocalyptic thought, as seen in 1 Enoch, a writing roughly contemporary with John: "In those days, whirlwinds carried me off from the earth, and set me down in the ultimate ends of the heavens. There I saw other dwelling places of the holy ones and their resting places too." (*1 Enoch* 39:3-4; from Boring, pp. 296-97, no. 460)

barley loaves. Somehow Jesus was able to make a feast out of the most meager of meals.

This evening had been no different. It was Passover season, a time to celebrate God's deliverance of Israel from bondage. They were so intent on the celebration that they had started a day early. That's how much Jesus enjoyed parties.

So if he was such a party animal, why was he suddenly being so maudlin? It just did not make sense. In fact, nothing that Jesus said was making any sense. The party was wearing on, the hour was getting late, the wine was still plentiful—and Jesus chose this time to get serious? The disciples were lost in the joys of the moment. But Jesus was beginning to look ahead to what would come next.

"I've got to be going soon," he said. "Well, don't worry," said Peter, "we'll all go with you. It's just about time for the party to end anyway."

The term "advocate" derives from forensic language. The concept is that God functions as a judge in his heavenly court. Humans come before God to plead their case and need an "advocate." Here the advocate has been appointed by God, and thus is a sign of God's mercy and compassion. The concept exists elsewhere in Jewish thought. Philo, for example, refers to the role of advocate played by various personified figures. "For he who has been consecrated to the Father of the world must needs have that Father's Son [that is, the cosmos itself] with all His fullness of excellence to plead his cause, that sins may be remembered no more and good gifts showered in rich abundance." (Philo, *On the Life of Moses* 2.134 [ca. 30–40 C.E.]; from Boring, p. 298, no. 463)

"No, what I mean is, I've got to go back where I came from. Later you can follow me there, after I prepare a place for you," said Jesus.

"Well, you'd better draw us a road map," said Thomas, "'cause you know how easily we get lost. Why just this afternoon Peter and I took a wrong turn on our way here and almost missed the party!"

"You don't need a road map," said Jesus, "but you do need to stop and ask directions every now and then to make sure you're pointed in the right direction."

"But Jesus," said Philip, "you know how we hate to stop and ask directions. Why don't you just tell us now how to get there. We can follow your directions. Right, fellows?" "Right!" they said.

"I've been giving you directions all along, in case you didn't notice," said Jesus. "As long as you have been attentive to me and my teachings, you have been pointed toward God."

"Oh," said Judas, as the light dawned in his eyes, "that's what you've been up to all this time." Then he caught himself. "Sure, we knew that. What makes you think we didn't know that? But, Jesus," he continued, "why don't you tell us the way once more, just to make sure we don't get lost."

"Tell you what," said Jesus, "why don't I send down a tour guide for you, to help you find the way?"

"Good idea!" said the disciples.

Then Jesus sighed and looked up to heaven. "God," he prayed, "time has just about run out. This is all I have had to work with. I've tried my best to get them ready. I just hope they are up to it." *(Dennis E. Smith)*

# Betrayal and Arrest

*Jesus is arrested in the garden.*

### The Story

AFTER this prayer, Jesus went out with this disciples across the Kedron ravine. There was a garden there, and he and his disciples went into it. The place was known to Judas, his betrayer, because Jesus had often met there with his disciples. So Judas made his way there with a detachment of soldiers, and with temple police provided by the chief priests and the Pharisees; they were equipped with lanterns, torches, and weapons. Jesus, knowing everything that was to happen to him, stepped forward and asked them, 'Who is it you want?' 'Jesus of Nazareth,' they answered. Jesus said, 'I am he.' And Judas the traitor was standing there with them. When Jesus said, 'I am he,' they drew back and fell to the ground. Again he asked, 'Who is it you want?' 'Jesus of Nazareth,' they repeated. 'I have told you that I am he,' Jesus answered. 'If I am the man you want, let these others go.' (This was to make good his words, 'I have not lost one of those you gave me.') Thereupon Simon Peter drew the sword he was wearing and struck at the high priest's servant, cutting off his right ear. The servant's name was Malchus. Jesus said to Peter, 'Put away your sword. This is the cup the Father has given me; shall I not drink it?'

### Comments on the Story

"This is the cup the Father has given me; shall I not drink it?" These are remarkable words of Jesus and they summarize quite well how Jesus' arrest is recounted here. The basic scene is the same as we find in the synoptic Gospels, but the story has been adapted to fit John's theological interests. The reference to the cup is a good example. In the other Gospels, Jesus prays that the cup, representing the suffering he is about to endure, might pass from him (as in Mark 14:36). There is no such agonizing prayer in the garden in John's story. Instead the Jesus of John's story presents what is effectively a rebuttal of the synoptic story and embraces his fate. There is no hesitation, doubt, or suffering in John.

The theme throughout John's passion narrative is that Jesus is in charge of his own death. It is a dramatization of the theological statement made in John 10:18, "No one takes it [my life] away from me; I am laying it down of my

136

own free will." This is unlike Mark, where the story is one in which Jesus accepts God's will that he die, but does so in agony and suffering. Here in John it is Jesus' own will that he die, and he directs the events to bring that about. It is a story that is built on the high Christology of John in which Jesus is fully divine and therefore responds as a divine being. For John, the effectiveness of Jesus' death as a saving event rather than just a good example or tragic story is derived from the identity of the one who died. He was not a normal human being; he was God incarnate.

Jesus went to the garden with his disciples because, as John puts it, it was a place where "Jesus had often met there with his disciples" (v. 2) though this is the only time it is mentioned in John's story. Since Judas knew that, he is able to lead the soldiers to him there. This is consistent with the point made earlier in John, that the Jewish leaders needed someone to tell them where he was so they could arrest him (11:57). Jesus had alarmed them because he was attracting such large crowds (11:48, 12:19), but he was no longer easy to find (11:54). They needed someone to tell them where he could be found when no crowds were around. That was Judas's job; that was what he betrayed.

The garden was located "across the Kedron ravine." It is the same area that the synoptics call Gethsemane. Only John calls it a garden, and he does not use the term Gethsemane.

Judas went to the garden "with a detachment of soldiers, and with temple police provided by the chief priests and the Pharisees" who carry "lanterns, torches, and weapons" (18:3). The reference that they had lanterns and torches is a nice touch, because it brings to our attention that these events are taking place at night. This relates to John's regular use of the symbolism of night and darkness to represent evil

The choreography of the arrest is dramatic and theologically rich. The one who initiates it is Jesus himself. The narrator sets the scene by reminding us once more that Jesus "[knew] everything that was to happen to him." On that basis he stepped forward and asked them, "Who is it you want?" They answer him, "Jesus of Nazareth." He responds, "I am he," or, more properly, "I AM." In Greek the response of Jesus carries both of these meanings. Jesus' response thus has a double meaning—it is the form for a normal statement as well as a divine epithet.

The arresting party responds appropriately, as the narrator takes pains to point out, for when they hear the phrase "I am he" ["I AM"] they draw back and fall to the ground. At this point, they are not responding to Jesus as a human being but as a god. Jesus repeats the question, they give the same response, and he once more identifies himself with the same epithet. He then requests that they let his disciples go, which the narrator tells us was to fulfill his own words that none of "his own" would be lost (6:39, 10:28).

In John's version of the story, Judas's role is rather minor. There is no kiss or other identification of Jesus by him. Here Jesus identifies himself; all Judas does is lead them to him and remain in their midst when Jesus makes his pronouncement of his identity (18:5). His role is played down because John's emphasis is on Jesus' own control of the situation. Yet Judas is no less a traitor in John's view.

When Jesus identifies himself with the words "I AM" he uses a phrase of the most profound significance. In fact, it is the phrase used to indicate the very name of God in the Greek version of the Bible. God's name is given to Moses in the well-known story in Exod. 3:13-14. Like other ancient names, it has a derivation, but it is an obscure one. It is a name formed off of the verb "to be." When translated into Greek, it becomes "I AM," which is both a statement about God and the name of God. When Jesus uses this term, which is at the same time an innocuous, simple expression ("I am he") and a divine name, he is identifying himself with God, even though it is in an ironic form, since the term can carry two meanings in this context.

After Jesus identifies himself for the second time, Peter steps forward, draws a sword, and strikes one of the individuals arresting Jesus. He ends up cutting off the ear of the servant of the high priest whom the narrator tells us was named Malchus. The use of the name here gives verisimilitude to the story.

Once more Jesus must restrain the impetuous Peter, telling him to put away his sword. He is ready to follow the course the Father has set for him. Peter's role is once more that of one who believes, but who wants to make things happen in his own way. Jesus reminds him that it is God's will that he must follow, not his own. What is especially striking here is that God's will is not consistent with the taking up of the sword. Peter's dilemma is one that has been faced time and time again by Christian believers. In times of doubt and confusion, when we are surrounded by those who threaten us, how are we to discern God's will? Peter's response seemed appropriate to him at the time, yet the sword was not the instrument God had chosen. Peter's doubt and confusion will continue after this. Though Jesus told him the sword was not the way, Peter's subsequent actions will suggest that he is still troubled and confused about what God has planned for humanity.

## Retelling the Story

> So Judas made his way there with a detachment of soldiers . . . and Judas
> the traitor was standing there with them. (John 18:3a, 5b)

It was not a gunshot, but it was just as deadly. Nor was a knife used, but it drew blood, cutting to the heart. No word was spoken, only a look exchanged. That was all it took to set in motion the terrifying and deadly trajectory of betrayal.

But let me return to the beginning of my story. It was a day like any other. I had gone to the church early to catch up on the reports we have to give to our superiors. It is soul-killing work, I assure you, and the only one that rivals the church at such trivialities is the military. A knock came at the door, but instead of being irritated, as I would have been had I been studying my texts for Sunday or preparing my sermon, I was glad for the diversion.

When I opened the door to my study I was met by a young man who was so clearly distraught that he could hardly speak. I invited him in to sit down and when he was finally able to utter a word, it was in such a whispered voice that I could hardly hear him. "Speak up! What is it?" I almost shouted hoping to bring him out of his trance.

Finally he said in a quiet, but distinct voice, "They've done it. The word came on the radio that the authorities in Vichey have ordered all Jews to be rounded up and sent to work camps."

The boy could not have left me more stunned if he had struck me with his fist. Not that I didn't expect such news. I did. It was only a matter of time before Petain and the other Nazi puppets in our so-called government would begin to round up Jews to be sent to death camps. It was just that I was overwhelmed for a moment by the realization that I would now have to take a stand that could mean my life.

"What shall we do?" The young man, Jean, was a member of the youth group in our congregation. He knew very well where I stood on such matters. His question was no longer a rhetorical one, the subject of a program for the youth or a talk at the women's society. It now must be answered by action.

> To prostrate oneself before the divine name is an appropriate response in Jewish lore, even for a king. In Dan. 2:46, Nebuchadnezzar prostrates himself before Daniel in homage to the God of Daniel who has revealed the secret of his dream. In a midrash on the story of Moses attributed to Artapanus, a first-century B.C.E. Jewish writer, Pharaoh is said to have fallen speechless to the ground whenever Moses uttered the divine name. (Brown, *The Gospel According to John*, 2.818)

"We will take them in and hide them, of course." My voice was calm but inside I was trembling.

"Of course," he responded, and a nervous smile crossed his lips. "Will we fight them, the police or the Germans?"

"With the weapons of the Spirit, my boy." My answer sounded too pat, too glib even for me to take seriously.

"I will do whatever it takes to fight them off, and I bet the Jews we hide will join me in the fight." Well, the refugees did come and we hid them as best we could. We housed some with the farm families in our area. Who would notice an extra child or two among an already large family? No one we asked refused to take in another mouth to feed, even though they knew it could mean death if they were caught. We are Huguenots, you see, and are familiar with religious persecution. This could have been us, they told me, it could just as easily have been us. We welcome the stranger because we were strangers and sojourners, as it says in the Book.

Before many months had passed, about one-third of our religious school was Jewish. We had guarded discussions about how we should respond if the authorities appeared one day and ordered us to identify our "guests." Some contended that we should stockpile arms and "give them a dose of their own medicine." Jean always weighed in on this side of the discussion, as did several of the Jewish youngsters. When I would say to them, "Then they kill more of us and we kill more of them. Where does the violence stop?" I was answered with looks that I knew meant that Jean and his compatriots thought I was irredeemably unrealistic.

Then one day we got a chance to try out our theories concerning how we would act under duress. The students had practiced keeping their eyes straight to the front, for if one student even glanced at another, it might give them all away to investigating officials. We thought that if it were the regional police who came to us we would have a very good chance of coming through their interrogation without losing anyone. As long as we did nothing to cause them to reflect poorly before their superiors they would usually let things pass. I know for a fact that many were sympathetic to us and our cause.

The officers entered the classroom and asked if we had seen any suspicious strangers recently. We knew that these words were their code for Jews. Everyone stared to the front and was silent. Everyone, that is, but Jean. "We would hide them if we did," his words startled us all.

"Oh, you would, my little hero," the lead officer spoke French with a decidedly German accent. "I suppose you are willing to fight for these cowardly Jew curs. They are afraid to fight for themselves. Would you do that for them too?" I knew that the officer was baiting us to see if he could force one of us to break down.

As I said, it was neither a gun nor knife but a look that betrayed. Jean merely glanced at one of our Jewish students as he said, "They are not cowards." He looked away as soon as he realized what he had done, but it was too late. The officer grabbed the student by the collar and threw him to the floor. "This is not the last you will hear from us," the officer growled as he led the student outside the room.

That day marked the end of our school. Before we could leave our classroom, more soldiers came and we were all arrested. The students that were suspected of being Jewish were sent to camps in other countries, places whose names are now synonymous with torture and horrific deaths. The rest of us

140

were parceled out to jails and detention centers mostly in occupied France. I could never determine what happened to our Jewish students though I surmise that few survived. I was able to gather a few stories of the other students and their fate.

Jean was sent to a detention center that was known to have a very low death rate. Though the treatment there reportedly was humane, it could not save Jean from himself. He blamed himself for the suffering of the rest of us, and that combination of guilt and self-contempt was lethal. He survived less than three months. I never spoke to him after that tragic day, though I have no idea whether my tiny corner of insight on the events of that day would have saved him.

The one thing I do know is that the tragedy ran both ways. I can only guess that the Jewish student did not survive the death camp. Jean did not survive his own guilt, but I live with mine knowing that it could have just as easily been any of us who looked. It could just as easily have been me.

*(Michael E. Williams)*

Jesus' reference to "the cup the Father has given me" uses the drinking of the cup as a symbol for accepting his fate. It is a direct reflection of the prayer at Gethsemane in the synoptic Gospels in which Jesus prays, "take this cup from me" (Mark 14:36). The symbol of the cup draws on rich Old Testament imagery in which the cup represents that which God metes out to humankind. For the people of God, there is the cup of God's blessings: "my cup brims over" (Ps. 23:5). For the wicked, there is the cup of God's wrath: "For the LORD holds a cup in his hand, and the wine foams in it, richly spiced; he pours out this wine, and all the wicked on earth must drain it to the dregs" (Ps. 75:8). Yet the persecutions of Israel can also be designated as the cup of God's wrath: "From the LORD's hand you have drunk the cup of his wrath, drained to its dregs the bowl of drunkenness; . . . Thus says the LORD . . . I take from your hand the cup of drunkenness. Never again will you drink from the bowl of my wrath; I shall hand it to your tormentors" (Isa. 51:17-23). The cup Jesus must drink is not the cup of God's wrath. But perhaps the symbolism of the cup in Isaiah 51 has been combined with the symbolism of the suffering servant of Isaiah 53, who suffers and bears the sins of the people. For the cup that Jesus must drink is the cup of suffering. It is the cup that God has designated for him in order that he might "[give] himself as a sacrifice for sin" (Isa. 53:10).

# Trial and Denial

*Jesus is tried before Annas while Peter denies him in the courtyard.*

## The Story

THE troops with their commander, and the Jewish police, now arrested Jesus and secured him. They took him first to Annas, father-in-law of Caiaphas, the high priest for that year—the same Caiaphas who had advised the Jews that it would be to their interest if one man died for the people. Jesus was followed by Simon Peter and another disciple. This disciple, who was known to the high priest, went with Jesus into the high priest's courtyard, but Peter stayed outside at the door. So the other disciple, the high priest's acquaintance, went back and spoke to the girl on duty at the door, and brought Peter in. The girl said to Peter, 'Are you another of this man's disciples?' 'I am not,' he said. As it was cold, the servants and the police had made a charcoal fire, and were standing round it warming themselves. Peter too was standing with them, sharing the warmth.

The high priest questioned Jesus about his disciples and about his teaching. Jesus replied, 'I have spoken openly for all the world to hear; I have always taught in synagogues or in the temple, where all Jews congregate; I have said nothing in secret. Why are you questioning me? Question those who heard me; they know what I said.' When he said this, one of the police standing near him struck him on the face. 'Is that the way to answer the high priest?' he demanded. Jesus replied, 'If I was wrong to speak what I did, produce evidence to prove it; if I was right, why strike me?'

So Annas sent him bound to Caiaphas the high priest.

Meanwhile, as Simon Peter stood warming himself, he was asked, 'Are you another of his disciples?' But he denied it: 'I am not,' he said. One of the high priest's servants, a relation of the man whose ear Peter had cut off, insisted, 'Did I not see you with him in the garden?' Once again Peter denied it; and at that moment a cock crowed.

## Comments on the Story

"Question those who heard me; they know what I said." These words of Jesus to his interrogator set the tone for this trial. It draws in the hearers of the story and challenges them to stand alongside Jesus and respond to those who would judge him.

This first interrogation of Jesus takes place before Annas, father-in-law of the current high priest Caiaphas and a former high priest himself. John notes that Caiaphas is the one who earlier "had advised the Jews that it would be to their interest if one man died for the people" (see 11:49-52). This reminder helps to establish the ironic nature of the story. We are thereby made aware of a meaning of the story of which the characters themselves, save for Jesus, are unaware.

All of the Gospels include a Jewish interrogation in their trial narratives, but the actual judgment that Jesus must die is clearly a Roman decision because crucifixion is a Roman form of capital punishment. Unfortunately, Christian theology has often used texts like these to buttress anti-Semitic tendencies by blaming the Jewish nation eternally for the death of Jesus. The story speaks of Jewish leaders, however, not the entire Jewish nation, for all of the early Christians were Jews as well. In fact, the characters of Annas and Caiaphas, like other characters in John, are stereotypes. In John's world, they represented voices of opposition to the fledgling Christian community. In other contexts, they can represent those of any age whose attempts to protect the established religion is so strong that they are in danger of denying the very essence of what worship of God is all about.

John introduces another character who is only found in his version of this story. Peter, he says, is accompanied by "another disciple" who was an acquaintance of the high priest and thus could gain access to the courtyard and get Peter in as well. This odd detail functions not only to explain how Peter got in, it also brings into the picture once more the ubiquitous unnamed disciple, whom we call the Beloved Disciple, who keeps turning up at odd points in John's Gospel. There is an intriguing parallelism between this text and John 21, another text where Peter and the Beloved Disciple are brought together. Whereas here there is a threefold denial of Jesus by Peter, in John 21 there will be a threefold confession.

Here and elsewhere in John, the unnamed disciple seems almost to be a surrogate for the author. He observes the action, but does not always respond to it, as is the case here. When he does respond, it is often with a greater insight than that of the other disciples. He is a bridge between the author and the story world. As such, he provides a unique window on the action for the hearer of this story, a privileged position, so to speak, from which the true understanding of events can be observed.

Another storytelling device found here is one that is actually shared with all of the Gospels. This is the interweaving of the story of Jesus' interrogation before the high priest with the story of Peter's denial in the courtyard. This is clear by the way the stories are set up. First we are told that Jesus was taken before Annas (18:12-14). Then we are told that Peter followed and began to deny him in the courtyard (18:15-18). Then while we are aware of Peter's presence in the courtyard, we skip once more to the interrogation (18:19-24). Then we skip back again to Peter's final denial in the courtyard and the crowing of the cock (18:25-27). This interweaving of the two stories causes the reader/hearer to compare Jesus' interrogation with Peter's denial. It is a perspective that was not available to the characters in the story, because the events were taking place simultaneously in two different locations. It gives us, the hearers of the story, a privileged position from which we can properly observe the action of the story and understand its true meaning.

Thus when Jesus says, "Question those who heard me; they know what I said," we are able to see that statement being fulfilled elsewhere. In fact, the prime apostle, Peter, is being questioned about Jesus at that moment in the courtyard. Here is his big chance. But instead of confessing Jesus, he denies him. In this way the trial is effectively shifted from Jesus to Peter.

Along with Peter stood the Johannine community. They were facing interrogations of this sort by the Jewish authorities in their world, and expulsion from the synagogue was an ever-present reality. In such a moment of crisis, how were they going to respond? Would they be like Peter, and deny Jesus? Or would they have the faith to confess him as Peter was later able to do? It is a question faced in varying degrees by every community of faith that has claimed this Gospel as its own.

## Retelling the Story

One of the high priest's servants, a relation of the man whose ear Peter had cut off, insisted, 'Did I not see you with him in the garden?' Once again Peter denied it; and at that moment a cock crowed. (John 18:26-27)

I was warming my hands by the fire when I saw him, the big Galilean I had seen on the Mount of Olives that evening. I watched as he, too, warmed his hands, occasionally rubbing them nervously against his rough cloak and stealing glances at the window of the high priest.

Yes, he was the one. It had been dark in the garden, but not so dark that I couldn't recognize him now in the flickering glow of the courtyard fire. He'd been the one who had drawn first blood. It had been he who had rushed to defend the one they called Jesus.

A feminine voice cut the silence. "You are one of the man's disciples, aren't you?" The woman who stood by the gate was talking to the big man. My muscles tensed.

"No. I am—not," he replied. I could see sweat on his palms as he held them in front of the fire. He was a disciple all right—as bound to his master as I was to mine, although perhaps not in the same way. That was why he risked staying so close now.

Why? Why had he stayed when the others had run? He could have run, too. Maybe what they said about this Jesus was true. I'd seen him once before—heard him speak. There was something different about him. And when he spoke, it seemed like he was speaking to me. And yet, tonight, I had arrested him.

I had told myself I had no choice; I was only doing my job. But I couldn't get him out of my head. His words, the gentleness in his voice echoed inside me.

I hadn't wanted the arrest to happen, but I knew what he said threatened my master and others like him. So they had come for him as they said they would, and now he would be silenced forever.

But his words had made sense to me! It seemed as though for the first time in my life, things made sense! He spoke of a God who could love even me—and I believed him! Why had I blindly obeyed and arrested him? I had to tell him. I had to ask his forgiveness! I looked at that hulk of a man across the fire from me and thought, "Maybe, I still have a chance. If this really is his disciple, he can help me."

I swallowed hard. "You are one of his disciples, aren't you?" I asked intently.

"No! I am not!" he denied, more strongly than before.

Although I didn't dare speak it aloud, inside I raged. "Don't you under-

Josephus, the first-century Jewish historian, refers to the trial of Jesus in a famous passage in his *Antiquities of the Jews.* Here he describes the Jewish involvement in Jesus' death as an accusation delivered to Pilate by "men of the highest standing among us." "About this time there lived Jesus, a wise man, if indeed one ought to call him a man. For he was one who wrought surprising feats and was a teacher of such people as accept the truth gladly. He won over many Jews and many of the Greeks. He was the Messiah. When Pilate, upon hearing him accused by men of the highest standing amongst us, had condemned him to be crucified, those who had in the first place come to love him did not give up their affection for him. On the third day he appeared to them restored to life, for the prophets of God had prophesied these and countless other marvelous things about him. And the tribe of the Christians, so called after him, has still to this day not disappeared" (*Antiquities* 18.63-64). Josephus was not a Christian, but this passage professes Christian belief. Most scholars conclude that Christians, who frequently referred to this passage, had, over time, added the statements of belief in Jesus as more than a man, as the Messiah, and as the one prophesied by the prophets.

The noncanonical Gospel of Peter, which includes traditions that date from the first to third centuries C.E., presents another version of the story of Jesus' trial, death, and resurrection. It shares much in common with the canonical Gospels but tells the story differently. Here it is Herod, the Jewish king, not Pilate, who condemns Jesus, and it is the Jewish people who carry out the execution. The theme is to place total blame for Jesus' death on the Jews: "But of the Judeans no one washed his hands, neither Herod nor any one of his judges. Since they were unwilling to wash, Pilate stood up. Then Herod the king orders the Lord to be taken away, saying to them 'Do what I commanded you to do to him' " (1:1-2). Then the people, not Pilate, carry out the mocking and execution: "And he [Pilate] turned him [Jesus] over to the people on the day before the Unleavened Bread, their feast. They took the Lord and kept pushing him along as they ran; and they would say, 'Let's drag the son of God along, since we have him in our power.' And they threw a purple robe around him and sat him upon the judgment seat and said, 'Judge justly, king of Israel.' And one of them brought a crown of thorns and set it on the head of the Lord. And others standing about would spit in his eyes, and others slapped his face, while others poked him with a rod. Some kept flogging him as they said, 'Let's pay proper respect to the son of God.' And they brought two criminals and crucified the Lord between them" (2:3-4:1). (from Miller, 396-97)

stand? I don't want to hurt you; I want your help! Don't you see? Someone else may have betrayed your master, *but I captured him!* I need his forgiveness! Help me!"

"Man," I said under my breath, hoping that he would grasp my urgency. "Didn't I see you in the garden with him?"

I waited, scarcely able to breathe. But when he looked up at me, I knew. His eyes were clouded with tears and fear, and I knew there would be no grace for me, no reconciliation with the Man from Galilee.

"I do not know him," he said.

And the cock crowed.                                        *(Phyllis Williams Provost)*

146

# The Trial Before Pilate

*Jesus is tried by Pilate while his enemies wait outside.*

**The Story**

**[SCENE ONE]**    FROM Caiaphas Jesus was led into the governor's headquarters. It was now early morning, and the Jews themselves stayed outside the headquarters to avoid defilement, so that they could eat the Passover meal. So Pilate came out to them and asked, 'What charge do you bring against this man?' 'If he were not a criminal', they replied, 'we would not have brought him before you.' Pilate said, 'Take him yourselves and try him by your own law.' The Jews answered, 'We are not allowed to put anyone to death.' Thus they ensured the fulfilment of the words by which Jesus had indicated the kind of death he was to die.

**[SCENE TWO]**    Pilate then went back into his headquarters and summoned Jesus. 'So you are the king of the Jews?' he said. Jesus replied 'Is that your own question, or have others suggested it to you?' 'Am I a Jew?' said Pilate. 'Your own nation and their chief priests have brought you before me. What have you done?' Jesus replied, 'My kingdom does not belong to this world. If it did, my followers would be fighting to save me from the clutches of the Jews. My kingdom belongs elsewhere.' 'You are a king, then?' said Pilate. Jesus answered, '"King" is your word. My task is to

bear witness to the truth. For this I was born; for this I came into the world, and all who are not deaf to truth listen to my voice.' Pilate said, 'What is truth?'

**[SCENE THREE]**    With those words he went out again to the Jews and said, 'For my part I find no case against him. But you have a custom that I release one prisoner for you at Passover. Would you like me to release the king of the Jews?' At this they shouted back: 'Not him; we want Barabbas!' Barabbas was a bandit.

**[SCENE FOUR]**    Pilate now took Jesus and had him flogged; and the soldiers plaited a crown of thorns and placed it on his head, and robed him in a purple cloak. Then one after another they came up to him, crying, 'Hail, king of the Jews!' and struck him on the face.

**[SCENE FIVE]**    Once more Pilate came out and said to the Jews, 'Here he is; I am bringing him out to let you know that I find no case against him'; and Jesus came out, wearing the crown of thorns and the purple cloak. 'Here is the man,' said Pilate. At the sight of him the chief priests and the temple police shouted, 'Crucify! Crucify!' 'Take him yourselves and crucify

147

him,' said Pilate; 'for my part I find no case against him.' The Jews answered, 'We have a law; and according to that law he ought to die, because he has claimed to be God's Son.'

**[SCENE SIX]**    When Pilate heard that, he was more afraid than ever, and going back into his head-quarters he asked Jesus, 'Where have you come from?' But Jesus gave him no answer. 'Do you refuse to speak to me?' said Pilate. 'Surely you know that I have authority to release you, and authority to crucify you?' 'You would have no authority at all over me', Jesus replied, 'if it had not been granted you from above; and therefore the deeper guilt lies with the one who handed me over to you.'

From that moment Pilate tried hard to release him; but the Jews kept shouting, 'If you let this man go, you are no friend to Caesar; anyone who claims to be a king is opposing Caesar.'

**[SCENE SEVEN]**    When Pilate heard what they were saying, he brought Jesus out and took his seat on the tribunal at the place known as The Pavement (in Hebrew, 'Gab-batha'). It was the day of preparation for the Passover, about noon. Pilate said to the Jews, 'Here is your king.' They shouted, 'Away with him! Away with him! Crucify him!' 'Am I to cru-cify your king?' said Pilate. 'We have no king but Caesar,' replied the chief priests. Then at last, to satisfy them, he handed Jesus over to be crucified.

## Comments on the Story

This story is one of the most dramatic in all of John. It divides clearly into seven scenes, just as does the counterpart story of the blind man in John 9. It is a story built on irony, for even though it purports to tell of the trial of Jesus, it is actually Pilate and "the Jews" who are on trial here. Though Pilate thinks he is in charge, it is Jesus who holds the power (19:11).

The division into scenes is indicated by the movement of Pilate back and forth between Jesus inside the praetorium and the Jewish leaders outside the praetorium. His dilemma mirrors that of one who must choose between Jesus and the world.

The praetorium or governor's residence is where Pilate resided when in Jerusalem. The traditional location is the Fortress Antonia, located on the east-ern hill of Jerusalem. It is here that the modern-day "way of the cross" begins. More recent investigations have suggested that the Fortress Antonia may have been built after Jesus' time. A more likely location for the praetorium may be the Herodian Palace located on the western hill of the city. The residence itself was a place where the prefect could be consulted, but it was at a nearby instal-lation, called the bema or "tribunal," where judgment would be rendered. This was an open-air platform with a bench upon which the official sat when giving judgment. John utilizes these details in his story by locating Pilate's interrogation of Jesus in the praetorium and his final judgment on the bema (19:13). Those details provide a historical backdrop for John's story that would make sense to his readers.

Scene one (18:28-32) takes place outside the praetorium ("Pilate came out to them" [18:29]). The scene is set up by noting that the Jewish leaders cannot enter the praetorium in order that they will not be defiled and precluded from eating the upcoming Passover meal. This keeps the action moving between outside and inside. It is a detail that derives from Jewish custom, since ritual purity for the Passover could be compromised if one entered impure gentile space. But it also shares in the overall irony of the entire story, for these same individuals who are being so careful to keep themselves pure are, in fact, being defiled by implicating themselves in the death of the Messiah.

The overall plot of this story has the Jewish leaders pressing for the death of Jesus while Pilate vacillates. That plot begins here, for Pilate at first attempts to avoid the entire issue by telling them to judge Jesus by their own law. Here John inserts another intriguing detail, for the Jewish leaders then claim they "are not allowed to put anyone to death" (18:31). John sees this as a major point, for it is the basis for the fulfillment of Jesus' own words that he would die by Roman, not Jewish, execution. Had it been a Jewish execution, he would have been stoned. Whether it was true that the Sanhedrin, or Jewish court, had been forbidden use of the death penalty by the Roman occupiers is a debatable point. For example, see the stoning of Stephen in Acts 7:57-58. For John's story, however, it is an essential detail. For even though Jesus dies on a Roman cross, John operates from the thesis that "the Jews" were responsible for his death.

"The Jews," however, are characters in John's story, and caricatures of the Jewish leadership who were opposed to John's Christian community. It is the term John uses when he wants to speak of those of "his own people" who reject Jesus. John uses the term Israel, however, as a positive term (as in 1:49), for, after all, John's Christian supporters were also Jews. Therefore, it should be borne in mind when one reads John that "the Jews" is a polemical term that arose out of the special circumstances of John's situation. It cannot function as an indictment of the entire Jewish nation, unless we have diabolical purposes. We should avoid reading John as a source for modern-day anti-Semitism. In fact, the irony is that it is the anti-Semites who today are most like the crowd that calls for the death of Jesus, thus attempting to suppress what Jesus was all about, all in the name of true religion.

In scene two (18:33-38*a*), Pilate goes inside to talk to Jesus. He inquires whether Jesus is, in fact, king of the Jews. His questions fit very nicely into John's theology, for that is the ultimate question, whether Jesus is king of the Jews. Jesus responds that his kingdom is not of this world, indicating that it represents a different understanding of kingship than that of the world. Then he says that he came into the world to testify to the truth "and all who are not deaf to truth listen to my voice" (18:37). It is a perspective that is consistently followed throughout John, that those who "see the glory" rather than the flesh are the ones with true vision (see 1:14). Pilate's response indicates where he is on this scale, for he can only reply, "what is truth?" He neither affirms nor denies what Jesus has said; he is still vacillating.

In scene three, Pilate goes out to the Jewish leaders once more (18:38b-40). He announces that he finds nothing against Jesus and allows them to choose Jesus' fate. In reference to the custom that a prisoner be released to them at Passover season, Pilate asks with pointed irony, "Would you like me to release the king of the Jews?" The crowd says no, thereby rejecting their own king. At this point, they are carrying the primary guilt, yet Pilate is implicated as well by his vacillation.

Scene four, as the central of the seven scenes, contains an interpretive key to the story. Here Jesus is flogged and then robed in purple like a king and crowned with a crown of thorns. The soldiers then mock him with the words, "Hail, king of the Jews!" Yet the entire scene is an ironic one, for he not only is in fact the king of the Jews, but it is precisely their act of mocking and his resulting suffering and death that we acknowledge as his coronation.

In scene five (19:4-7), Pilate once more goes out to the Jewish leaders, only this time he brings Jesus, robed in purple and wearing the crown of thorns. Once again he announces that he finds nothing wrong with Jesus. They respond that he must die according to their law "because he has claimed to be God's Son" (19:7). It is not clear whether John understands this to be a false charge or a true charge. But the irony of the statement takes it as true. For, in John's view, it is according to the law, that is, in fulfillment of scripture, that the Son of God must die.

In scene six (19:8-12), Pilate now begins to waver once more. The identity of Jesus as son of God strikes home with him. He then asks a leading question but in doing so speaks the language of John's Gospel, "where have you come from?" In John, the origin of Jesus is, in fact, the key to his identity. It is at this point that Jesus resorts to silence, a trial motif used in all of the Gospels as a reflection of Isa. 53:7. Pilate responds that he has the power to release or crucify him. But Jesus responds that he has no power unless it had been granted by God. The entire trial has been something of a charade. Jesus is choosing his own death and is really in charge of the events. Pilate is the one who is on trial here. He tries once more to release Jesus (19:12), but the crowd, as if they can read his mind, responds as if from backstage, "If you let this man go, you are no friend to Caesar; anyone who claims to be a king is opposing Caesar." They play their final trump card, reminding Pilate of the political realities of his situation.

So Pilate takes Jesus out once more (scene seven [19:13-16]) to the bema or tribunal. The phrase that is translated "he took his seat on the tribunal" is obscure in the Greek; it could refer either to Pilate or to Jesus. The judgment is really Pilate's, so he should be the one taking the seat. But if read the other way, Pilate is seen to place Jesus, still robed in the purple robe and wearing the crown of thorns, in the judgment seat and then proclaim, "Here is your king." The irony is that it is true. The Jewish leaders, in order to avoid accepting Jesus as their king, then make a statement that is truly blasphemous, "We have no king but Caesar." Their sin is complete; they have ended up renouncing their God.

In 19:11, Jesus makes a statement that is key to the meaning of this story. He said, "The deeper guilt lies with the one who handed me over to you." The phrase "handed over" is the same phrase as "betray." Theologically, then, guilt for the death of Jesus is carried by this term. The term is first imputed to Judas (18:2). Then in 19:11 it is imputed to the Jewish leaders. But Pilate too will not escape guilt. Though he has vacillated and tried to release Jesus, he finally "handed Jesus over to be crucified" (19:16). Therefore, in the end he shared the guilt for Jesus' death as well.

### Retelling the Story

Pilate said, "What is truth?" (John 18:38*a*)

"In the case of the Empire versus Jesus of Nazareth: I examined the accused at length and found no specific laws he has broken. But he has caused an uproar among the people, and, as I am charged to maintain public order, it has become necessary to look into his case in more detail."

Pilate paused in his dictation and sighed. The scribe looked up and waited for him to continue. Pilate hated this backwater assignment, especially during the religious festivals of the rabble over which he had been given authority. He longed for the civilized life he could live in Caesarea-by-the-Sea. Now there

John's story of Jesus' trial before Pilate has an underlying theme of fulfillment of scripture. To a significant extent, it draws upon a midrash of Psalm 2. This is a royal psalm that speaks of the coronation of a king of Israel in the face of opposition from the "kings of the earth" (2:1-2). Here in John, Jesus' coronation as king is underway in the face of opposition from the rulers of the earth, though here it is a coronation in an ironic mode. In the psalm, "he who sits enthroned in the heavens laughs" and says, "I myself have enthroned my king on Zion, my holy mountain" (2:4-6). Here in John, Jesus proclaims, "my kingdom does not belong to this world," but he will die as "King of the Jews." In Psalm 2, the Lord proclaims to the anointed one, "You are my son, this day I become your father" (2:7). This is a favorite messianic text in Christian preaching, and forms the background for John's emphasis on Jesus as Son and God as Father. (adapted from Crossan, 82-85) was a city that befit a Procurator. Though a number of Jews lived there, it was anything but a Jewish city. It was known throughout the Empire for its fine coliseum and amphitheater, its sewer system that flushed with the tides, its spectacular harbor, its fine public buildings—all built to honor Caesar by Herod, Caesar's king of the Jews. Pilate especially missed the open thoroughfares and the view of the sea out his window. He could hardly wait to get back to civilization.

"He was first brought before me on such vague charges that no clear action could be taken," Pilate continued. "I then returned him to his own authorities with the reminder that they too are responsible for public order. The religious courts responded by charging him with a capital offense under their law, although they are not allowed under Roman law to execute such a punishment. I then reexamined him to determine if additional charges under Roman law could be assessed."

Pilate fell silent again and walked to the window overlooking the city.

The tendency to blame the Jews as a nation for the death of Jesus continued to grow in popular Christian literature. By the third century C.E., stories had grown up in which Pilate was completely exonerated of all guilt. By this time, the church was seeking to accommodate itself to the Roman world. At the same time, the latent anti-Semitism of earlier stories had now emerged as a primary theme. One version of this tradition tells of Pilate being brought before the Emperor Claudius to account for his impious deed in crucifying Jesus. Pilate defends himself: "Great King, I am innocent of these things. The rashness and guilt belong to the multitude of the Jews." Caesar then tells him, "When they delivered him to you, you should have kept him in strict security and sent word to me, and you should not have been persuaded by them to crucify this righteous man who did such beneficent signs, as you indicated in your report. For from these signs it is clear that Jesus was the Christ, the King of the Jews." At these words of Caesar, the images of the pagan gods all crumbled into dust. Caesar then ordered the Jews to be punished by sending a company of soldiers to "scatter them into the Diaspora . . . and enslave them." He then ordered Pilate to be beheaded. Before his beheading, Pilate prays for forgiveness. A voice from heaven responds, "All the generations and families of the Gentiles will bless you, because all things spoken about me by the prophets were fulfilled by you. And you yourself, as my witness, shall appear at my Second Coming, when I am about to judge the twelve tribes of Israel and those who do not confess my name." The text continues: "The prefect cut off Pilate's head, and behold, an angel of the Lord took it up." (*Paradosis of Pilate*; from Cartlidge and Dungan, 88-90)

Everything in Jerusalem was so crowded and cramped, and the various odors of Semitic dishes wafted through the streets so that one could not escape them. Everything about the city was oppressive. All he had wished was that the season of his servitude in this wretched place would pass without controversy. Apparently that was too much to ask. Now his stay was wrecked, and over what? Nothing!

"People say he claims to be a king, but when I questioned him about imperial aspirations," Pilate continued, "he pursued a rather evasive line of response. When asked whether he was king of the Jews, he asked me whether I had come up with that idea myself or whether someone else suggested it to me. My response to his impertinence was to clarify our roles in the interrogation. Each time I thought I had obtained a reasonable response, he would divert the conversation in some other direction. He claims that he and his followers have no violent intentions. But I am not at all sure that is the case."

Pilate ceased speaking once again and stared off into space. This fellow was as cagey as a philosopher. You couldn't get a straight answer out of him to save your life. Instead of confirming or denying that he was a king he babbled some nonsense about his reign taking place somewhere other than this world. Pilate's line of questioning had been intended to entrap Jesus, to get him to admit to imperial aspirations. In that case, he would be making himself a rival to Caesar, and would be guilty of treason and deserving of death. But this claim about an otherworldly kingdom was obviously a ruse. He wanted it both ways. But Pilate was too clever for him.

Pilate rubbed his eyes wearily and resumed his dictation. "The testimony given before me this day has not been especially productive. He has not been a cooperative witness. It has been difficult to get to the truth of this situation."

"Truth! What is truth?" That was the question Pilate had asked him. But it was a question Jesus either couldn't or wouldn't answer. Things would have gone better with this backwoods rabbi if he would have at least attempted an answer. But, no. He just stood there in

> Flogging before crucifixion was apparently a standard procedure and is often mentioned in crucifixion stories. Of special interest are stories of Jews who were crucified under the Romans. Philo tells of an officially sponsored Jewish pogrom in Alexandria in 38 C.E.: "[Jews] were arrested, scourged, tortured and after all these outrages, which were all their bodies could make room for, the final punishment kept in reserve was the cross" (*Against Flaccus* 72). The Roman general Titus crucified hundreds of Jewish prisoners during the siege of Jerusalem in 70 C.E.: "They were accordingly scourged and subjected to torture of every description, before being killed, and then crucified opposite the walls." (Josephus, *Jewish War* 5.446)

silence. Well, enough time had been wasted that day on a case that should have been resolved before it ever came to the Procurator. King or no king this man was causing too much of a stir among the people. The crowd needed to be brought to their senses. So Pilate had given them a choice. Did they want him to release the terrorist, Barabbas, or their king, Jesus? They recognized the stakes in this deadly game right away. To accept Jesus as their king would have aligned them against Caesar. Innocence or guilt was not the question. Pilate had them either way.

"In any case, it has seemed expedient to preserve public order at all costs. Therefore, in accordance with my responsibility as Caesar's representative in Judaea to preserve the Pax Romana, and in concurrence with the decisions reached separately by the local religious courts and by the representatives of the people, I have pronounced a sentence of death by crucifixion upon the aforementioned Jesus of Nazareth.

"Signed, Pontius Pilate, Procurator of Judaea."

Pilate ended his dictation and received the completed scroll from the scribe. With a voice reflecting both irritation and weariness, he said aloud, to no one in particular: "What is truth, indeed. This is truth, inscribed on this scroll. I have decreed that Jesus of Nazareth must die and no power in heaven or on earth will stop it." *(Michael E. Williams and Dennis E. Smith)*

# The Crucifixion

*Jesus is crucified at Pilate's command.*

## The Story

J ESUS was taken away, and went out, carrying the cross himself, to the place called The Skull (in Hebrew, 'Golgotha'); there they crucified him, and with him two others, one on either side, with Jesus in between.

Pilate had an inscription written and fastened to the cross; it read, 'Jesus of Nazareth, King of the Jews.' This inscription, in Hebrew, Latin, and Greek, was read by many Jews, since the place where Jesus was crucified was not far from the city. So the Jewish chief priests said to Pilate, 'You should not write "King of the Jews," but rather "He claimed to be king of the Jews."' Pilate replied, 'What I have written, I have written'.

When the soldiers had crucified Jesus they took his clothes and, leaving aside the tunic, divided them into four parts, one for each soldier. The tunic was seamless, woven in one piece throughout; so they said to one another, 'We must not tear this; let us toss for it'. Thus the text of scripture came true: 'They shared my garments among them, and cast lots for my clothing.'

That is what the soldiers did. Meanwhile near the cross on which Jesus hung, his mother was standing with her sister, Mary wife of Clopas, and Mary of Magdala. Seeing his mother, with the disciple whom he loved standing beside her, Jesus said to her, 'Mother, there is your son'; and to the disciple, 'There is your mother'; and from that moment the disciple took her into his home.

After this, Jesus, aware that all had now come to its appointed end, said in fulfilment of scripture, 'I am thirsty.' A jar stood there full or sour wine; so they soaked a sponge with the wine, fixed it on hyssop, and held it up to his lips. Having received the wine, he said, 'It is accomplished!' Then he bowed his head and gave up his spirit.

## Comments on the Story

How Jesus dies says a lot about who he is and what his death means. Every storyteller knows that, and each Gospel writer tells the story a bit differently to fit his own picture of Jesus. John's version fits John's overall picture of Jesus. In John, Jesus is a divine being, Word become flesh. Throughout the passion narrative, he is shown to be in charge, directing events according to a preordained script. The passion in John is not so much a tragedy as it is a divine drama.

The theology behind John's telling of the story is expressed in John 10:17-18, "I lay down my life . . . no one takes it away from me; I am laying it down of my own free will." Thus John's story emphasizes that when Jesus is taken away to be crucified, he is "carrying the cross himself." No one helps him with the burden in John's story, unlike the version found in the other Gospels. Further, when Jesus finally dies, the manner of his death is true to form. Whereas in Mark, Jesus cries out as if in agony (Mark 15:33-37), the theme of suffering has been sublimated in John. Here Jesus chooses the time of death and, literally, chooses to die: "Having received the wine, he said, 'It is accomplished!' Then he bowed his head and gave up his spirit."

There is a certain nobility to the manner of Jesus' death in John. This fits the irony of the story as John sees it. Not only is this the Word of God who dies on the cross, but he is also "King of the Jews." Pilate, in an act of supreme irony, puts the sign on his cross stating that. Pilate, of course, does not mean it to be true; he rather sees it as an indication of Jesus' crime, that he claimed kingship that was not his. The irony known to the reader, however, is that the statement is true. Indeed, the act of dying on the cross is the act that makes Jesus "king." In the world of John's irony, then, the crucifixion is Jesus' coronation as king.

Intricate details of John's are identified as fulfilling scripture. This supports the view that the story John tells is a pre-scripted divine drama. That is the function of the odd detail concerning how the soldiers handled his clothing. They did as the scripture said, casting lots for the tunic (Ps. 22:18), because it was of such a quality as a seamless garment that it should not be divided up. Even when Jesus asks for a drink, he is said to do so not so much because he is suffering, but rather "in fulfillment of scripture" (see Ps. 69:21). At the moment when he actually chooses to die, he does so because he can say, "It is accomplished," as if to say that the pre-scripted story has now been accomplished. The idea that this story follows a pattern ordained by God and foretold in scripture elevates it to a level of meaning above the ordinary.

Jesus is identified earlier in John as "the Lamb of God who takes away the sin of the world" (1:29). The story of his death carries out that theme by invoking numerous parallels to Passover tradition. In this way, Jesus' death is defined as redemptive, since it parallels the sacrifice of lambs at Passover. In effect, Jesus becomes our Passover lamb, as Paul puts it (1 Cor. 5:7), or, in the language of John, "the Lamb of God." Thus Jesus dies at noon on the Day of Preparation, that is, the day prior to the evening Passover meal; this is the time when the Passover lambs are normally slaughtered (19:14). This detail is found only in John's version of the death of Jesus; Jesus dies on the day after the Passover meal in the other Gospels. Another allusion to Passover sacrificial tradition is the reference to a sponge of sour wine being placed on hyssop to be raised to Jesus' lips (19:29). Hyssop is a strange choice for this procedure, since it is such a small, flimsy plant, though of symbolic importance for the storyteller since it is the prescribed plant used to sprinkle blood on the doorpost at Passover, thus assuring the deliverance of the firstborn of Israel from the avenging angel (Exod. 12:22-23). The hyssop is an agent of deliverance in the original Passover tradition. Here the theme of deliverance has two potential referents. As the firstborn, Jesus will indeed be delivered from this death. And as the Lamb of God, he will be the means to deliver humanity from death.

Perhaps the most enigmatic episode in this section is the conversation of Jesus from the cross with the Beloved Disciple and Jesus' mother. This story is unique to John. Its meaning has been variously debated. Some would take it literally, as a poignant story telling how Jesus saw to it that his mother would be cared for after his death. Certainly the story draws on such logic in order to be a good story; that is to say, it is the kind of thing one might imagine happening. But John is much too symbolic for this to be no more than that. Furthermore, both the Beloved Disciple and Jesus' mother, neither of whom is ever identified by name in John, are given symbolic roles elsewhere in John's Gospel. Consequently, those interpretations suggesting a symbolic meaning to this story seem more correct. An often repeated interpretation is that Jesus' mother here represents the church, which has now been given into the safekeeping of the Beloved Disciple, who would here symbolize the leadership of John's Christian community.

I propose another interpretation. In the only other story where the mother of Jesus appears, in the story of the wedding feast at Cana (2:1-11), she has a role as one who participates in bringing about the mission of Jesus. She is not like other characters in John who have to go through a process of faith; she is already in the know. In fact, she operates virtually as a partner in Jesus' mission on that occasion at the beginning of Jesus' ministry. Now at the end of his ministry, when he is about to depart, he entrusts his "partner" to the Beloved Disciple. In doing so, he symbolically appoints the Beloved Disciple, and all who would follow him in a leadership like his, to be the agent of his mission on earth in his absence. In this sense, the Beloved Disciple becomes symbolic of pastoral leadership in the church in any generation. His role at the foot of the cross is to interpret events correctly, utilizing the spiritual insight symbolized by the mother of Jesus, an insight made accessible to succeeding generations by the stories presented in this very Gospel.

## Retelling the Story

And to the disciple [he said], "There is your mother"; and from that moment the disciple took her into his home. (John 19:27)

Of all the gifts that had come to him from Jesus' hand, a new mother was the last thing John had expected. Even from the distance that separated him from the distant figure on the cross he could feel Jesus' eyes fixed on him. John knew that the words were meant for him. "Son, look to your mother," Jesus had said.

Mary was so shaken in her grief, so blinded by her tears that John wondered if she had even heard her son's words to her, "Mother, look to your son." From this Friday, John knew, everything he did must say to Mary that he looked upon her as his own mother.

It was a great honor, true enough, and John would have done anything within his power that Jesus asked of him, especially something as important as caring for Jesus' mother. He knew he could never measure up to the son she was losing, but he would be another, lesser son in his own way. He watched Mary cease crying for a moment, look up and hold perfectly still as if listening to a distant voice that only she could hear. John knew that his own loss would never begin to sound the depths of pain that this mother felt as she stood helplessly beside him while her son was tortured and killed in the most cruel fashion Roman ingenuity could devise.

Crucifixion was a public execution intended to serve as a deterrent to other criminals. In Jesus' case, the sign on the cross meant that others were to be deterred from political insurrection against the state. Roman law specified how a crucifixion was to function: "That the sight might deter others from such crimes and be a comfort to the relatives and neighbors of those whom they have killed, the penalty is to be exacted in the place where the robbers did their murders" (*Digest* 48.19.28.15). "Whenever we crucify the guilty, the most crowded roads are chosen, where the most people can see and be moved by this fear. For penalties relate not so much to retribution as to their exemplary effect." (Quintillian, *Declamations,* 274 [first century C.E.], from Hengel, 50)

There was never yet a son born who could replace a son lost, even one lost to God. John moved closer to Mary. When he touched her arm she came out of her trance and looked into his eyes. "Why?" she asked. John was unsure whether he had actually heard Mary's voice or whether he had simply read the question from her eyes. In either case he heard his own voice speak the most unsatisfactory answer, "I don't know."

"I feel so helpless," Mary was actually speaking now. "I don't think . . . " her voice trailed off into tears.

"He loved you, you know." John wanted to transport Mary from this terrible scene. "Remember when he was first starting out? Things were easier then. We were joyful then. Each day we awoke wondering what new light Jesus would shed on our lives that day. Every day was a wedding. Remember the wedding at Cana? Jesus never would have shown himself if you hadn't insisted. He loved you as a son should love a mother."

"He didn't always speak to me as a son should speak to a mother. That day was the first time he had ever called me, 'Woman.' I thought I knew what he was about then. He would be the kind of teacher around whom wonderful, miraculous things happened. He would make me proud, I just knew it that day. Then he called me, 'Woman,' and I knew by the tone of his voice that something strange and different was going on. Soon the joy of the occasion overcame me, and it was one of the best days of my life. At that wedding I began looking forward to the day of his marriage and the arrival of my grandchildren and. . . . "

Her voice broke and did not return again to pick up her hopes and dreams for Jesus where she had left off. Instead, John heard the choking sounds of her sobs and felt her body trembling with grief as he placed an arm around her shoulders. He still did not know what to say. He could find no comfortable words for Mary or for himself. He settled for, "None of us expected it to come to this."

Around them stood the symbols of Roman power: the soldiers with their weapons and, of course, the cross. What a hated image that was for any of Rome's occupied people. That would now be the last memory Mary had of her son. What could ever wipe such a horrific image from a mother's mind? What could ever redeem such a cruel memory for any of Jesus' disciples who stood there wishing they could be anywhere else instead. In fact, many were gone. The other male disciples, other then John, were hiding out, so he stood today as a lone man among the women followers of Jesus.

"I don't think I really understood anything then, at the wedding, that is." John had been so deep in his own thoughts that he hadn't realized that Mary's sobs had quieted and she was again speaking to him. "How does such joy lead to such pain, John? What kind of God would expect this of my son? Or of me? I can't go on."

Only a God who would be willing to climb up on the cross with Jesus. Only a God who would suffer and die, too. Only a God who knows from the inside what that would feel like. John thought these things but did not speak them. "Come home with me now, Mother" he heard himself say. (*Michael E. Williams*)

Chrysostom interpreted Jesus' care for his mother to be the action of a dutiful son. But, he notes, some might wonder why Jesus did not concern himself with the other women who were present. "Yet, why was it that he made no mention of any other woman, though others also were standing there? To teach us to give more to our mothers than to any others." (Chrysostom, *Homilies on John* 85 [late-fourth century C.E.])

# The Body on the Cross

*Soldiers find Jesus already dead, leave his legs unbroken, and pierce his body with a lance.*

### The Story

Because it was the eve of the sabbath, the Jews were anxious that the bodies should not remain on the crosses, since that sabbath was a day of great solemnity; so they requested Pilate to have the legs broken and the bodies taken down. The soldiers accordingly came to the men crucified with Jesus and broke the legs of each in turn, but when they came to Jesus and found he was already dead, they did not break his legs. But one of the soldiers thrust a lance into his side, and at once there was a flow of blood and water. This is vouched for by an eyewitness, whose evidence is to be trusted. He knows that he speaks the truth, so that you too may believe; for this happened in fulfilment of the text of scripture: 'No bone of his shall be broken.' And another text says, 'They shall look on him whom they pierced.'

### Comments on the Story

In a normal crucifixion, the person would hang on the cross for days, dying a slow and painful death, with his body remaining on the cross even after death as an example to the populace. In the story of Jesus, however, he dies and has his body removed after only one day on the cross. Why he dies so quickly is not explained, except in theological terms. Here in John, for example, he dies at his own choice after he notes that all has been accomplished as prescribed in scripture (19:30). But there is a reason why his body is taken down so quickly after his death. The day of Jesus' death is the day of preparation, that is, the day before the Sabbath, and it would offend Jewish sensibilities to leave the bodies there on the Sabbath. Thus the Jewish leadership requests of Pilate that the crucified men's bodies be taken down. Only in John does their request include the breaking of the legs of those who hang on the crosses.

Crucifixion was intended to be a long, drawn out, painful death. To break the legs would actually be an act of mercy, since it would evidently hasten the death. That seems to be the logic here. The Jewish leaders request that the bodies be removed; they cannot be removed until they are dead; so to hasten their death the soldiers are sent to break their legs. This they do to the two who are crucified with Jesus, but when they come to Jesus and find he is already dead,

160

they do not break his legs. Instead, one of them thrusts at him with a lance. This action is not intended to kill him, but only to prick him to make sure he is dead. But these actions of the soldiers are not incidental; rather they are embued with theological irony.

The storyteller explains to us that what the soldiers do actually fulfills details from the scripture. This makes the soldiers actors in the divine drama. Without knowing it, they are seen to be carrying out precise actions that have been preordained by God. Thus in the story, the soldiers unknowingly provide testimony to the divinity of Jesus.

The fact that Jesus' legs were not broken, we are told, fulfills the scripture that says, "No bone of his shall be broken." The exact text in mind here is unclear, but it is most likely a reference to the tradition that no bone of the Passover lamb was to be broken (Exod. 12:46, Num. 9:12). This correlates with the theme throughout John that Jesus is "the Lamb of God who takes away the sin of the world" (1:29). The Passover imagery is alluded to throughout John's story of the death of Jesus. For instance, Jesus dies at the hour when the slaughter of the Passover lambs for the evening meal was to begin (19:14). The notation that his legs were not broken, while those crucified with him did have their legs broken, further confirms the Passover connection. The quotation from scripture makes this clear. It is a detail that John's readers would have understood immediately.

The second of the scripture texts that John quotes comes from Zech. 12:10, a text that speaks of the mourning for the inhabitants of Jerusalem who have suffered: "Then they will look on me, on him whom they have pierced, and will lament over him as over an only child, and will grieve for him bitterly as for a firstborn son." In this way the piercing of Jesus' side is also seen to be following a scriptural pattern, one that has messianic overtones for John because it refers to "an only child . . . a firstborn son."

But there is another level of meaning to the piercing of the side of Jesus— the fact that from it there came "a flow of blood and water" and there was a believer present who witnessed this and testified to it. Clearly John's readers were supposed to understand immediately what this reference meant. Since we do not live within the symbolic thought world of John, it is sometimes more difficult for us. But the meaning has to be connected with the purpose of the testimony, "that you too may believe." What the witness testifies to, therefore, is not the fact of these events, but their meaning. To paraphrase 1:14, the witness sees with the eyes of faith and therefore, unlike, say, the soldiers who do not respond at all to these events, the witness sees not the "flesh" but the "glory" of the "Word." In other words, this text makes sense as a testimony to the salvific power of the death of Jesus. We are therefore to understand blood and water as symbolic. What they are symbolic of is not as clear to us now as it must have been to the original readers, but there are various possibilities. Since the Passover imagery is so strong here, the blood of Passover may be the intended reference, for the blood of the lamb on the doorpost is that which saves those who are within the house. Water is also a frequent symbol in John, and often stands for salvation itself, as in the reference to Jesus as the one who gives "water of life" and "living water." When these two ideas are put together—blood of the Passover lamb and water of life—we get a strong image attesting to the saving power of Jesus' death.

What are we to make of the unnamed witness? This is one of the few texts in all of the Gospels in which an eyewitness testimony is claimed; otherwise the stories of Jesus are told in an anonymous third-person format typical of a storyteller's style. It should be noted that the storyteller and the witness are not the same person here, and that the storyteller elsewhere in John presents the story of Jesus without reference to first-person testimony. Yet clearly the author considers all of the stories in John to be of equal validity and worth; he even says as much in 20:30-31. If eyewitness testimony were considered essential to these stories, it would be utilized more often. Clearly it is not. So why is it here?

To say that this story is here because it actually happened that way is only half an answer, because it then raises the question about why are there not more such stories? Why only this one? Is this all they had? John would not have intended us to raise such questions, nor would he have intended the eyewitness nature of this story to lead us to doubt stories that do not claim eyewitness testimony. Thus we must resort once more to a symbolic reading. To "see" in John is a metaphor for faith, as is evidenced, for example, in 1:14 and in chapter nine. The eyewitness to these events at the cross provides testimony for what the true believer is supposed to see. The bystander would see a horrible punishment taking place, either of one deemed deserving or one deemed innocent. But the believer sees events whose meaning is found on the divine level. The unnamed eyewitness provides a window for every believer since then, allowing all of us to look to the cross and see not a tragedy but a story of salvation.

## Retelling the Story

'They shall look on him whom they pierced.' (John 19:37)

Three people came down the road on that dark day. Behind them, you could see the three crosses rising stark against the darkening sky. Each person told the story in his own way.

The first two people came walking side by side. They each had the hard look of the professional soldier. They were met by a traveler. "What did you see?" the traveler inquired.

"What did we see?" said the first soldier. "What do you think? It was a crucifixion, just like many others I have observed. It is a dirty business, but that's our job."

"I saw three insurrectionists getting their just rewards," said the second soldier. "We were sent to hasten their deaths. If it were up to me, I would make sure they died as slowly as possible. That's what they deserve, after all. And the people here in this god-forsaken land need to get a clear signal that you just don't mess with the Roman government. But the locals have some kind of superstition about leaving dead bodies on the cross on a holy day, so we were sent to break the legs of the victims so they would die faster and could be taken down.

"Everything went as planned with the first two. In fact, I rather enjoyed it. At least I got to inflict a little more pain. Scum like that deserve to suffer."

The Roman philosopher Seneca argued that a quick death by any means, such as suicide, would be preferable to the long drawn-out suffering of crucifixion. "Can anyone be found who would prefer wasting away in pain dying limb by limb, or letting out his life drop by drop, rather than expiring once for all? Can any man be found willing to be fastened to the accursed tree, long sickly, already deformed, swelling with ugly tumours on chest and shoulders, and draw the breath of life amid long-drawn-out agony? I think he would have many excuses for dying even before mounting the cross!" (*Epistles*, 101 [first century C.E.], from Crossan, 164)

"Funny thing about that third one, though," said the first soldier. "He seemed to be dead already. Now that just does not seem right. No one should die that quickly. The whole idea is for them to hang there and suffer. That's the

The Gospel of Peter [mid-second century C.E.] refers to the breaking of legs as a means of hastening death, but in this case, applies it not to Jesus but to one of the criminals crucified with him: "And they [the people] brought two criminals and crucified the Lord between them. . . . But one of those criminals reproached them and said, 'We're suffering for the evil that we've done, but this fellow, who has become a savior of humanity, what wrong has he done to you?' And they got angry at him and ordered that his legs not be broken so he would die in agony" (4:1-5). It has often been argued that breaking the legs would hasten death by asphyxiation, but there are conflicting studies about the cause of death in crucifixion. In any case, further trauma could not help but bring on a quicker death. (Brown, *The Death of the Messiah*, 2.1090-92) way the crucifixion is designed to work. And we are professionals—we know how to prolong the suffering.

"Somehow this guy managed to beat the system and die before he was supposed to. It's almost as if he decided for himself when he was going to die. I hate it when that happens.

"Just to make sure, I gave him a little prick with my lance. There was a little blood, but no response otherwise. Clearly, he was dead already, so we left him there."

"We did our job," said the second soldier. "We'll let the locals clean up the mess." The two soldiers then continued down the road.

Close behind them, but carefully keeping his distance, was a third person. At first it was difficult to see his face because he had pulled his cloak close around his head. But when the traveler approached him, the stranger turned so that his face could clearly be seen. What the traveler saw shocked him. The stranger had an odd look in his eyes, almost a look of triumph. It seemed strangely out of place at a crucifixion. What kind of man was this, to take such perverse delight in such a gruesome event?

"What did you see?" the traveler asked the stranger.

"What did I see?" replied the stranger. "Why, of course, I saw a crucifixion, but also much more. That was not a mere Galilean peasant on the cross—that was the King of the Jews, the Lamb of God who takes away the sin of the world. He did not merely die, he ascended back to the heavens from which he had descended.

"Whatever filled your head with such ideas?" asked the traveler.

"Because I saw the sign—I saw the holy water and blood flow from his side when the soldier opened it with his lance. That was God's sign that this death was acceptable to God and redemptive for us."

"But," the traveler said, glancing in the direction of the crucifixions, "when I look at the cross, I see only a tragic death of a poor peasant."

"Pah!" said the stranger. "You see nothing. Your eyes are closed to the truth. Who are you going to believe, me or your own eyes?" *(Dennis E. Smith)*

The flow of blood and water from the side of Jesus was commonly interpreted in sacramental terms in the early church. "It was not accidentally or by chance that these streams came forth, but because the Church has been established from both of these. Her members know this, since they have come to birth by water and are nourished by flesh and blood. The mysteries have their source from there, so that when you approach the awesome chalice you may come as if you were about to drink from his very side." (Chrysostom, *Homilies on John* 85 [late-fourth century C.E.])

# The Burial

*Jesus is buried by Joseph of Arimathea and Nicodemus.*

## The Story

AFTER that, Joseph of Arimathaea, a disciple of Jesus, but a secret disciple for fear of the Jews, asked Pilate for permission to remove the body of Jesus. He consented; so Joseph came and removed the body. He was joined by Nicodemus (the man who had visited Jesus by night), who brought with him a mixture of myrrh and aloes, more than half a hundredweight. They took the body of Jesus and following Jewish burial customs they wrapped it, with the spices, in strips of linen cloth. Near the place where he had been crucified there was a garden, and in the garden a new tomb, not yet used for burial; and there, since it was the eve of the Jewish sabbath and the tomb was near at hand, they laid Jesus.

## Comments on the Story

Normally, a crucified body would remain on the cross to be eaten by carrion birds and dogs. That was part of the ignominy of the act of crucifixion. Sometimes, however, special permission might be given to bury the body. We now have archaeological evidence that this happened because the remains of a crucified man, with a nail still imbedded in his ankle, have been found buried in a first-century tomb in Jerusalem (Zias and Sekeles). Such permission was probably rare. Nevertheless, the Gospels tell such a story about Jesus.

According to Paul, the burial was an original part of the early Christian confession (1 Cor. 15:4). The stories told by all of the Gospels note that Jesus' closest followers, "the twelve," had forsaken him and were not present at his crucifixion. In fact, none of his followers are present except a group of women, and, attested only in John, the unnamed "Beloved Disciple" (19:25-27). None of these, however, not even the women, are the ones who bury him. Rather, a character is introduced who is otherwise unknown in the Gospel stories: Joseph of Arimathea. In John's version of the burial story, Joseph is accompanied by another individual who is known elsewhere in this Gospel—Nicodemus.

John's story is more than just a description of Jesus' burial. It is also a story of discipleship. Joseph is identified as "a disciple of Jesus, but a secret disciple for fear of the Jews" (19:38). He fits the pattern of the individual of faith whose com-

165

mitment has been found lacking. There are several such individuals in John. They tend to be individuals who believe in the signs, but whose faith is not substantial enough that they can be trusted (2:23-25). They often flocked to Jesus, but they seemed to misunderstand what he was about. One such group wanted to make him king, for example (6:15). More often than not, such individuals exhibited a failure of nerve, and refused to acknowledge their faith for "fear of the Jews," like the believers in Jerusalem (7:13) or the parents of the blind man (9:22).

Such individuals are in the story because they exemplify the problems of discipleship that were present in the world of the storyteller, that is, in the world of John. "The Jews" that they feared did not represent the nation of Judaism as a whole, because the Christians in John's community were Jewish also. Rather they represented the Jewish leadership of their day who had begun to consolidate Judaism into one set of beliefs and were now expelling from the synagogue all those who confessed Jesus to be the Messiah (9:22). So "fear of the Jews" was well-founded in their world, for they were in danger of losing contact with the only religious community they had ever known—the synagogue.

John's Gospel is written as a warning to these kinds of individuals, the "secret believers." And exhibit A for such believers was Nicodemus. When we first meet Nicodemus, in John 3:1-21, he has come to Jesus "by night," a dead giveaway that he is indeed an example of those to whom Jesus could not trust himself (2:23-25). For darkness is what Jesus, as the "light of the world," came to dispel. But even though Nicodemus is a believer in the signs of Jesus, he cannot quite accept what that belief demands. His problem is not an intellectual one, it is a problem of commitment. As Jesus summarizes at the end of the Nicodemus episode: "the light has come into the world, but people preferred darkness to light because their deeds were evil" (3:19).

Yet Nicodemus continues to hang around at the fringes of the Jesus movement. He shows up once more when the Jewish council deliberates about the necessity that Jesus must die. Nicodemus, a member of the council, tries to argue against such rash actions, but his words are ignored (7:50-51). Now here he is again. But he is still the same old Nicodemus. The storyteller reminds us that he is "the man who had visited Jesus by night"—and once more Nicodemus operates in the safety of the darkness. On one level his commitment is profound, for the amount of myrrh and aloes he has brought would fill a small room. He has obviously overdone it, and we are made to wonder if this is not an attempt to salve his conscience.

Joseph and Nicodemus function as important benefactors for the church. They are men of wealth and influence and they use their power to provide a profound service to the church. Without them, the story could not have proceeded as it did. Yet even so, the fact that they continue to inhabit only the fringes of the faith hangs like a cloud over them. They are like many who must have existed in John's world and have existed in the church ever since—individuals who perform great acts of service to the church by exercising their wealth and influence, without whom the church could not survive, yet who still refrain from full, public commitment. There is a sad poignancy to this story. Their actions are profound and the need they fill is great, but in the end their great monetary gifts cannot substitute for the one gift that God desires most of all—the gift of the whole person.

## Retelling the Story

So Joseph came and removed the body. He was joined by Nicodemus. (John 19:38b-39a)

It was a new tomb, and the stench of rotting flesh and spices did not offend the nostrils when the men entered it. It was extraordinarily clean for a room hewn out of stone and dirt. There was a shelf of sorts on which the body would lay. "It looks almost comfortable," he thought, then laughed quietly to himself at the thought of the dead worrying about the comfort of their resting place. Besides, the body wouldn't be there forever. After the flesh had decomposed, the bones would be placed in an ossuary. This reminded Nick that he would have to arrange for one of the nicer bone boxes, as well. But there would be time for that later on.

There were so many things to think of. If Jesus didn't die by sundown on Friday then no burial preparations would take place, since the Sabbath would have already begun. The men might not even get him into a tomb by then. This would present an even greater difficulty. The Romans were notorious for leaving corpses hanging on their crosses to remind the populace of the fate of those who crossed the Empire. That simply must not happen with Jesus. Perhaps Nick could approach the religious authorities, among whose number he was

In the ancient world, the final indignity that could be imposed on one's enemies was to leave them unburied, to be eaten by carrion birds and beasts. This is how Octavius treated those who had murdered Julius Caesar: "To one man who begged humbly for burial, he is said to have replied: 'The carrion birds will soon settle that question'" (Suetonius, *The Deified Augustus* 13:2 [early second century C.E.]). Because a crucifixion was such an ignoble death, leaving the body on the cross without burial was considered the norm. "The vulture hurries from dead cattle and dogs and crosses to bring some of the carrion to her offspring" (Juvenal, *Satires* 14.77-78 [early second century C.E.]). In recounting how a slave was to be treated, Horace noted: "[If a slave were to say to me,] 'I never killed anyone': [my reply would be,] 'You'll hang on no cross to feed crows.'" (*Epistles* 1.16:46-48 [late-first century B.C.E.], from Crossan, 160-61; Hengel, 50) supposed to belong, and ask that they do everything in their power to assure that death would come as quickly as possible.

Nick realized that neither he nor Joe had spoken a word since they had arrived at the tomb. The conversation that had been raging in his head had been silent, overheard by no one.

Jewish tradition specified that a dead body should not hang on a cross overnight. This was based on Deut. 21:22-23: "When someone is convicted of a capital offence and is put to death, and you hang him on a gibbet [that is, impale him], his body must not remain there overnight; it must be buried on the same day. Anyone hanged is accursed in the sight of God, and the land which the LORD your God is giving you as your holding must not be polluted." Although the text originally applied to the impaling of the body after death, it came to be applied to crucifixions as well: "the Jews are so careful about funeral rites that even malefactors who have been sentenced to crucifixion are taken down and buried before sunset" (Josephus, *Jewish War* 4.317). Rulers would not always be agreeable, however. Philo notes that Roman rulers in the past had often allowed crucified bodies to be removed and buried by their kin in honor of pagan festal occasions, but the evil Flaccus nevertheless did not allow this to be done with the bodies of the Jews whom he had crucified. (*Against Flaccus* 83, from Crossan, 163-67)

"It's beautiful here." Joe had broken the silence, and Nick wondered if the quiet had weighed on his friend. For Nick it had been a relief.

"Yes, it's pretty. But he won't care. Why create unseen gardens for the dead who won't have occasion to appreciate them?" Nick was resentful of anything that seemed merely decorative when the man he admired most in the world was being executed.

"I suppose so," Joe replied, then fell silent once more. When he spoke again he sounded tired. "From whom do I get permission to take the body down?"

"Pilate, I suppose, since it's a Roman execution. But you won't get it until they're sure he's dead." Nick hated the nitty-gritty details of life, especially those that surrounded death. This was even worse: an execution. The political and religious factions would be watching closely to see who took care of the body. Jesus' friends would surely be watched closely and might even face execution themselves. This fact weighed on Nick's mind, since it meant his own life could be in danger.

"If he's not dead by the beginning of Shabbat? What do we do then?"

"I don't know. He'll be dead in time." Nick's confident tone of voice didn't convince even himself that he believed the prediction he had just spoken. Now he had other things occupying his mind. He had to arrange for the purchase of aloes and myrrh and the other spices that would be needed for the burial. He knew a merchant who could keep his mouth closed. Nick might have to pay a bit more, but cost was not a factor in this arrangement.

"Do they know about you?" Joe was whispering now.

"Who?"

"Your powerful friends in Jerusalem. Do they know you are a follower of the Rabbi?"

"In the first place they are my colleagues, not necessarily my friends. And second, it's none of their business what I do on my own time." Nick sounded more defensive than he intended.

> Later Christian popular legend expanded on the story of Joseph of Arimathea. The *Acts of Pilate* tell of his arrest by the Jews and his defense before the chief priests, in which he recounts how Jesus appeared to him while he was in prison. Stories from the medieval period tell of Joseph traveling to England where, in Glastonbury, he built a church in honor of Mary, thus giving England a church founded in apostolic times. (Brown, *Death of the Messiah*, 2.1233)

"The time will come when we may have to declare ourselves. I've talked to no one so far. I'm not sure exactly what I'll do when that time comes."

"Sooner or later the news will come out about our making the arrangements for his burial. You realize that, don't you?" Nick had defended Jesus publicly. If the authorities came for him, how much doubt would be in their minds about where his loyalties lay?

"Are you willing to die, if it comes to that?"

Nick waited a long time before responding. "The first time we met, Jesus talked about being born from above. I couldn't make heads or tails of what he was saying then. Since I've had some time to think about it, though, it has become clearer to me. I can't say it exactly, but what he called being reborn had to do with this death. Don't ask me how exactly, but it may have a lot to do with our dying to be reborn."

"That doesn't make any sense."

"I know."

The two walked on in the silence, watching the sun moving toward Shabbat. The evening had begun to enfold the two dark figures like a still, small voice pulling them along toward a future they could not imagine.

*(Michael E. Williams)*

# JOHN 20:1-10

# The Empty Tomb

*Mary Magdalene, Peter, and the Beloved Disciple encounter the empty tomb.*

## The Story

EARLY on the first day of the week, while it was still dark, Mary of Magdala came to the tomb. She saw that the stone had been moved away from the entrance, and ran to Simon Peter and the other disciple, the one whom Jesus loved. 'They have taken the Lord out of the tomb,' she said, 'and we do not know where they have laid him.' So Peter and the other disciple set out and made their way to the tomb. They ran together, but the other disciple ran faster than Peter and reached the tomb first. He peered in and saw the linen wrappings lying there, but he did not enter. Then Simon Peter caught up with him and went into the tomb. He saw the linen wrappings lying there, and the napkin which had been round his head, not with the wrappings but rolled up in a place by itself. Then the disciple who had reached the tomb first also went in, and he saw and believed; until then they had not understood the scriptures, which showed that he must rise from the dead.

So the disciples went home again.

## Comments on the Story

When Paul in 1 Corinthians 15 reviews the early Christian "creed" as he knew it, he mentions death, burial, and resurrection as evidenced by numerous resurrection appearances, but he makes no mention of the empty tomb. All of the Gospels, however, present the empty tomb as the first event of the resurrection. In the basic passion narrative that the Gospels have in common, the empty tomb story functions as the transition to the resurrection appearances proper. In the basic passion narrative, all of Jesus' male followers have forsaken him and are not present at the cross. It is a group of women followers who witness the crucifixion, note where he is buried, and then discover the tomb empty on Sunday morning. They then pass this information on to the leading male followers who then experience the resurrected Lord for themselves.

That basic outline is adapted by each Gospel writer to fit his own theological purposes. The same is true of John, whose empty tomb and resurrection stories are elaborate and unique to his Gospel.

The first episode is this one, in which the empty tomb is discovered by Mary Magdalene who then passes on the information to Peter and the Beloved Disciple. Unlike the story in the synoptic Gospels, where a group of women come to the tomb to anoint the body, here Mary Magdalene comes alone and no reason is given for her coming. A group of women at the foot of the cross, including among them Mary Magdalene, had been mentioned earlier (19:25), but none of the others accompany Mary to the tomb in John's version of the story.

Mary's role is to discover the empty tomb and then report it to the others. When she arrives at the tomb, the narrator says that she saw that the stone had been removed from the entrance of the tomb. It is not mentioned that she looked into the tomb, but what she reports to the disciples is that someone has taken the body from the tomb and no one knows where it is. That she jumps to this conclusion, that the body was taken away by someone, shows how far she was from comprehending the resurrection.

It is a standard theme in the resurrection preaching of the early church that Peter was the first to experience the resurrection (1 Cor. 15:5). This is clearly a reference to Peter's position as the acknowledged leader of the early church. Consequently, resurrection appearance stories functioned not only to buttress the faith of the community but also to direct our attention to its leaders. That is the function of this story in John as well.

It is the two rivals for leadership in the world of John, Peter and the Beloved Disciple, to whom Mary reports the discovery of the empty tomb. What follows is a fascinating and intricately choreographed competition between the two to see who will emerge as the rightful leader. The operative presupposition is that Peter is the acknowledged leader of the church. What the story seeks to do through subtle means is present a challenge to Peter's leadership.

Upon hearing the news from Mary, the two disciples run to the tomb, but the Beloved Disciple is faster than Peter and arrives there first. This is not a comment on his athletic ability but on his passion for the faith. Upon arriving at the tomb, he looks in and notes the arrangement of the grave wrappings. He therefore becomes the first to observe the empty tomb, since in John's story, Mary has not yet looked inside.

Though he looks in, the Beloved Disciple does not go into the tomb, for it is not his role to usurp the position of Peter. Thus he steps aside and lets Peter enter first. Peter enters and observes the details of the grave wrappings that indicate that the body is gone but the wrappings have been left. Only then does the Beloved Disciple enter, and the storyteller notes once more that he was the first to reach the tomb, thus reminding us of his superior passion for the faith.

Next the narrator notes that the Beloved Disciple "saw and believed." To this point, he is the only one who believes, and he does so on the basis of the empty tomb only. Not only is his passion greater, but his faith is as well. For he arrives at authentic resurrection faith by only observing the empty tomb itself. Others,

Peter included, will need an appearance by Jesus. In this way the Beloved Disciple becomes a model for the faith of the community, for he believes without experiencing a direct appearance of the resurrected Lord. That will also be the only form of faith available to the community (and subsequently to us as well).

Not only does the Beloved Disciple exemplify resurrection faith, but he also stakes a claim on leadership in the church. The claim is a subtle one. Peter is still the acknowledged leader, but the Beloved Disciple is promoted as comparable. This intriguing interaction between the two as authority figures in the community of John will also be addressed in chapter 21.

The Beloved Disciple is never named in John, but his identity seems to be known to the readers. He enters the story during the passion narrative, first appearing at the table during the Last Supper (13:23). There, also, he is found to be closer to Jesus than Peter is. That closeness to Jesus is explicitly noted by his identifying epithet: "the disciple whom Jesus loved." It is not known who he was, but he is claimed in John as a founding leader of John's Christian community. Theirs was an isolated community in many respects, and their leader was one whom they alone claimed. He became the authoritative figure for them, surpassing even Peter, even though they acknowledged that Peter was the acknowledged leader elsewhere in early Christianity. In this particular story, John's community acknowledges Peter's leadership but also affirms that of their own traditional leader, the Beloved Disciple.

Though the Beloved Disciple believes, the story goes on as if to ignore that point. The conclusion to the story is that the disciples in general did not yet believe because they did not yet understand the scriptures pertaining to the resurrection. This notation leads up to the scenes that follow, in which resurrection faith officially comes to the apostles when they witness a resurrection appearance of the Lord.

Unlike the synoptic Gospels, John says that Jesus' body was properly anointed before burial (19:40). Why then did Mary come to the tomb? Jewish tradition spoke of a time of mourning of up to three days, during which the body could still be visited at the tomb. John may have been assuming that Mary came to the tomb to mourn. (Brown, *The Gospel According to John,* 2.981-82)

### Retelling the Story

Until then they had not understood the scriptures, which showed that he must rise from the dead. So the disciples went home again. (John 20:9-10)

Mary had only been gone for a short time, but it still seemed too long to the two worried, jittery men who were waiting for her. They had told her not to go; it was too dangerous. But she insisted that she needed to go to the tomb to check on things. She assured them she would be okay. Now they sat there at the table, Peter and one of the other disciples, hoping against hope that she was okay.

They had good reason to worry, considering what had happened. And it all happened so fast. It was only three nights ago that they had been happily enjoying a party with Jesus. Everything seemed fine then. Of course, Jesus did seem a bit somber that night. He kept saying gruesome things about needing to go somewhere ominous. Peter assured him that he would not have to go alone—Peter would see to that. But that did not seem to satisfy Jesus. He acted like Peter didn't mean what he said.

Perhaps that is why Peter did what

The type of tomb envisioned here is a rock-hewn type, probably what archaeologists call the *loculi* style of tomb. This type has been found in the Jerusalem area. These tombs usually consisted of a central chamber just large enough for a man to stand in. Side chambers were dug for placement of the remains of the deceased. The entrance to the tomb was often closed by rolling a stone into the opening, as indicated in John. (from Hachlili, "Burial, Ancient Jewish," *Anchor Bible Dictionary*, 1.789-94)

he did, to prove to Jesus that he did mean it. Because when they came to arrest him, it was Peter who tried to prevent it—with his sword. But once more, Jesus rebuked him as if Peter was not understanding the things that must happen.

Then everybody scattered. But Peter and the disciple who waited with him now had followed the crowd that had apprehended Jesus. But they stayed well back at a safe distance, lest they be spotted and arrested too. Peter even had to lie to a few people about who he was, but it was only in self-defense. If he had not done that, he would probably not be alive today. Then what use would he have been to anyone?

But he never expected things to go so far. He and the others hid out, thinking that Jesus would soon be released and would be rejoining them. Instead, they heard to their horror that he had been crucified! Crucified! The very thought of that sent goosebumps down their spines! Now they knew they were in real danger of death as insurrectionists. That is why none of them had ventured out very far from the house, and why they were so worried when Mary had left.

Suddenly, Mary burst into the room. "The tomb . . . ," she said, panting.

"Yes," Peter said, "what about it?"

"The tomb . . . it's . . . it's . . . "

"It's what? Come on, Mary, tell us!"

"It's . . . EMPTY!"

The two of them looked at her incredulously for a moment. Then, in the next moment, they had both bolted for the door, only to find that it was not wide enough for the two of them to go through at the same time.

"After you."

"No, after you."

"No, after you."

Finally, they extricated themselves and ran for the tomb.

Now, in his time, Peter had been quite an athlete. He could usually hold his own in any footrace. But today, somehow his feet felt like lead. What did it all mean? Why were they doing this? What dangers awaited them at the tomb?

The other disciple got there first, but Peter came soon after.

"After you."

"No, after you."

"No, after you."

Well, what was Peter supposed to do? Who wanted to be the first to go inside a tomb that had been mysteriously opened, for crying out loud? Finally, Peter took the plunge, and went in. But he didn't plan to stay long. So he glanced about wildly to confirm that there was no body there, then he grabbed the arm of his companion and said, "I don't like the looks of this. Let's get out of here."

They walked swiftly out, arm in arm, glancing neither to right nor left, hoping no one had seen them leave.

"Do you think they saw us?" Peter asked nervously.

"Naw, we weren't there that long," said the other.

"Tombs give me the willies. How about you?" said Peter.

His companion nodded, but said nothing.

"What do you make of it?" said Peter.

His companion looked thoughtful, but again he was silent.

"I'll tell you what I think," said Peter. "I think it's a plot. They're trying to trap us. We'd better lay low and hope they forget we even exist. The less said about this, the better."

*(Dennis E. Smith)*

The "scriptures which showed that he must rise from the dead" are not entirely obvious to us. Possibilities include Hos. 6:2 ("on the third day he will raise us to live in his presence"). There is also a general pattern in scripture in which persecution is followed by vindication. For example, Psalm 2 tells a story of a royal figure against whom the nations have conspired, much as the nations, in the guise of Pilate, conspired against Jesus. The story concludes with vindication, in which God says to the anointed one: "You are my son . . . ask of me what you will: I shall give you nations as your domain, the earth to its farthest ends as your possession. You will break them with a rod of iron" (2:7-9). This pattern in scripture would have led the discerning student of the Bible to conclude that God's anointed would ultimately prevail, despite having suffered at the hands of the nations. (adapted from Crossan, 190-91)

# The Appearance to Mary

*Jesus appears first to Mary Magdalene.*

### The Story

So the disciples went home again; but Mary stood outside the tomb weeping. And as she wept, she peered into the tomb, and saw two angels in white sitting there, one at the head, and one at the feet, where the body of Jesus had lain. They asked her, 'Why are you weeping?' She answered, 'They have taken my Lord away, and I do not know where they have laid him.' With these words she turned round and saw Jesus standing there, but she did not recognize him. Jesus asked her, 'Why are you weeping? Who are you looking for?' Thinking it was the gardener, she said, 'If it is you, sir, who removed him, tell me where you have laid him, and I will take him away.' Jesus said, 'Mary!' She turned and said to him, 'Rabbuni!' (which is Hebrew for 'Teacher'). 'Do not cling to me,' said Jesus, 'for I have not yet ascended to the Father. But go to my brothers, and tell them that I am ascending to my Father and your Father, to my God and your God.' Mary of Magdala went to tell the disciples. 'I have seen the Lord!' she said, and gave them his message.

### Comments on the Story

Resurrection can be misinterpreted. That is what happened to Mary. But through her experience, we are brought to a clearer understanding of the meaning and purpose of the resurrection.

Mary Magdalene had not been introduced to the reader of John prior to 19:25, where she is found to be among the group of women at the foot of the cross. She is clearly a believer and must have been famous in early Christianity, since all of the Gospels mention her prominently in the story of Jesus. John has taken this well-known character and given her a key role in exemplifying what resurrection faith is all about.

The story has elements of the resurrection tradition found in the other Gospels, but the details have been rearranged and expanded to fit John's story. Mary had been the first to find the empty tomb and report it to Peter and the Beloved Disciple. They then went to the tomb and inspected it, but came to no understanding of the resurrection.

Now that Peter and the Beloved Disciple have left, Mary is left to examine the tomb more closely. She begins to weep and decides to look inside. There she sees two angels. This is the first time they have been noted; they must not have been there before.

"Why are you weeping?" the angels ask her. It is a key question, for Jesus asks her the same question moments later and adds, "Who are you looking for?" These questions operate on an ironic level and focus on Mary's lack of spiritual vision. She sees the angels, but it does not register what they mean. She sees Jesus and thinks he is the gardener. She observes the graveclothes carefully laid aside, but has not yet comprehended what they mean. At this point she shares the condition of the other disciples, "until then they had not understood the scriptures, which showed that he must rise from the dead" (20:9). If she had understood, she would not be weeping. She would not be looking for a corpse that had been moved, but for a Lord who had risen.

"Mary," Jesus says. And with that one word, Mary recognizes him. Suddenly she knows; this is the "Teacher." It is a touching, poignant moment. Indeed, this scene reenacts a moment from the parable of the Good Shepherd: "He who enters by the door is the shepherd in charge of the sheep. . . . he calls his own sheep by name, . . . and the sheep follow, because they know his voice" (10:2-4). What is the sound of that voice? It is the call of the Shepherd, who knows each of the sheep intimately by name. When Mary hears Jesus say her name, she knows who it is because no one else says her name quite the same way. When the storyteller, or public reader of the Bible, comes to that point in the story and must verbalize what Mary hears in that voice, the tone will not express command but intimacy and compassion.

"Do not cling to me, for I have not yet ascended to the Father," says Jesus. Mary had recognized the Teacher come to life, but she had not yet grasped the significance of it all. Though Mary wants him to stay with her just as he is, that cannot be. As he explained in the last discourse, he must ascend to the Father in order that the process will be complete and his followers' fate will be secured (14:1-3; 16:7).

Mary went through three phases of faith, and in doing so mirrored the experience of Christians in John's world as well as Christians today. First she failed to factor in the resurrection. Then, when faced with the resurrection, she misinterpreted it. What had she missed? At first, she wept because she thought all was lost. The divine messengers were incredulous. Why should anyone weep? Look around you and see the signs of God's victory. Then, when she recognized the fact of the resurrection, she wanted to capture the moment and hold it. She looked for a way to escape the fact that this moment of experience would pass. She tried to make the resurrection real for herself in the present moment. It is an approach that will be utilized by generations of gnostics after her, who will claim that the resurrection is directly available for the believer in present time, which allows an escape from the present life. But Jesus responds that she cannot cling to him. Things have changed. Yes—she and other believers now have access to eternal life. But that does not mean that they can escape their mission in this life.

Finally, when the meaning of the resurrection has become clear, Mary moves to the third and final level of faith. She runs to announce the news to the others that the Lord had risen. She thus exhibits an appropriate faith in the resurrection, for she now sees it not as a means of escape but as a means for redefining life in the present. Once more John uses a woman to represent the highest level of faith and model it to the still uncomprehending disciples. In this way John promotes a view in which church leadership is envisioned for all social levels within the membership, and not just for those who follow Peter (see comments on John 20:1-10).

## Retelling the Story

> So the disciples went home again; but Mary stood outside the tomb weeping. (John 20:10-11)

Mary was weeping again. She tried not to, but she couldn't help herself. What had come over her? She had always been the strong one, the one everyone else depended on. But now, with Jesus gone, she felt so devastated. What would they do without him?

Mary of Magdala, they called her. It was a distinctive name, because it was unusual for a woman to be known by the city she came from, rather than by the family she was connected to. But Mary was a successful merchant, and had achieved a reputation as her own person.

There were many other resurrection stories in the early church besides those that made it into the canon. One of the most elaborate is found in the Gospel of Peter. Here we also find a reference to two angels, but, whereas they make only a brief and obscure appearance in John, they have a specific purpose in Peter: It is their job to bring the resurrected Jesus from the tomb. "They [the soldiers guarding the tomb] saw the skies open up and two men come down from there in a burst of light and approach the tomb. The stone that had been pushed against the entrance began to roll by itself and moved away to one side; then the tomb opened up and both young men went inside . . . While they [the soldiers] were explaining what they had seen, again they see three men leaving the tomb, two supporting the third, and a cross was following them." (Gospel of Peter, 9:3-4, 10:2; from Miller, 399)

Mary was a tall, sturdy woman with a steady gaze and a commanding presence, the kind of woman that you did not trifle with. She had been the oldest of nine children. Her mother died giving birth to the ninth child, so Mary had taken over the role of mother for her siblings. Then when her father died, she had had to take over supporting the family.

> In Jewish literature, visitors from heaven were often dressed in "magnificent attire" (2 Macc. 3:26). The type of garment could be linen (Ezek. 9:2, Dan. 10:5) or simply a dazzling white raiment (1 Enoch 87:2).

Magdala was a small village near Tiberias on the Sea of Galilee and was known for its fishing industry. Her father had been a fish merchant, but she had to find another way to make a living. She had always been known for the fine cloth she could weave, and had even begun to sell some of it at the marketplace to make extra money. Now she turned that avocation into a business, and through hard work and a business acumen that until then she did not know she had, she soon became a successful merchant.

Her business took her all over Galilee. It was on a trip to Capernaum that she first saw Jesus. His reputation had preceded him. He was known as a healer; not just any kind of healer but a healer of souls. She was intrigued by what she heard, for, unlike the usual holy man, Jesus had a reputation as one who would accept a wide variety of people. He was even known to include women among his followers. That appealed to Mary, so she decided to check him out.

She was not disappointed. She quickly found herself caught up in his movement to reform their ancestral religion. And Jesus soon came to rely on her as one of the people who could get things done. She was a behind-the-scenes person, helping with the logistics of the Jesus movement. Through her travels as a merchant, she had made connections throughout Galilee. She became a kind of advance person for the movement as its members traveled from village to village.

When they decided to take the annual pilgrimage to Jerusalem for Passover, she went along—she knew she would be needed. In fact, there were several women in their group, including Jesus' mother. That it how they all happened to be there when their festive spirit so quickly turned to tragedy. In the blink of an eye it seemed, he was arrested, and then, when all the rest had forsaken him, the group of women found themselves standing at the foot of the cross—his cross—watching as his life ebbed from him.

It was a scene Mary would never forget. The scene of that cross stayed with her even as she watched them remove the body for burial. And it was still with her as she went to the tomb three days later to grieve for him once more.

But when she found the tomb empty, she did not think she could bear it. How could she grieve when she did not even know where the body was? She was distraught and confused. And she began to weep uncontrollably.

"Why are you weeping?" two strangers asked. What an insensitive question! Didn't they understand anything? And who were these odd figures anyhow? "Why are you weeping? Who are you looking for?" Now it was the gardener asking stupid questions. Surely he knew what was going on, or did he? Had the whole world gone mad? Why was she weeping? What else could she do? What else could anyone do?

Then suddenly, she heard that voice calling her name, "Mary," and immediately she recognized who it was. And in that instant, her grief and confusion left her. It was a moment of crystal clarity. No one else said her name that way, with such warmth and compassion. It could be no one else but him. And intuitively she knew that this must be it—this must be the resurrection. All that came to her in a flash of insight with the simple act of his saying her name.

Chrysostom interpreted Mary's response to be just like a woman: "How tender-hearted and inclined to sympathy is womankind. I am mentioning this that you may not wonder why in the world it was that, while Mary was weeping bitterly at the tomb, Peter displayed no such emotion." (Chrysostom, *Homilies on John* 86 [late fourth century C.E.])

"Mary," he said, and she recognized once more the need in his voice. She was the one he always depended on, and now he had another job for her. "Yes, Lord," she said, "I will do it." And to her was given the task to be the first to proclaim: "He is risen!"  *(Dennis E. Smith)*

# Appearances to the Disciples and Thomas

*Jesus appears to the disciples in a locked room and later to Doubting Thomas.*

## The Story

L ATE that same day, the first day of the week, when the disciples were together behind locked doors for fear of the Jews, Jesus came and stood among them. 'Peace be with you!' he said; then he showed them his hands and his side. On seeing the Lord the disciples were overjoyed. Jesus said again, 'Peace be with you! As the Father sent me, so I send you.' Then he breathed on them, saying, 'Receive the Holy Spirit! If you forgive anyone's sins, they are forgiven; if you pronounce them unforgiven, unforgiven they remain.'

One of the Twelve, Thomas the Twin, was not with the rest when Jesus came. So the others kept telling him, 'We have seen the Lord.' But he said, 'Unless I see the mark of the nails on his hands, unless I put my finger into the place where the nails were, and my hand into his side, I will never believe it.'

A week later his disciples were once again in the room, and Thomas was with them. Although the doors were locked, Jesus came and stood among them, saying, 'Peace be with you!' Then he said to Thomas, 'Reach your finger here; look at my hands. Reach your hand here and put it into my side. Be unbelieving no longer, but believe.' Thomas said, 'My Lord and my God!' Jesus said to him, 'Because you have seen me you have found faith. Happy are they who find faith without seeing me.'

There were indeed many other signs that Jesus performed in the presence of his disciples, which are not recorded in this book. Those written here have been recorded in order that you may believe that Jesus is the Christ, the Son of God, and that through this faith you may have life by his name.

## Comments on the Story

The resurrection was not only a glorious end to the story of Jesus, it was also the beginning of another story—the story of the church. It was a transition event. This story addresses that issue. All of the things Jesus spoke of in the last discourse come to focus here. Now the disciples must be prepared for life on earth without the physical presence of Jesus.

The story opens with the disciples meeting much like the church of John's day might meet—on "the first day of the week," "behind locked doors" and "for fear of the Jews." This they do even after Mary has announced to them that she has seen the Lord. Clearly the implication of her announcement has not sunk in yet. At this point, they are acting out the same kind of borderline faith as is often found in John, where fear has leached the commitment out of them. In the case of the community of John, their fear of "the Jews" represented the conflict they were experiencing with the local Jewish leadership. The church was also Jewish and was facing the quandary of what to do now that it no longer had a home in the synagogue. At such an indecisive moment in their lives, this story spoke to them the message of the risen Lord. Like the disciples in the story, John's church needed to reunderstand the meaning of the resurrection and its significance for their present circumstance.

Though they were behind locked doors, Jesus still appeared among them. The miracle here, that Jesus could pass through a locked door, does not correlate well with the motif that Jesus' body is still a physical body, with the marks of death still there to be seen and felt. But that point does not worry John. Perhaps there is another point to be made by the appearance to them while they are behind locked doors. Though they had insulated themselves and virtually gone into hiding, the risen Lord could still seek them out. They may not have access to the trappings of power in the physical world, but they had unlimited access to the power of God spiritually.

The message of the risen Lord echoes the promises he made in the last discourse. "Peace be with you," he says, for he had promised, "Peace is my parting gift to you, my own peace, such as the world cannot give" (14:27). The point is not that they will be magically released from the necessity of the locked doors. Rather it is a spiritual peace that Jesus offers that will sustain them even when they can find no peace in the world. "As the Father sent me, so I send you" fulfills Jesus' prayer, "As you sent me into the world, I have sent them into the world" (17:18). The disciples' mission will mirror Jesus' mission; as he was hated by the world, so they will be hated (15:18; 17:14-16).

Jesus next breathes on them and says, "Receive the Holy Spirit!" "Spirit" and "breath" are the same words in Greek as well as Hebrew, so this action of Jesus as a means of passing on the Spirit makes sense in their language world. The Spirit had been promised in the form of the "advocate" or "Spirit of truth" (14:16-17; 15:26; 16:7-11). Indeed, it is necessary that Jesus ascend to the Father so that the advocate can come. As Jesus says, "it is in your interest that I am leaving you. If I do not go, the advocate will not come, whereas if I go, I will send him to you" (16:7). Now that time has come, and the Spirit is dispensed to the disciples. This story does not speak of individual possession of the Spirit, but rather of the possession of the Spirit by the community as a whole when it gathers as a community. Thus as this story is told in the Christian community, it functions as a confirmation that the Spirit is indeed present among them even in the face of the powerlessness they experience in regard to the outside world.

181

What they receive from this gift of the Spirit is not understood to have anything to do with such manifestations as speaking in tongues. That will occur in another church in another context (see 1 Corinthians 12 and 14). Rather, what they experience is power to represent God's judgment to the world. As Jesus said, "When he [the advocate] comes, he will prove the world wrong about sin, justice, and judgement: about sin, because they refuse to believe in me; about justice, because I go to the Father when I pass from your sight; about judgement, because the prince of this world stands condemned" (16:8-11). That action of the advocate is mirrored in the statement of the risen Lord here: "If you forgive anyone's sins, they are forgiven; if you pronounce them unforgiven, unforgiven they remain." Though their experience was of powerlessness in their world, in God's terms they had the power of the risen Lord on their side. The judgment they would pronounce would be exhibited by the simple act of membership in their community. Those who rejected them would be rejecting God as well.

This is a harsh message that does not always fit the church in every generation, because it can so easily lead to a holier-than-thou judgmentalism. But it fit well the sectarian situation that John's church found itself in, because they were experiencing such a severe dissonance between their identity as the people of God and their experience as the persecuted of the earth. They needed the reassurance that their estranged position vis-à-vis the world, a position they did not choose but which had been forced on them, constituted a judgment of God on the world. It was a theology that helped give affirmation to an oppressed minority. It is misused if applied by a group in power to oppress those who are different.

In the next segment of this story, we meet Doubting Thomas. He had not been present when Jesus appeared to the others, and despite their proclamation, "We have seen the Lord," he is not convinced. "Unless I see the mark of the nails on his hands, unless I put my finger into the place where the nails were, and my hand into his side, I will never believe it," he says. The position of Thomas serves as a bridge between the faith of the disciples and that of all later generations. What Thomas demands might well be demanded by all later generations of believers as well. But that is not to be. Yet in the story Thomas gets his wish, and is able to see and feel the body of Jesus. In this way, the story affirms the physical nature of the resurrected body. But later generations must believe without the physical evidence, and their faith is praised by Jesus, "Happy are they who find faith without seeing me."

Later generations cannot see as Thomas did, but they can still "see" with the eyes of faith. That is because they now have the story, and when the story is told it will bring to them the testimony of the signs of Jesus. That is why this book was written, as the author states immediately after the Thomas story, in a rare address directly to the reader. Here the author points out that this book has presented a selection of Jesus' signs so that the reader might believe and "have life by his name." Though the physical experience of Jesus is no longer possible for those who read this book, faith that is nevertheless sufficient for salvation, or signs faith, is available. That is because readers can confront Jesus and his signs through the telling of the stories found within. When these stories are told, then the signs come to life once more, and the eyes of faith will see through the signs to the glory of the one they reveal.

### Retelling the Story

But [Thomas] said, "Unless I see the mark of the nails on his hands, unless I put my finger into the place where the nails were, and my hand into his side, I will never believe it." (John 20:25*b*)

Welcome, sahib. Please make yourself at home. You asked about the origins of our church and I would be more

> According to the apocryphal writing, *Acts of Thomas*, Thomas's mission work carried him as far as India, where he was martyred, and where he came to be revered as a patron saint of the Christian Church.

> What kind of resurrection body could show physical signs of the manner of death and yet still appear in a locked room? Chrysostom explains the anomalies in the text in this way: "But, one might understandably be puzzled as to how an incorruptible body could show marks of the nails and be capable of being touched by a mortal hand. However, do not be disturbed, for the phenomenon was an evidence of Christ's condescension. To be sure, a body so tenuous and unsubstantial that it entered through doors that were shut was entirely lacking in density. But Christ made His appearance as He did so that the Resurrection would be believed and so that they would know that it was He—the very one who had been crucified—and not someone else who had arisen instead of Him. That is why he arose with the marks of the crucifixion still evident and it was for this reason that He partook of food. In fact, the Apostles repeatedly cited this as a proof of the resurrection and said: 'We who ate and drank with Him' [Acts 10:41]. Therefore, just as when we saw Him walking on the waves, before the crucifixion, we did not say that body of His was of a nature different from ours, so when, after the Resurrection, we see that He still has His wounds, we do not say that He is, therefore, still mortal. It is for the sake of the disciple that He is making His appearance in this way." (Chrysostom, *Homilies on John* 87 [late-fourth century C.E.])

than happy to tell you. Allow me to pour you some tea. I see you take it like an American. Most of our visitors are from Britain. I suppose that is because of our historic, and very tragic, colonial tie. For that reason, perhaps, I find it easier to be open with those visitors with whom I do not share that particular history.

I will begin at the beginning. Our church was founded not long after the death of our Lord by the apostle Thomas. We believe that our Savior chose Thomas to be the one to bring his gospel to India. I realize that in the West, Thomas is viewed as a poor example, as one who doubted while the other apostles believed. You must remember, though, that the other disciples gathered in that room had experienced the presence of our Lord. Thomas was simply requesting the privilege of seeing what his fearful brothers had already seen. He is not doubting Jesus, you see, but the testimony of his cowardly disciples could hardly be taken at face value, now could it?

John repeatedly refers to Thomas as "the Twin," or *Didymos* in Greek. Indeed, the name "Thomas" itself may derive from an Aramaic term meaning "twin." John never specifies why Thomas was called "the Twin," but there was a popular belief that developed in the early church, particularly in Syria, that Thomas was the twin brother of Jesus. Thomas became in effect the patron apostle of Syrian Christianity, and numerous stories circulated about his deeds. He was known as "Judas Thomas Didymos" in Syrian Christian circles, as evidenced in the *Gospel of Thomas* and in the *Acts of Thomas*. It is the third-century *Acts of Thomas* that identifies him as the twin of the Lord. Here the Lord appears in the form of Thomas but explains, "I am not Judas who is also Thomas, I am his brother." (*Acts of Thomas* 11)

For us, Saint Thomas was the only one among the disciples who was not so filled with fear that he was unwilling to leave the disciples' hiding place. Perhaps that is the reason he was not afraid to leave his home and travel here to bring the Word of life to our ancestors. We might better call him Fearless Thomas than Thomas the Doubter.

For us, Saint Thomas is the disciple who was honest enough to express his doubts to his brothers and his faith to his Lord. We believe that Jesus rewarded this honesty by showing Thomas his hands, feet, and side. He even offered them to Thomas to touch, though the Bible does not say that Thomas actually touched his Lord. His reward was the simple offering by Jesus of his wounds. Is this not greater proof, even more so than signs, miracles, or teachings that Jesus is, indeed, the chosen one of God? Our Lord offers the evidence of his wounds suffered for Thomas in his doubt, suffered for the other disciples in their fear, and suffered for us who live in doubt and fear much of the time.

So when the Lord called Thomas to

go to a country foreign to him and to preach the good news to people who spoke another language and lived in a very different manner than the one to which he was accustomed, Thomas went before kings and fearlessly told them of an even greater king to whom they must learn to be servants.

He spoke to outcasts and told them of an outcast named Jesus who died so that they might know they are children of a great king. He described to them a great spiritual teacher who washed his disciples' feet, something they could not imagine even with tremendous effort. Such a teacher was never known among them before. Do you have such teachers in your part of the world?

So, you see, for us Thomas is truly a saint, a man of faith who planted a seed of holiness in our hearts. I now ask you, Could a doubter such as what you believe Thomas to be do that? Or perhaps doubt such as what Thomas expressed is part of the very fabric of our faith. Without a measure of holy doubt we would fall victim to those unscrupulous people who would take advantage of our gullibility for their profit. I believe there are many such on television programs in your country. Perhaps such fearless, honest, doubting faith is the weft that adds color and interesting patterns to the theology that provides the warp of our faith.

Thomas's story puts us on trial, my friend, not him. The apostle's fearlessness and honesty raises the question, "Could I say 'My Lord and my God' when I see Christ's wounds wherever they appear in my world?"

*(Michael E. Williams)*

Chrysostom, like most early Christian interpreters, considered Thomas's refusal to believe to be a sign of obstinacy. "Just as it is an indication of gullibility to believe easily and carelessly, so to scrutinize and examine immoderately before believing is the mark of an obstinate will. That is why Thomas is blameworthy. For he refused to believe the Apostles when they said: 'We have seen the Lord,' not so much because he did not trust them, as because he considered the thing an impossibility—that is, resurrection from the dead. He did not say, 'I do not believe you,' but, 'Unless I put my hand into his side, I will not believe.' " (Chrysostom, *Homilies on John* 87 [late-fourth century C.E.])

# The Appearance by the Sea

*The risen Lord appears by the sea, brings about a miraculous catch of fish, then serves a breakfast of charcoal broiled fish.*

## The Story

SOME time later, Jesus showed himself to his disciples once again, by the sea of Tiberias. This is how it happened. Simon Peter was with Thomas the Twin, Nathanael from Cana-in-Galilee, the sons of Zebedee, and two other disciples. 'I am going out fishing,' said Simon Peter. 'We will go with you,' said the others. So they set off and got into the boat; but that night they caught nothing.

Morning came, and Jesus was standing on the beach, but the disciples did not know that it was Jesus. He called out to them, 'Friends, have you caught anything?' 'No,' they answered. He said, 'Throw out the net to starboard, and you will make a catch.' They did so, and found they could not haul the net on board, there were so many fish in it. Then the disciple whom Jesus loved said to Peter, 'It is the Lord!' As soon as Simon Peter heard him say, 'It is the Lord,' he fastened his coat about him (for he had stripped) and plunged into the sea. The rest of them came on in the boat, towing the net full of fish. They were only about a hundred yards from land.

When they came ashore, they saw a charcoal fire there with fish laid on it, and some bread. Jesus said, 'Bring some of the fish you have caught.' Simon Peter went on board and hauled the net to land; it was full of big fish, a hundred and fifty three in all; and yet, many as they were, the net was not torn. Jesus said, 'Come and have breakfast.' None of the disciples dared to ask 'Who are you?' They knew it was the Lord. Jesus came, took the bread and gave it to them, and the fish in the same way. This makes the third time that Jesus appeared to his disciples after his resurrection from the dead.

## Comments on the Story

Now that the resurrection is over, what are the disciples to do? Is there a letdown after this big event? One would think so, since Peter decides that it is time to go fishing, and the other disciples follow the leader.

To be sure, Peter is not pictured here as a slacker. Fishing for him is not a vacation but a vocation. He is not avoiding life—he is going about his business. Yet there is a missing dimension, so Jesus appears and brings back the proper focus. With the presence of Jesus the catch is superabundant.

Fishing has become a metaphor here, but not in the sense of the synoptic Gospels. It does not stand for evangelism or fishing for people, as we find, for example in Mark 1:17. Evangelism is not the concern of this chapter. Instead the rest of the chapter focuses on the spiritual life of the community, on discipleship, as we will see in the second half of this story. Consequently, fishing would seem to be a metaphor for the life of the church. At first, Jesus' followers seem to drift aimlessly, accomplishing little. With the appearance of Jesus, however, they suddenly have access to a superabundance of spiritual power. It is a reminder that when the church taps into the power of the risen Lord, rather than drifting aimlessly, it will have access to a power beyond human measure.

When Peter realizes it is the Lord, he covers his nakedness and dives into the water, evidently to swim to shore. This almost comical scene exhibits the skill of the storyteller. The discovery that they are mere humans in the presence of the Divine must be acknowledged. Peter's burlesque actions do exactly that.

When they have come ashore, they find that Jesus has prepared a fire and is cooking a breakfast of fish for them. He sends them to bring some of the fish they have caught to add to the meal. He then serves them a meal of bread and fish.

What a meal this would have been—miraculous fish cooked and served by the risen Lord! The story is rich with symbolic overtones. The words at verse 13 suggest eucharistic language: "Jesus came, took the bread and gave it to them, and the fish in the same way." Although John has no eucharistic words of Jesus in his Last Supper story, these words echo the miraculous meal of loaves and fish at John 6:1-13. That text is not specifically eucharistic either, but it does include eucharistic imagery. In this text also, while eucharistic overtones are present, there is more to the text than that. For example, fish is present at the meal, yet fish is not a normal part of the Eucharist. But fish is a highly symbolic food, and often represents the food of the gods in ancient belief. That tradition fits well here, for this is not a normal meal, nor was the fish secured by normal means. It is a meal of "numinous" or divine food that the disciples enjoy.

When they gather for this meal, "none of the disciples dared to ask 'Who are you?' They knew it was the Lord." The recognition scene is over; now they gather as community fully focused on the risen Lord. The scene would certainly recall a community Eucharist, but it is more than that. The symbolism of the bounteous banquet of heavenly food, the so-called "messianic banquet," is not just realized when the community comes together for the Lord's Supper. It is also realized in the life of the community as a whole.

Now that the resurrection is over, what is the community to do? It is to go about its task of being the children of light in a world of darkness. But Christians do not drift alone in a barren sea. They have access to the risen Lord, who provides the spiritual nourishment that brings life and empowers the church on its faith journey in a hostile world.

Chrysostom interpreted the responses of Peter and the Beloved Disciple (whom he identified as John) to be true to character: "Now, in recognizing Him, the disciples Peter and John once again showed the traits peculiar to their respective characters. For, Peter was more ardent, John, more spiritual; Peter was more impulsive, John, more cautious. Therefore, John was the first to recognize Jesus, while Peter was the first to go to him." (Chrysostom, *Homilies on John* 87 [late-fourth century C.E.])

## Retelling the Story

'I am going out fishing,' said Simon Peter. 'We will go with you,' said the others. (John 21:3)

Thomas awoke that morning to face a gray day. It fit his mood exactly. In fact, the entire group of disciples seemed listless and unfocused. That is why they jumped at the chance to go fishing when Peter brought it up. At least it was something to do.

The problem was, they had a bad case of the postresurrection blues.

"What are we gonna do, now that the resurrection is past?" thought Thomas. He reflected back on recent events. There had been a lot of excitement for a while. Why, they had stood in the presence of the divine! Thomas himself had touched the holy body. They had all experienced a spiritual high like no other. "It just doesn't get any better than this," he thought at the time.

But now, he had awakened to find that the world was the same as it had always been. Nothing had changed. That spiritual high was gone. In its place was a bad case of the postresurrection blues.

"What are we gonna do, now that the resurrection is past?" Thomas said to Peter. Peter merely scowled and turned back to his work. He was preparing the boat for their fishing trip. Usually he enjoyed his work, but today was different. Today he saw for the first time how futile it all was. Nothing had changed, and it seemed to him that it never would.

Perhaps more than any of the others, Peter had had big dreams. He saw visions of the triumph of God over evil throughout the world. Injustice would be obliterated and justice would prevail for all of God's people. Wasn't that what the resurrection was supposed to mean?

But here he was, preparing his fishing boat as he had always done, and as he would always do. Was it all a dream? Had he just imagined the resurrection? Certainly it had left no traces in the real world, that was clear. Once he had thought the triumph of God was near, but now he just had a bad case of the postresurrection blues.

"What are we gonna do, now that the resurrection is past?" They all carried that thought with them as they set out in the boat. The entire crew seemed listless and moody. They knew it shouldn't be this way. They were supposed to be basking in the glow of the glory of God. Instead, they were fighting mosquitoes and cursing the heat like nothing had changed.

To top it all off, there were no fish to be found. It was a wasted trip. They had a bad case of the postresurrection blues.

But just when they thought it couldn't get any worse, he came back once more. And suddenly the world changed, and the fish were abundant. "Yesss!" thought Thomas., "This is how it is supposed to be!"

It was as if he had come back for an encore, for one last party, before leaving for good. And what a party it was! They forgot all about the blues as they feasted and celebrated once more. "It just doesn't get any better than this," said Thomas as he raised a cup in celebration.

But he knew they had to look to tomorrow. What then? Would they go back to singing the blues as soon as he left? Is that all they had to look forward to?

Slowly the lesson began to sink in. "You are in the world, but not of the world," he had said. Now they began to understand what that meant. The world was the same—they were the ones who were different. They now knew that they had a superabundance of spiritual nourishment available to them. But the world would stay the same unless they shared that abundance.

What were they going to do, now that the resurrection was past? Shed those postresurrection blues! Share the party—feed the sheep!

*(Dennis E. Smith)*

The heavenly banquet at the end of time, or messianic banquet, would represent a celebration of God's victory over evil. Jewish speculation about this event often made reference to the ancient myth of the sea monster, Leviathan, whose defeat by God represented victory over chaos. That myth goes on to speak of Leviathan then providing nourishment for the victory banquet. This is one likely source for the symbolism of fish at the banquet prepared by the risen Lord. A representative text is 2 Bar. 29:1-8, where not only are the land and sea monsters provided as food, but also manna and abundant wine: "It will happen that when all that which should come to pass in these parts has been accomplished, the Anointed One will begin to be revealed. And Behemoth will reveal itself from its place, and Leviathan will come from the sea, the two great monsters which I created on the fifth day of creation and which I shall have kept until that time. And they will be nourishment for all who are left. . . . And those who are hungry will enjoy themselves and they will, moreover, see marvels every day." (from Boring, pp. 249-50, no. 375)

189

# Feed My Sheep

---

*The risen Lord commissions Peter to care for the flock.*

---

## The Story

After breakfast Jesus said to Simon Peter, 'Simon son of John, do you love me more than these others?' 'Yes, Lord,' he answered, 'you know that I love you.' 'Then feed my lambs,' he said. A second time he asked, 'Simon son of John, do you love me?' 'Yes, Lord, you know I love you.' 'Then tend my sheep.' A third time he said, 'Simon son of John, do you love me?' Peter was hurt that he asked him a third time, 'Do you love me?' 'Lord,' he said, 'you know everything; you know I love you.' Jesus said, 'Then feed my sheep.

'In very truth I tell you: when you were young you fastened your belt about you and walked where you chose; but when you are old you will stretch out your arms, and a stranger will bind you fast, and carry you where you have no wish to go.' He said this to indicate the manner of death by which Peter was to glorify God. Then he added, 'Follow me.'

Peter looked round, and saw the disciple whom Jesus loved following—the one who at supper had leaned back close to him to ask the question, 'Lord, who is it that will betray you?' When he saw him, Peter asked, 'Lord, what about him?' Jesus said, 'If it should be my will that he stay until I come, what is it to you? Follow me.'

That saying of Jesus became current among his followers, and was taken to mean that that disciple would not die. But in fact Jesus did not say he would not die; he only said, 'If it should be my will that he stay until I come, what is it to you?'

It is this same disciple who vouches for what has been written here. He it is who wrote it, and we know that his testimony is true.

There is much else that Jesus did. If it were all to be recorded in detail, I suppose the world could not hold the books that would be written.

## Comments on the Story

One more issue remained to be dealt with in John. How was leadership to be passed on in the church? This issue had come to the fore because of the ambiguous position of this church in relation to other Christian groups on the subject of leadership.

The Gospel of John clearly represents a Christian sectarian group that existed in a hostile setting. They had developed a self-image as an insular group surrounded by enemies. They seemed to have little contact with the outside world, particularly with other Christian groups, though they had some knowledge of their existence. This explains the singular form of John's language and theology—they were not in conversation with other forms of Christianity. Yet somehow they were aware of the existence of other Christian groups and desired to identify with that larger heritage. They certainly knew that Peter was the acknowledged leader elsewhere. But their leadership, and its accompanying theology, had developed differently. Their distinctive theology was identified with their own special authority figure, the Beloved Disciple, an individual who is unnamed and therefore unknown elsewhere in Christian tradition. But in John, he emerges as a disciple with special access to Jesus and as a leader often equal to Peter. Those stories exist in order to justify the current form that the Johannine community has taken. In essence, this story serves an apologetic function, to establish a connection with the larger world of Christianity while still affirming the uniqueness of their own tradition.

The setting is "after breakfast," so we are to understand that this story is a continuation of the scene in which the disciples enjoyed a fish meal prepared by the risen Lord. Peter is directly addressed by Jesus, and three times is asked, "Do you love me?" To each inquiry Peter replies, "Yes, Lord, you know that I love you." And to each reply of Peter, Jesus responds, "Feed my sheep." The repetition of three seems odd until we remember that Peter had denied Jesus three times. In essence, Peter has been rehabilitated.

Peter's leadership role is clearly acknowledged here. As such, he represents leadership succession in the Christian community. So when Jesus says, "Feed my sheep," he refers to the role of Christian leaders to care for the community. It is his commission to all of the disciples through Peter. The use of the sheep metaphor reminds one of the Good Shepherd parable. Unlike the "hired man" who "abandons the sheep and runs away," Peter is urged to follow the lead of the good shepherd, who "lays down his life for the sheep" (see 10:11-12). The expression, "feed my sheep," draws also on the context here. Just as the disciples have been spiritually nourished by Jesus in the previous scene, so they are to do the same for their charges.

After this, Jesus foretells Peter's death and states that the Beloved Disciple will live even longer. Apparently, this section is here to resolve some issues in the recent history of the Christian community of John. We may assume that the Beloved Disciple had indeed outlived Peter and this was seen as another sign of his priority. By the time this is written, however, he, too, has died. Yet his legacy lives on, for he is claimed as the authority behind the writing of this book. Since the book does not use first-person testimony as the primary means for telling the story of Jesus, it makes most sense to interpret the writer to mean not that every story in John came from the Beloved Disciple, but rather that the overall theology of the book rests on the authority of the Beloved Dis-

191

ciple. He was a pastor who, like Peter, had fed the sheep of this community during a tumultuous period in their history. His pastoral skills are still exhibited in the Gospel that is his legacy to us today.

## Retelling the Story

> Peter was hurt that he asked him a third time, 'Do you love me?' 'Lord,' he said, 'you know everything; you know I love you.' Jesus said, 'Then feed my sheep.' (John 21:17)

When a guy decides to go off down the road with a dozen fellows in beards and sandals, he can expect some life changes, but when one of those guys turns out to be God, then what is he to do? It was a grand occasion—the first Easter dinner, a fish fry on the shore of Lake Galilee—and Peter was in a quandary.

You see, there was that rooster thing that had happened the night before the crucifixion. He hadn't exactly been exemplary in the way he stood up for his Lord, and he knew Jesus knew it. Now Jesus was back—and Peter was on God's short list. What would happen? Peter had read the scriptures. He knew the possibilities, and deep down, he was scared stiff.

The more he thought about it, the more worried he became, and the more worried he grew, the more his agitation grew. Then, just as the quaking of his insides was reaching a fever pitch, he looked up. Jesus was walking toward him!

What would he do? What would he say? Peter could only imagine the worst: "Peter, you've done it this time!" or "Peter! My Father wants a word with you. Now!"

"I've had it," Peter thought.

Jesus spoke quietly. "Simon."

Peter's heart sank. No longer was he being called by the nickname Jesus had given him. He had been right. The relationship was gone forever. He couldn't bring himself to look at Jesus' face. "Here it comes, and I deserve everything I get," thought Peter.

"Yes, Lord?" he said.

"Simon, do you love me more than these?"

It was concern that Peter saw in Jesus' eyes, not anger.

Peter didn't know what to say. They both knew he'd failed miserably. He'd shown his lack of love when he did

The reference in the text to the kind of death Peter was to die is thought to be a veiled reference to crucifixion. According to Christian tradition, Peter was martyred by crucifixion in Rome in the time of Nero. According to the third century C.E. apocryphal work Acts of Peter, he was crucified upside down at his own request. (*Acts of Peter* 9.37) what he said he never would—when he denied and deserted Jesus. But down in his heart of hearts, he *did* love Jesus more than anything—although he didn't know how he could ever make Jesus believe that. All he could say was, "You know I love you, Lord."

He waited for Jesus to yell at him. To throw the book at him. To cry out, "Then where were you when I needed you?" or "No, I *don't* know that!" or "Get out of my face—forever!"

But Jesus' response was soft. "Take care of my sheep."

Peter couldn't believe it! Could Jesus really be overlooking what he had done?

The ending of John at 21:25 uses a motif found elsewhere in ancient literature. For example, Porphyry ends a list of miracles of Pythagoras in this way: "Ten thousand other things yet more marvelous and more divine are told about the man, and told uniformly in stories that agree with each other. To put it bluntly, about no one else have greater and more extraordinary things been believed." (*Life of Pythagoras* 29 [late-third century C.E.]; from Boring, p. 308, no. 484)

"Simon, *do* you love me?"

Again, Peter's heart sank. "Not 'do you love me *most*' " thought Peter, "but 'do you love me *at all*?' "

His answer was as controlled as he could make it, but his voice wavered. "Lord, you know I love you."

He wanted to break—to throw himself at Jesus' feet and cry out, "*Please know I love you! Please tell me you forgive me!*"

"Feed my lambs."

"Feed *what* lambs?" Peter thought. He was still confused.

"Simon."

"Yes, Lord?"

"Feed my sheep."

And suddenly Peter *knew*! Jesus was not going to toss him aside, because not only did he know Peter still loved him, *Jesus still loved Peter*! He'd known Peter was going to fail and had loved him anyway.

Jesus didn't need to forgive him—he was already forgiven! Peter marveled at the wonder of it all.

"I think the fisherman's ready to become a shepherd," said Peter.

Jesus smiled. "I think he's been one for a long time."

*(Phyllis Williams Provost)*

# Selected Bibliography

References in the text are cited by author.

Boring, M. Eugene, Klaus Berger, and Carsten Colpe. *Hellenistic Commentary to the New Testament.* Nashville: Abingdon Press, 1995.

Brown, Raymond E. *The Gospel According to John.* 2 vols. Anchor Bible 29 & 29A. Garden City, N.Y.: Doubleday, 1966-70.

_____. *The Death of the Messiah.* 2 vols. Anchor Bible Reference Library. Garden City, N.Y.: Doubleday, 1994.

Cartlidge, David R., and David L. Dungan. *Documents for the Study of the Gospels.* Cleveland: Collins, 1980.

Corley, Kathleen E. *Private Women, Public Meals: Social Conflict in the Synoptic Tradition.* Peabody, Mass.: Hendrickson, 1993.

Crossan, John Dominic. *Who Killed Jesus?* San Francisco: HarperSanFrancisco, 1995.

Culpepper, R. Alan. *Anatomy of the Fourth Gospel: A Study in Literary Design.* Philadelphia: Fortress, 1983.

Duke, Paul D. *Irony in the Fourth Gospel.* Atlanta: John Knox, 1985.

Hachlili, Rachel. "Burial, Ancient Jewish," *Anchor Bible Dictionary.* 6 vols. Garden City, N.Y.: Doubleday, 1992.

Haenchen, Ernst. *John.* 2 vols. Hermeneia. Philadelphia: Fortress, 1984.

Hengel, Martin. *Crucifixion in the Ancient World and the Folly of the Message of the Cross.* Philadelphia: Fortress, 1977.

Kysar, Robert. *John's Story of Jesus*. Philadelphia: Fortress, 1984.

Martyn, J. Louis. *History and Theology in the Fourth Gospel*. Rev. ed. Nashville: Abingdon Press, 1979.

Miller, Robert J., ed. *The Complete Gospels*. Sonoma, Calif.: Polebridge, 1992.

Montefiore, C. G., and H. Loewe. *A Rabbinic Anthology*. Cleveland: World Publishing Co. [Meridian Books], 1963.

Zias, Joseph, and Eliezer Sekeles, "The Crucified Man from Giv'at Ha-Mivtar: A Reappraisal," *Israel Exploration Journal* 35 (1985): 22-27.

# Index of Readings from
## *The Revised Common Lectionary*

# Index of Parallel Stories

## OLD TESTAMENT

## OLD TESTAMENT PSEUDEPIGRAPHA

## RABBINIC LITERATURE

## GREEK AND ROMAN LITERATURE